Messenger

Messenger

THE INSPIRING STORY OF
MATTIE J.T. STEPANEK
AND HEARTSONGS

Jeni Stepanek

with Larry Lindner

HAY HOUSE
Australia • Canada • Hong Kong • India
South Africa • United Kingdom • United States

First published by Dutton, a member of Penguin Group (USA) Inc.
375 Hudson Street, New York, New York 10014, U.S.A.
Penguin Books Ltd, Registered Offices: 80 Strand, London WC2R 0RL, England

First published and distributed in the United Kingdom by:
Hay House UK Ltd, 292B Kensal Rd, London W10 5BE. Tel.: (44) 20 8962 1230; Fax: (44) 20 8962 1239.
www.hayhouse.co.uk

Published and distributed in Australia by:
Hay House Australia Ltd, 18/36 Ralph St, Alexandria NSW 2015. Tel.: (61) 2 9669 4299; Fax: (61) 2 9669 4144.
www.hayhouse.com.au

Published and distributed in the Republic of South Africa by:
Hay House SA (Pty), Ltd, PO Box 990, Witkoppen 2068. Tel./Fax: (27) 11 467 8904. www.hayhouse.co.za

Published and distributed in India by:
Hay House Publishers India, Muskaan Complex, Plot No.3, B-2, Vasant Kunj, New Delhi – 110 070. Tel.: (91)
11 4176 1620; Fax: (91) 11 4176 1630. www.hayhouse.co.in

A catalogue record for this book is available from the British Library.

ISBN 978-1-8485-0251-2

Printed and bound in Great Britain by CPI William Clowes, Beccles, NR34 7TL.

Permissions appear on page 322 and constitute an extension of the copyright page.

Interior photos: GMA: page 125 (left); Harpo Productions: page 124; Jim Hawkins: pages 60 (left), 125 (right);
IAFF: page 305 (left); MDA: pages 1, 44 (bottom), 142 (right), 162, 176 (bottom), 231 (top, bottom), 232 (right),
246, 247, 262 (bottom), 280 (left), 304; Sandy Newcomb: page 176 (top); Omar Pancoast: page 232 (left); Ben
Quinto: page 321; Mary Lou Smith: page 279 (top); Terry Spearman: page 91 (right); Jeni Stepanek: pages v, viii,
10, 11, 26, 27, 44 (top, left, right), 45, 59, 60 (right), 75, 76, 91 (left), 92, 108, 109, 141, 142 (left), 163, 176 (top),
177, 193, 194, 214, 215, 231 (middle), 262 (top), 263, 279 (bottom), 280 (right), 305 (right), 312, 313.

Photo insert: Nancy Hunt: insert page 7 (top left); Michael Mangone: page 8 (bottom); Sandy Newcomb: page 2
(top left, right), page 4 (middle), page 5 (top left), page 8 (middle); Nell Paul: page 4 (top right); Jane Stack: page 8
(top right); Jeni Stepanek: pages 1, 2 (bottom left, right), 3, 4 (top left, bottom right), 5 (top right, bottom left,
right), 6, 7 (top right, bottom left, right); Ed Tenney: page 8 (top left).

For Sandy Newcomb

Mattie's "VFABF"

—Very Favorite Adult Best Friend—

Contents

Maya Angelou and Mattie, April 2002

Foreword

by Dr. Maya Angelou

There is an old African American gospel song which asks the Creator directly, "Lord, don't move your mountain, just give me strength to climb it. You don't have to move that stumbling block, just lead me, Lord, around it."

In essence that was the theme of Mattie Stepanek's life. That person, young in years, small in stature and challenged physically, dared to say of life—"However you press me, and pain me, and dare me, I shall live you fully. I shall find peace in the storm of disease. I shall find joy in the heart of pain. My name is Mattie Stepanek and I shall be an ambassador of love."

This young poet asked to speak to me, and at first I was simply pleased. As I came to know him, his life, his mother and his poetry, I was honored to be a person who had encouraged and inspired him. Mattie Stepanek did not come from the ground like grass, he grew like a tree. He had roots.

Jeni Stepanek, who has seen all of her children succumb to the ruthless disease and watched her son, the poet, fight valiantly for each day of his life, for each ray of sunshine, and has, herself, been assailed by the same illness, is a root. She is planted deep in the earth. She has given strength to all her children, nurture and admiration to her son, the poet, and now she has given us this book, *Messenger: The Legacy of Mattie J.T. Stepanek and Heartsongs*.

I commend Jeni Stepanek for daring to live, for daring to give, and above all for daring to love.

Messenger

Prologue

International Association of Fire Fighters honoring
Mattie at his funeral, June 28, 2004

. . . I will revolve seasonally
When my death comes,
And children will remember
And share their Heartsongs,
Celebrating the gifts in the circle of life.[1]

A jar of jawbreakers, a crucifix, a SpongeBob pillow, a copy of *To Kill a Mockingbird*, the noisy half of a remote control fart machine. These were among the items Mattie had with him in his casket.

We had begun discussing what he would "take" nearly a year and a half earlier, in February of 2003. Mattie was in the Intensive Care Unit of Children's National Medical Center in Washington, DC, clearly having crossed the line from being a child with a life-threatening condition to a child who's going to die, probably sooner rather than later.

---

1 From "Eternal Role Call" in *Celebrate Through Heartsongs,* page 52.

I was about to open the game box with the Yahtzee dice and UNO cards when he looked straight at me and asked, "Mom, do you think people are going to come to my funeral?"

He was finding it difficult to breathe. In this latest health crisis, his airway had eroded; at times he felt like he was suffocating. His fingers bled, he coughed up blood and tissue from his tracheal lining, and a tracheostomy tube came out of the hole in his neck—ventilator and oxygen line attached.

Mattie had had life-threatening episodes before, but I had avoided having direct conversations with him about his death up until that point. "You know," he continued, "I'm going to be young when I die, and maybe people won't feel comfortable coming."

"Of course people will be there!" I answered reflexively. I hadn't actually thought about people coming to his funeral before that moment. Mattie was going to be the fourth child I buried as a result of a rare disease called dysautonomic mitochondrial myopathy, and I was, I suppose, trying to keep my distance from that inevitable day even while I was preparing for it somewhere within.

But this was going to be different. My other children died very young, all before the age of four. Mattie, on the other hand, was already twelve. He could participate in his own funeral arrangements. It was different, too, because Mattie had achieved renown. He had been on *The Oprah Winfrey Show*, *Larry King Live*, *Good Morning America*; he had written several books of poetry that had reached the *New York Times* bestseller list and sold millions of copies; he had become the National Goodwill Ambassador for Jerry Lewis's Muscular Dystrophy Association; he knew his heroes—Jimmy Carter and Maya Angelou—personally; he had given inspirational talks to thousands about peace, about being true to yourself and following your Heartsong, as he called it. My grief and the grief of those close to him was going to be private, but many others were also going to grieve and want to pay respects.

Most important, however, was that Mattie's funeral go the way he wanted. He asked if he could tell me some things he would like. I took out a piece of paper and a pen. He talked about what he wanted mentioned in various prayers, songs he wanted sung, who he wanted to do the readings, who he wanted to say his Mass. In the Catholic Church, a funeral Mass is a celebration, a spiritual send-off, and he wanted his celebration to go just right.

Mattie then went on: "Please don't send me to a morgue," which is standard procedure after someone dies. "I don't want my face covered with a shroud. I don't want to be put in a drawer. I know I'll be dead and it'll be meaningless then, but I'm alive now and I'm afraid of the dark. Please keep a light on in the funeral home, too."

He added that he didn't want to go from the funeral home to the church in a hearse, if that was in any way possible. In a hearse you're alone, with just a stranger driving.

I was thinking of Mattie's requests as we drove to his funeral, which occurred sixteen months later, on a warm day in late June 2004. I was going down a mental checklist to make sure I had honored all of his wishes. I don't know what Heaven is, but it has got to be good, and I was wondering, from that good space, is my son happy? Does he know I have done everything to make this the celebration he wanted?

I suddenly realized that I had forgotten to put his Black Belt in the casket. Before Mattie became too sick, he had earned a Black Belt in a Korean martial art called Hapkido, and he wanted the reward for that triumph with him. I felt horrible that I hadn't remembered.

Everything else that he requested was there, though—a photograph of him with his older brother, Jamie, the only other sibling alive by the time Mattie was born; a photograph of his other brother, Stevie, and his sister, Katie, both of whom he planned to meet for the first time in Heaven; a photo of Mattie and me; the baptism rosary of our little friend Kaylee, who called him "Uncle Mattie"; a camera with a flash because Mattie wasn't sure about "the lighting situation after death"; a small tape recorder "with extra batteries"; Mr. Bunny, a fleece puppet he had from the day he was born; his Muscular Dystrophy Association (MDA) business cards; a *Lord of the Rings* bookmark; Austin Powers memorabilia that Mike Myers had sent to him; some Legos; and a number of other items. Despite being Catholic, I bury my children like little Egyptians departing for the next life with their worldly goods, and Mattie, aware of that, wanted as much tangible that mattered to him as the casket would hold.

Others put in gifts of their own. There was the Native American offering of feathers; a white rose from the flower arrangement sent by Oprah Winfrey; a photo of Mattie and his friend Hope, whom he had known since he was five; a wooden plaque with a picture of Hermione from *Harry Potter*; other tokens of affection; and yes, the noisy half of his remote control fart machine.

I had refused to place it in myself, even though it was one of the last things Mattie asked for when we talked about his funeral. "You have to take it," he said. "Put the noisy half in the casket with me, keep the trigger half, and, before I'm actually buried, press it, so I get the last laugh." Mattie believed people should "remember to play after every storm"—this was his personal philosophy for life—and he felt this would allow mourners to begin playing again.

I told him I couldn't do it, that I was his mother and that I would be grieving and it wouldn't be right. So Mattie asked Devin Dressman, a research doctor who he had become close friends with, to do it.

A lot happened in the sixteen intervening months between Mattie's conversation with me and his death, even though we had not been optimistic that he would make it out of the hospital when we had that discussion. He published a fifth bestselling book of poetry. The Iraq War began, just weeks after then-President and Mrs. George W. Bush called Mattie to thank him for all he did for our world in the name of peace. He panicked new doctors on his team by drinking from a urinal that he had filled with apple juice. He started going to the hospital every other day for blood and platelet transfusions. He attended MDA Summer Camp and had the time of his life, mourned the death of his friend Racheal, turned thirteen, ate Maryland crabs with Christopher Cross, delivered a keynote speech for Rosalynn Carter's Intergenerational Caregiving Conference. His interest in girls went from prepubescent to adolescent. He discussed the concept of angels on *Larry King Live* as part of "an expert panel," slept at the local firehouse during a hurricane, underwent treatments to try to strip toxic levels of iron from his blood, did book signings, went into cardiac arrest—three times—fell into a coma, came out of it, saw the latest *Harry Potter* movie. . . .

The day he died, June 22, a terrific rainstorm kicked up in the moments after his heart stopped, with blasts of thunder and lightning. Afterward, as improbable as it may sound, a giant rainbow stretched itself across the sky and could be seen from different locations. I wasn't looking out the window, but kids at his summer camp three hours away saw it. Staff in the hospital saw it. Someone I don't even know wrote about it in the guest book at the funeral.

The storm delayed a visit to the hospital from Mattie's service dog, a golden retriever named Micah. I wanted Micah to see Mattie and know that he had died rather than abandoned him. But I had only a certain window of time. For Mattie to go straight to the funeral home and not to the morgue, which he wanted to avoid, the hospital said I needed to have the funeral home pick him up within three hours of his passing. He died at 1:35 in the afternoon.

Barely ten minutes had passed when people started coming by. A hospital public relations agent came to me and said, "I'm sorry, but we have every news station on the phone. Word has gotten out. Are you able to issue a statement?" By two o'clock, television stations were interrupting their programs to announce Mattie's death.

Micah didn't make it to the hospital until six that evening, the storm and traffic tangles made getting him there difficult. He jumped up on Mattie's bed, excited, licked him, sniffed him, then lay on the floor and just sighed and moaned. He smelled death, literally, and grieved rather than felt confused or abandoned. He lost twenty pounds in only weeks.

The funeral home attendees came by around seven. Nearly six hours had passed, but the hospital waited rather than calling the morgue. In accordance with Mattie's desire not to have his face covered or be left in the dark, the body bag was zipped only up to his face.

Once at the funeral home, the request to leave on a light all night was honored, and Mattie was put in a room with others who had died so he wouldn't be "alone." Nobody can explain it, but his body was still warm when I left the funeral home that night. He was gone; there was no doubt. It was not as if he had slipped into a deep coma. And the life support had been removed as soon as he passed. But seven hours after the time of death was called, the heat of a live person had not yet left him.

Four days after Mattie died, I arrived at the funeral home to finalize plans for the wake and funeral. He was lying there exactly as he had been left, wrapped in a blanket, holding his stuffed animal wolf, Grey Hero. Someone had pinned a note to his blanket: "My name is Matthew. I prefer to be called Mattie. Please leave me in a room with other deceased, and keep a light on for me. Please do not do anything. My mother will come and dress me."

Mattie liked dressing sharply when the occasion called for it, having once said, "I always breathe better in a tuxedo." With that in mind, I dressed him that day in a black tuxedo with a silver vest; Grinch boxers; Simpsons cartoon socks; his black light-up sneakers; his watch and glasses; and his trach tube, which he did not want removed. I also gave him a fresh haircut, fashioned with the number 3 trimmers instead of the usual number 2 trimmers because he wouldn't have wanted it to look *too* fresh.

The funeral home was about a twenty-minute drive from the church, Saint Catherine Laboure. I had never been there, but it was the largest church in our county, with a capacity of 1,350 people, and a large crowd was anticipated. Just how large I couldn't have imagined.

Mattie's casket, four and a half feet long and draped with a blue-and-white United Nations flag that had flown during a peacekeeping mission in Kosovo, was carried out of the funeral home by his pallbearers. Three of them were the children of my closest friend, Sandy Newcomb, who came to see Mattie when he was born and was in the hospital room when he died.

The pallbearers brought the casket to a fire truck decorated with swags of black crepe. The International Association of Fire Fighters is a major supporter of MDA, and Mattie had become good friends with a number of firefighters around the U.S. and Canada. The fire truck was their way of honoring Mattie's wish not to be taken in a hearse.

Out at the curb, the six family pallbearers handed over the casket to six firefighter pallbearers, whose specific job it was to lift the casket onto the truck. Two firefighters with whom Mattie had become particularly close friends, Bert Mentrassi from Greenburgh, New York, and Jim Jackson from Mississauga, Ontario (affectionately known as "Bubba" and "J.J."), rode on the ledge at the back of the truck. Mattie was being honored with the funeral of a fallen firefighter.

I wasn't prepared for the ride to the church from the funeral home. I had considered that, because Mattie had become a person of note, the church might be full. But major roads were closed to traffic. A police motorcade in front of us blocked access. Television newscast helicopters were flying above, along with other aircraft; the airspace above the church was being closely guarded because former President Carter was expected to attend.

Sandy drove my van, which followed behind the fire truck carrying Mattie's casket. From the radio we heard, "Mattie's funeral procession is starting now. They're making their way out of the funeral home." It is a surreal experience, listening to your life in real time while living through your raw grief. At the same time, I was so proud for the attention being paid to my little boy.

That attention turned out to be an even greater outpouring than I had anticipated. I had wanted to stare at the casket in front of me. But my eyes kept being pulled to the sidewalks. People were stopping, making the Sign of the Cross, bowing their heads, taking pictures as the fire truck went by. They put their hands on their hearts. As we came closer and closer to the church, signs were held up: "We love you, Mattie!" "You won't be forgotten!" "Our little peacemaker."

When we turned down the road that led to the church, we saw hundreds of people lined up—Harley-Davidson riders, another big MDA sponsor, in denim and leather; firefighters in dress blues; Muslim women in head scarves; nuns in traditional habits; men in both African dashikis and business suits; the governor of Maryland; country singing star Billy Gilman; homeless people; a U.S. senator; television celebrities; Mattie's former schoolmates; clergy. . . . In that moment, it felt like Mattie really had succeeded in bringing the world together in peace. He would have been thrilled. It was a central tenet of Mattie's message of hope that "we have to make peace a habit"—actually live it day to day in our own choices as well as bring it out to the larger world as a reality—share it "even with people with whom we disagree" or feel angry about or wronged by.

The line of people at the church doors wended down the sidewalk and out of sight around the far side of the building. Two and three thick, they slowly made their way forward. Those who couldn't fit inside stood on grassy hills and other areas nearby.

I sat in the van for fifteen minutes before getting out. During Mattie's final few years, when he existed in the celebrity spotlight, I had become accustomed to television cameras and interviews and chatting with people I didn't know who wanted to tell me that Mattie had somehow touched their lives, and it all made me feel wonderful. But I was going to be following my son's casket into the church. I couldn't face people even to receive expressions of sympathy, and certainly not reporters' questions that day. I knew that if I started talking, I might start crying and that "the mother's grief" would become news. I didn't want the focus shifted from Mattie. I left the van in dark sunglasses so as not to betray any emotion. Fortunately, not a single reporter came up to me the entire day, nor to any famous person there.

I and several others close to Mattie, including Sandy and her mother, were wearing purple. A song he had written that was going to be sung during the funeral service talked about purple being one of the colors of hope, and we wanted to wrap ourselves in Mattie's vision of what hope looked like.

Inside the church, three people gave pre–funeral Mass tributes. One was Jann Carl, a correspondent for *Entertainment Tonight* and also a cohost for the annual *Jerry Lewis Labor Day Telethon*. She read a poem written for Mattie by Jerry Lewis, who couldn't be there because he was quite ill at the time. She talked about "that sparkle" in Mattie's eye, "that innocent yet mischievous grin . . . the way he would push his glasses back to the bridge of his nose." She also said that Mattie "left us a blueprint . . . step-by-step instructions, to not only mend our broken Heartsongs, but to make the world a better place"; that he taught people to play, which "brought back a touch of innocence in all of us. And from that innocence, hope. And from hope, the elusive peace."

Another speaker was Dr. Murray Pollack, director of the Pediatric Intensive Care Unit at Children's National Medical Center, who reminded those in attendance of Mattie's "wit and his wisdom" and reiterated Mattie's advice to "play after every storm." Dr. Pollack said, "Medical failure with Mattie was inevitable . . . yet his spirit and enthusiasm made it oh-so-easy to try. He was a world-class prankster. He really did put apple juice in the urine cup. . . . He really did watch *Ferris Bueller's Day Off* just to get some inspiration. He really did make liberal use of his fart machine. . . . He had adult thoughts—he brought people together—but he was a child. . . . And that was, in large part, his magic."

Oprah Winfrey, who had become a close friend and confidant to Mattie, spoke also. She told the crowd how she "fell in love with him" from the very first moment she met Mattie, and called him "my guy" during phone calls and e-mails. "It's not often that we find people in our lives who create magic," she said. "I found him to be magical. I could not believe so much wisdom, so much power, so much grace, so much strength and love could come from one young boy. . . .

"With Mattie," Oprah said, "the light of his life shined so brightly that every one of us who knew him, who were honored and had the grace to meet him, will feel the glow for the rest of our lives.

"I loved his desire to be known for his work," she commented, "and not just to be famous." She cited an e-mail exchange from a few years earlier in which Mattie talked about some kids he knew who said to him that because he became famous, he should *always be happy and never sad.*" But Mattie added:

> I don't think they understand what it's like to know you
> have to live your life so fast . . . my life here won't
> last. . . . I get scared about the pain of dying and about
> what I will miss because I love living so, so, so much. . . .
> I want to leave so many gifts for people to have when I'm
> not here anymore. . . . I want people to remember me some
> day and say, "Oh, yes! Mattie! He was a poet, a peace-
> maker, and a philosopher who played."

Oprah also talked about how Mattie loved sunrises, about how he had seen magnificent sunrises during beach vacations in North Carolina. She told him that most people wouldn't bother to wake for a sunrise because they like to *sleep* on vacation. That didn't wash for Mattie. In living fast, he wasn't rushing so much as relishing, getting as much out of every moment as he could.

He wrote her that he *"can't understand why everybody wasn't out on the pier at sunrise . . . can't figure out why people would want to miss"* such a miracle. . . .

Jeni and Mattie, Outer Banks, North Carolina, July 1992

CHAPTER 1

Sunrise on the Pier

Mattie celebrating life on Jockey's
Ridge, North Carolina, July 1999

*. . . The sky grows
Shadows, rising
With the passing of time. . . .
The sky sighs,
Ebbing with tides
Of pre-dawn nothingness,
And yet,
Seas of everything created,
Tucked into waves
The sun rises
Caressing spirits
With the passing of time
And the promise of hope
And the belief of life*

That gets better with age
As we edge into
The day that once was
Our distant tomorrow.[1]

Nell was getting more and more soaked each time the water sprinkler circled back around. She had fallen off the boardwalk into the beach grass on her way back from the ice cream shop and was now unable to get up, afraid she might have broken her leg. She also had a painful abrasion on her forehead.

Still, she was laughing to herself. While she waited for help getting to the emergency room, the sprinkler system came on automatically, and she knew the sight of her sitting there dripping wet was ridiculous—even more so because Mema, who had gone with her for ice cream, kept running off each time the *ch ch ch ch ch* of the sprinkler circled around. Mema had wanted to stay right by Nell's side while others in the group went for help but had her hair done that day and didn't want it ruined. So she would jump back with each spray, apologizing from a distance about her visit to the beauty parlor. This made Nell laugh even harder.

We were toward the end of our annual week at the beach on North Carolina's Outer Banks. Mattie and I had been coming every year since 1992, when he was two, courtesy of my dear friend Sandy Newcomb and her parents, Mema and Papa (whose real names are Sue and Henry Newcomb). They always stayed in a two-story condo right by the water—a crazy flophouse with red and purple walls and more air mattresses and foldout sofas than bedrooms—and they had us down for a week or more every July.

The summer of 2000 had been better than ever in the sense that all our *kin* were able to make it for at least a couple of days. By "kin," Mattie and I meant the family with whom you didn't necessarily share blood but

---

1 From "Night Light" in *Reflections of a Peacemaker: A Portrait Through Heartsongs*, page 29.

with whom you're related through life. These relationships were always wonderful to him, whereas blood relations could be sweet or sour.

Our "immediate kin" consisted of Sandy, who by that point had become more like a sister to me and like a favorite aunt to Mattie; Sandy's daughters, Heather and Jamie Dobbins, and her son, Chris Dobbins (all were teenagers or young adults then); and Mema and Papa. We playfully called this group the "Step'obbi'comb Fam"—combining Stepanek, Dobbins, and Newcomb into one "kinship unit."

Some "extended kin" were also a part of this beach vacation, including Mattie's best friend, Hope Wyatt; Hope's mother, Susan (Susan's husband, Ron, on a peacekeeping mission in Kosovo at the time, was the one who brought Mattie the United Nations flag); and Nell Paul and her husband Larry. Sandy had met Nell in a La Leche class when they were both expecting their first children, and through her I had become good friends with Nell, too. Mattie called us the *Three Granny'olas*.

It turned out Nell hadn't broken her leg after all. And although the gash on her forehead was a nasty one, it wasn't anything time and some pain medication wouldn't heal.

Nell had been a source of humor all week. The night we arrived, she explained that she was having health problems that made it difficult for her to stand on her feet too long. But she offered to help Sandy make a chicken tetrazzini dinner that night by calling out, without a hint of irony, that at least while sitting at the table, she could very easily "cut the cheese." When we all burst out laughing, she responded with some amount of confusion and indignity that "not being able to walk around a lot has nothing to do with my ability to cut the cheese"—which only made us roar.

Nell grew up a preacher's daughter in the South in the 1940s and 50s and simply didn't know certain idioms and other common wordplays. We had such fun teasing her all week about the T-shirts you see at the beach with suggestive double entendres and such. We entitled that vacation "The Education of Nell," playing practical jokes on her as we went. One day I looked sidelong at Mattie with a mischievous gleam and said to her, "I suppose you've never heard the phrase 'duck on the head.'" Mattie went along and called out, "Mom, I can't believe you'd even tell her that.

That's, like, rude." I then said to Nell with feigned indignation, "Never mind, we aren't going to go there."

Later in the week, Mattie and Hope staged a tattling scene wherein Hope accused Mattie of saying "duck on the head," and Mattie "defended himself" by responding that he was only telling Hope why she shouldn't say it, and I "scolded" both of them. Nell felt terrible. She had been repeating the phrase here and there in the belief we had been pulling her leg and thought it was she who got the kids going. We didn't disavow her of this notion. Then, on one of our last days there, we all tied tiny stuffed ducks to our heads and went around the side of the pool where Nell was sitting, quacking at her.

Mattie was having the time of his life. Chris would throw him into the deep end of the pool, and he'd soon be bobbing to the surface, yelling to be thrown in again. He also began interviewing all the kin for a fun book he and I were envisioning, *The Unsavable Graces*. He wrote goofy poems and went to the top of a giant sand dune called Jockey's Ridge. He went with me to Mass recited in Spanish, which we did every summer; doing so allowed us to really think about the essence of God in rituals rather than just recite prayers from rote. He and Hope, both blond, ambushed Chris, also blond, while Chris was trying to flirt with a pretty girl in an orange-pink bikini, saying, "Daddy, we're hungry, and Mommy said it's your turn to fix us lunch." Chris later married that girl, Cynthia, and Mattie was best man at their wedding.

Mattie's disability had progressed since the previous summer, but we were used to that and always found ways to accommodate his condition without letting it ratchet down the fun. For instance, when Mattie was six and seven, he could walk to the pool, do backward flips into the water, swim laps, and dive down ten feet to the bottom to grab pennies. As long as he remained attached to a tank of oxygen, he would be fine. We would rig a twenty-five-foot tube that connected the nasal cannula in his nostrils to the tank so he could swim anywhere in the pool and never be without the supplemental oxygen. When he wasn't in the water, he would drag the tank behind him on a cart, sometimes using his cannula and tubing as a jump rope and letting other kids take turns as he swung it.

When Mattie was eight, he needed a wheelchair with the oxygen on the back of it to get to the pool but could still move around pretty well once he was in the water. The summer he turned nine, he went from one oxygen tank to two, but as long as he had the extra oxygen, he didn't have the frequent feeling that he was suffocating.

This time around, Mattie was too weak to swim much—he would come up gasping—but he could still enjoy Chris throwing him into the deep end. To compensate, we bought a ten-foot blow-up alligator float that Mattie could hang on to in the water. The object was always to continue the fun no matter the challenge. There was always another solution, another fix.

Granted, this year there had been changes that were more marked than in previous summers. At night, Mattie now had to be on a BiPAP machine, short for bi-level positive airway pressure. It involves wearing a mask over your nose or mouth or, in Mattie's case, both, that helps you breathe easier when you're short of breath. Mattie also had to wear it during the day if he felt exhausted, such as right after pool time. This was in addition to the pulse oximetry and cardiorespiratory monitors to which he was connected anytime he was sitting or lying at rest since the day he was born, which would let us know if his heart or lungs weren't doing what they were supposed to. The *dysautonomic* in *dysautonomic mitochondrial myopathy* means things in the body that should happen automatically don't always. For example, when someone switches from physical activity to sitting, the heart self-regulates by beating more slowly. But Mattie's heart could overshoot the mark and start to "forget" to keep beating while he was at rest rather than simply slow a bit; the fine-tuning just wasn't there. If his heart rate fell too low, the machine triggered an alarm that would signal someone to jiggle him or provide other tactile stimulation or remind him to breathe more deeply for a minute until his heart could receive the "signal" and get its pumping back in sync with his body's needs.

Understanding this condition and how to deal with it came slowly, across the lifespans of all four of my children. The medical community didn't even have a name for it until my two eldest had died. It was simply called *dysautonomia of unknown cause*, and early on I was told that subsequent children would not be affected. Not until Mattie was two years old and my third child was months from death did doctors understand that it was a condition of faulty mitochondria—an essential component of every cell in a person's body.

I was actually diagnosed first—with the adult-onset form—then the children. Two years later, after my third child died and Mattie was only four, I was in a wheelchair. Now we were all too familiar with the condition's devastating effects.

We were used to adding supports and medical machinery to compensate for the detrimental effects of this progressive condition, and then we would keep going. But that summer, the changes weren't just in the BiPAP machinery or even in the fact that Mattie didn't have the energy to really swim. Hope, who was two years his junior, was now several inches taller than he was. Mattie's shoe size, in fact, was the same as in kindergarten—a child's 11. Growth taxed Mattie's autonomic system, and somehow his body knew that. In addition, he could not walk across the beach to the ocean. Mattie didn't need his wheelchair because he was incapable of walking; he needed it in large part because he would tire so easily.

In previous years, he had the energy to walk across the sand to the waves so he could bodysurf (always attached to his oxygen). He had to. We didn't always have a special beach wheelchair that could get traction over the sand. But this summer, after the first day of walking out to the water, he said he couldn't go back; it took too much out of him.

We did have a rented beach wheelbarrow that got me down to the waves that first day, and I told him he could hop on while someone pushed. But he said no. He was aware that he lacked the energy to handle the waves. And he knew he wasn't up to getting overheated on the hot sand; his condition also compromised his temperature stability, so that once he became too hot or too cold, his body had a hard time readjusting to normal.

Mattie didn't have the strength to climb Jockey's Ridge, either, a massive sand dune in the middle of the Outer Banks that offers stunning views of the barrier island chain from the top. Park rangers drove us up in a jeep that year. He was still his charismatic self, chatting up the rangers and people who had hiked up to fly kites. But instead of turning cartwheels at the top, as he had done the year before, he sat on a lawn chair.

We treated all of Mattie's limitations as challenges to be gotten around rather than game changers. Of course anybody could see that they were. But my aim was to help Mattie live on a day-to-day basis as though the assaults on his body could always be taken in stride, that any new weakening or new machinery were just part of life rather than shifts that called life into question. I even managed to convince myself much of the time that no symptom of illness was something a combination of medical help, ingenuity, and prayer couldn't overcome.

Mattie was ahead of me, though. Even on the first day of that vacation, he let me know. For fun, he went around asking everyone why they had come to the beach house that summer, either videotaping their responses or writing them down. It was all note-taking for the *Unsavable Graces* book. Everyone gave silly answers. Sandy said she came to learn Braille for a course she was taking and not get sick; the summer before, she had come down with an awful case of bronchitis and was laid up most of the time. Nell said she had been planning on thinking three deep thoughts but had already done that in the car so was at a loss as to what she was going to do the rest of the week. Chris said he was a plumber and had come to fix the sink, code for being on the hunt for pretty girls.

Then I turned the tables and asked Mattie what *he* was there for, figuring he'd give as ridiculous an answer as everyone else. But he just looked at me and said, "I really need to consider the meaning of life this summer, because life is changing."

Caught off guard and wanting to keep away from that subject, and not wanting to spoil the others' fun, I chided him. "Mattie, we're all clowning around, and you're being serious and philosophical." Immediately, I saw the hurt in his eyes—and have regretted to this day the words that fell out of my mouth at that moment. He was headed someplace else, even on day one.

Mattie remained ahead of me, however. After that exchange, he kept what he needed to say bottled up throughout the week, making sure his words mirrored the general festive mood. He jumped into as much physical activity as he could handle. He participated in the practical jokes.

He played board games with the rest of us. Even when he had to take breaks more frequently than he used to, he would beg off joining in some group fun as casually as possible and go to his room to read or write poetry (and then end up falling asleep, even in the middle of the day—his fatigue was that overpowering). Not that he didn't truly enjoy himself to the hilt. He did. But it wasn't until our sunrise on the pier that he spoke his heart.

Sunrise on the pier was a ritual Mattie and I engaged in, without fail, the morning of our last full day at the beach every year. It was our *thin space*. A preacher once described thin space to me as that place where your spirit and God are in closest contact. Generally, we're all aware we have a spirit, an essence, that's deep inside us. At your thin space, the veil separating your essence from your being becomes transparent enough that the spirit becomes undeniable. Instead of being a silent voice, your spirit more or less shows itself to you; you know it intimately rather than simply being aware of it.

All of the beach was thin space for Mattie and me. Where we stayed on the Outer Banks was not an arcade-laden, honky-tonk resort spot with some sand and waves that happened to be nearby. It was where, on an island jutting into the ocean, the sea met the sky and the earth; past, present, and future converged in an absence of measured time; and what we felt actually became something we could behold.

I had been coming to this stretch of beach since 1976, long before Sandy invited me to join her on family vacations. I didn't meet Sandy until 1989, but by coincidence, we had both fallen in love with the same place. After my first two children died, I even pitched a tent down on the sand near the pier to try to catch my spirit up to my life. When you lose a child, your body keeps moving, but your spirit doesn't want to come along. It drifts behind. At the beach, my spirit told me there's still more there. It allowed me to feel the essence of my children and the presence of God, which put it back in sync with my body and allowed me to go forward.

Now the beach, this pier, was the place where my spirit and Mattie's could talk to each other directly, without anything muffling what got said or what got heard, even between parent and child.

It never mattered whether it was a cloudy sunrise and the sun didn't show. An *unrise*, as we called such mornings, was just as significant.

We always came down to the pier before five A.M., at least a full hour before the sun actually rose. We had to start when the stars were still out, when it was still dark and time was taking a last look backward before moving *forthward*, as Mattie called it.

That morning, no breeze stirred as we made our way to the edge of the pier. The two of us wheeled out together across the warped wood, slowly, slowly, sounding a soft, almost rhythmic bumpedy-bump on the weathered planks, so we wouldn't be jolted out of our seats.

Mattie's ability to handle the chair on the rickety wood slats was something of a small marvel, considering his wheelchair beginnings. Fine and visual motor skills were never his strong suit, and he had to learn little by little how to navigate with the chair's joystick. When he first started using it, I took him to the first floor of a mall department store and had him circle around while I waited at the juncture of mall and store. I told him not to move out of anybody's way, to just stop where he was if someone came toward him, because he wasn't ready to back up or steer to the side.

After a few turns around the bank of escalators that stood in the middle of the floor, he said he had the hang of it and was ready to "step" aside should anyone come toward him. I said okay, with misgivings, and the next thing I knew he was wheeling gleefully from the store into the mall exclaiming, "Mom, Mom, I did it! I backed out of someone's way!" At the same time, however, alarms were going off. It turns out that in backing up, he had hooked on to a lingerie cart and had left the store with a bevy of unpaid lady's undergarments in tow.

Because the pier was so long and because we had to go so slowly, it felt like we had been rolling hours out to the middle of the ocean by the time we reached the edge. In previous years, we'd make our way to the end of the pier holding hands and laughing, but not that day. In the dark that morning, Mattie started out quiet.

We began our talk the way we always did, with Mattie asking about his sister and brothers. "Tell me about Katie," he would implore. "Tell me about Stevie, about Jamie. Tell me about how Jamie took care of me, how

I took care of him and became the big brother to him when he got sick."
Mattie used to "read" to Jamie. Mattie couldn't speak when he was a
toddler because the trach tube he had in his neck at the time limited the
use of his vocal cords. But he got around it by communicating with
American Sign Language. Jamie, for his part, couldn't see what Mattie
was signing because two years before he died, he lost meaningful use of
his vision. Yet Jamie would sit there and smile as Mattie signed for him
the illustrated stories in children's books. They had found their own thin
space between them.

These reminiscences were crucial to Mattie. When he was about
seven years old, he started crying hard, seemingly out of the blue, and
when I asked him what was wrong, he told me he was beginning to lose
his memories of Jamie. He remembered sitting in Jamie's bed and squeak-
ing his little yellow caterpillar in his brother's ear after Jamie had lost use
of his sight, Jamie smiling in response. And he remembered the two of
them sitting in each other's chairs for fun and my reading to the two
of them together, and Jamie's little white casket with the contents I put
in that he would take with him to Heaven—but not much more, and it
frightened him as well as saddened him to be losing touch with memories he held sacred.

He was saddened, too, about not having known Katie or Stevie, and
would tell me on the pier that he missed not ever getting to hear them
laugh, or to kiss or touch them. In 1993, when Stevie would have turned
six, Mattie told me he did not know whether to sing a nursery rhyme for
the baby Stevie was when he died, or to talk about fishing and other life
discoveries that would have interested the little boy Stevie would have
become by then. Mattie was three at the time.

When Mattie finished talking about his siblings, he asked me what I
wanted to be when I grew up. It was part of our pier ritual, our way of
moving by degrees from what was to what will be. And I always told him
the same thing—that I wanted to be eighty-three. He would laugh and
respond by saying that you couldn't be a number, and I'd answer, "Okay,
then, I want to be a beach chair philosopher, thinking deeply by the
ocean and sharing thought-provoking stories."

This would lead to my asking Mattie what *he* wanted to be. In years past, Mattie always talked about wanting to be a daddy—not simply a father, who wasn't necessarily close, but a daddy. He was going to have seven children and had already named them. The oldest was a namesake, Matthew Joseph Thaddeus Stepanek, Jr., who would be called Tad. Second would come Kathryn Hope, to be called Katie Hope after his sister, Katie, and his favorite word (and also his friend Hope, who he was fine with being his children's mother). Third and fourth would be Steven Blaine and Jamie, after his brothers, Stevie and Jamie. Since "Jamie" was not just his brother's name but also one of Sandy's daughter's names, she'd be a girl. Her middle name would be Margaret after his great-aunt Margaret, who died around the time he was born but had been very good to me while I was growing up. Mattie liked that he and I played Parcheesi with the same dice Margaret and I had rolled when I was a child.

Fifth came Patrick Noah ("Patch," for short), followed by Theresa Rose, or Tessie, which was going to be Mattie's name had he been a girl. Mattie planned on giving Tessie to me, and when I'd tell him his wife wasn't going to like that, he always explained that he'd make it up to her by letting her name the seventh child whatever she wanted, with the proviso that if she didn't choose a name within thirty days, the right to give a name would revert back to him, and in that case he would choose Sophie and Sadie since the youngest children would then be twin girls.

Pure fun as all this was, the idea of Mattie's fathering children wasn't totally in the realm of fantasy, and he knew that. Mitochondrial diseases like his are invariably handed down through the mother because virtually all of a person's genetic code for mitochondria comes from the egg—there's essentially none in the sperm. Thus, Mattie knew that if he made it through adolescence—and one doctor had even told him that adolescence would be a make or break point for him because the body goes through so many changes at that time—he could have children and not risk passing on his disease.

But as night shifted toward dawn that morning on the pier, Mattie didn't talk about having children. Instead, he went "off script" and said that sometimes he worried about what he would do if I died before him. He told me that if something happened to me first, he'd go into his room and stay there until he could come out and cope, that he'd end up having to shave a very long beard because that's how long it would take him to be able to move on. But he *would* move on, he said, because "you can't lie down in the ashes of another person's life." He talked about how after a time it would be okay to laugh again, to play with friends, to have fun.

Of course I nodded in agreement while he spoke, and did what a mother does in my situation—told him that I'd stay here as long as I could. While a prognosis is something of a moving target, the one I had been given left me with a vague "six months to ten years." But Mattie wasn't looking for an answer from me. He was setting me up.

"If I die first," he said, "you have to do the same thing—move on—because I could go before you, Mom."

I wanted to pull Mattie away from this line of thinking. His whole life was spent on the edge, yet we had always managed to skirt it, to find some semblance of stable footing and keep our focus on daily living. Now here he was looking over the edge, but he was just a boy; it was my responsibility to keep him looking in the other direction.

"Mattie," I joked with him, "you have at least until you're seventeen. We've had the signs." Mattie was born on the seventeenth day of the month, in the seventeenth minute of the seventeenth hour (5:17 P.M.), measuring seventeen inches and weighing 2,017 grams, and I had always used that to calm his fears—not to mention hang on to it myself as if it were a prophecy. Mattie nearly died minutes after he was born. Seventeen years of age sounded pretty good.

He wouldn't let it go, though. "Maybe I wanted to have kids," he said, "because you want to leave behind lessons, leave behind everything that matters to you. That's how you touch the world. But I have to reconsider what it's like to leave a legacy. I think my life is the opposite of what it says on your coffee mug."

On my coffee mug it said, "I may have to grow old, but I don't have to grow up." Mattie said, "I think I may have to grow up without growing old." He went on: "I think we're going to have to define differently what I'm going to be. We're going to have to define my growing up differently.

"I want to be remembered as a poet, a peacemaker, and a philosopher who played," he added after a pause. He had mentioned those things before in various contexts, and even at the pier in prior years. But that was the first time he had strung them together in a definitive way, under-lined them, so to speak.

I didn't want to hear Mattie creating an epitaph. At the same time, I had to let him talk. His mortality was facing him, and I couldn't pretend otherwise. I had already shortchanged him earlier in the week.

Now I understood why he reacted so strongly a few days earlier when Nell had to go to the emergency room. He had been really worried, cry-ing and praying for her, afraid that something was very wrong. I felt I understood at the time—Mattie's whole life was filled with loss, with visits to emergency rooms that ended with long stays in the hospital and life-altering compromises. But what I realized on the pier was that even while I was aware he was losing ground, he was sensing it in a way I wasn't able to see. As close as I could possibly be, I was an outsider look-ing in.

It wasn't as if once he brought up living a truncated life, we aban-doned all that was ritual in our visit to the pier. We still spoke, as we did every year, about choice—about how you can't choose whether you're going to have a disability, or your mother is going to be in a wheelchair, or your parents are going to be divorced, or you're going to be so without means at times that you have to stand in line for handouts at a church food pantry. Mattie lived a life in which these and so many other things happened that would never have been anyone's choice that we made it a point to list the things you *could* choose: whether to talk about someone behind his back, whether to be your best self and do your best work, whether to focus on what you do have instead of what you don't, whether to go forward despite challenges or sink into despair.

We also assessed our week as we always did, reviewing all the practi-cal jokes and shenanigans with everyone. We talked, too, about Mattie's poetry, which was so important to him.

But there was a new urgency about it, about the poetry and about the future. He said he needed to get his books of poems published. He had written several volumes of Heartsongs poetry by that point, "Heartsong" being a word he coined for himself to get at a person's essence—the longings and hopes and feelings that both describe and stir each of us. It is our charge, Mattie said, to take what we wish for in our Heartsong, package it in the best way we can, and offer it to others. In giving the gift you want most, he felt, you get it back. Mattie's package was his poetry; his Heartsong, a passion for hope and peace that grows from happiness, in a life that medicine kept dictating held no promise of hope.

Mattie also said he needed to talk to his role model, Jimmy Carter, to find out "if I'm doing peace right," and that he needed to get his message of hope and peace on *Oprah* so that it could be spread.

He had been talking about these things for a while, but previously they had seemed like the kind of yearnings all kids feed off of sometimes. Now they sounded like goals for an adult who needed to figure out how to make them happen.

"Mom," he said, "I need to live everything that matters to me quickly. I need to do everything I want without growing old. If I can get my poetry published, it'll be like I'm having children." Mattie and I had talked in previous years about a person's creating something that lasts beyond his life span—his echo, his silhouette. That day, he was addressing it more as a plan than a philosophical musing.

Then he said, "I don't think I'm ever going to be back here. March thirtieth is a dark day for me."

I felt a kind of nauseating ache start to rise. My daughter, Katie, was only twenty months old when she died, but the day before, she put away all her toys and refused to play with them. "Bye-bye," she said. "All through."

"What are you talking about, Mattie?" I said. "You've always been on machines. There are tons of things that can still be done."

"No, Mom," he answered. "I don't see next July. I don't see this pier in my future." The pier marked time for us. It was a kind of punctuation mark to our lives, a breather to go over where we were at that point and how we were going to move forward, how we were going to celebrate. It was where we planned our "what nexts."

The pit in my stomach rose higher. "You've got summer camp next year," I told him, although it was more like pleading. "You've got holidays." After a moment, I added, "Do you think you're going to die on

March thirtieth? Because we'll watch. We'll take extra care to watch you around that time." I had debated whether to say it out loud, considering that if the thought remained unspoken, I might be able to hide it, keep it from having a chance to become reality.

"I'm just saying I can't see past March thirtieth," he said. "I can't fit anything after that into a context."

"Don't you see anything at all after that day?" I asked. "Easter? Your birthday?"

"Maybe Thanksgiving at Sandy's house," he answered finally. "But I'm not sure if I'm seeing it, or just wanting it."

"Well, what do you see? Do you see people? The table? Do you see Christmas after that?"

"Mom, please let's hush. Let's just sit here. I have to memorize this."

"But, Mattie, we're videotaping this," I said. Mattie always liked to tape a minute of sunrise, shut the camera for ten minutes, then tape another minute so that everyone back at the beach house could see what they had missed.

"No, I'll remember what this looks like, what it sounds like. I have to memorize what this *feels* like," he countered. His voice had no trace of sadness or melancholy. It was more like an expression of "Wow, I'm really going to miss this," an anticipatory loss.

By now the sun was almost fully risen. It was one of the gorgeous, brilliant sunrises, not at all a gray and muted shift into the day but a ruby pink with shades of orange. Mattie commented that it looked more like a sunset than a sunrise—a gift from God, he said, because it combined his favorite color, the color of sunset, with his favorite time of day, sunrise.

I stopped trying to reassure myself, and we just sat quietly and looked out to the horizon. I put my hand on top of Mattie's and told him I loved him. We said that to each other a hundred times a day, every day, and we meant it; it wasn't just words. But it especially needed to be said then.

Everything looked as wonderful as it ever did—blue, cloudless sky; sun sparks dancing on the waves; strong, bright light. We even began to see movement in the water—dolphins. It was a common sight on the Outer Banks, but one that always delighted us. Except this time we saw water spouting up. It wasn't dolphins but whales! Water was spouting out of their blowholes—calves and their mothers. We could even hear their beautiful, haunting song.

We watched the whales as they moved farther and farther away from land and finally swam out of sight. Then we sat just a minute more before slowly turning around to roll back.

The next morning, after a last day of diving into vacation giddiness with the others, we loaded our things into the van and headed for home. It was Mattie's tenth birthday.

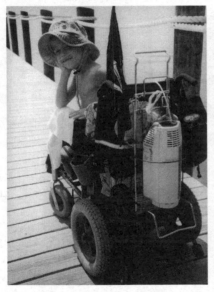

Mattie headed out to watch the sunset, Outer Banks, North Carolina, July 1998

Mattie taking in the sunrise, Outer Banks, North Carolina, July 1999

CHAPTER 2

Morning Coffee

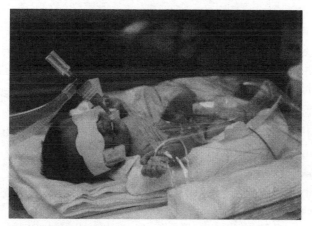

Mattie, July 17, 1990

> *The cold melon skies of morning*
> *Slowly streak through milky clouds*
> *As the orange juice sun rises*
> *Behind coffee and burnt toast branches.*
> *I would like to stop and share*
> *Magic-star cereal with*
> *The few winter birds,*
> *But the hands on the clock*
> *Keep pointing to the day saying,*
> *"Hurry up, or you'll miss the bus!"*[1]

Mattie topped off my coffee, then poured a cup for himself. We had already showered and had a look at the *Washington Post*. After chat-

---

1 From "Morning Crunch" in *Reflections of a Peacemaker: A Portrait Through Heartsongs*, page 7.

ting about items in the paper, discussing the day prior and making plans for the day ahead, homeschooling would start at seven.

Mattie had been drinking coffee since he was in second grade. It wasn't something I'd planned. One morning during the winter when Mattie was seven, it was bitterly cold, and although I turned up the heat the minute I started the van for us to be on our way, his teeth continued to chatter even after we were a couple of miles down the road. His lips turned blue.

It was his temperature instability getting the best of him again. Sometimes when Mattie felt cold, he could warm up, but sometimes he couldn't. The colder he became, the slower his heart would beat.

"Drink your hot chocolate," I said to him.

"I'll warm up," he said. But he didn't.

Again I told him to take of sip of his cocoa, at which point he answered, "I forgot it."

"Why didn't you tell me?" I asked.

"Because it was my responsibility to remember it," he answered.

Every morning, Mattie had certain responsibilities in getting ready for the day. He had to get himself washed and pack his homework. He had to make sure he took his inhalers and nebulizers for his asthma, his syringes with liquid medicines, and the prescription pills placed for him on the kitchen counter and put them in the fanny pack attached to his portable oxygen tanks. He had to fill those tanks from the huge liquid tanks lined up against the wall and make sure they were working properly—if a valve froze, oxygen wouldn't get through. He needed to pack a spare nasal cannula (the plastic piece that fed oxygen into his nose) in case the one he was using split. And if he was going with me for the hour drive to the university rather than to school, as he was that day because school was closed, he had to remember to take his travel mug filled either with hot chocolate or herbal tea. I always left it on a little table by the door.

I believed that Mattie needed to balance his privileges with responsibilities and also needed to be able to take care of himself. If he was in school, I wasn't going to be there to check on his medical apparatus, and given my diagnosis, it wasn't clear how long I'd be there to take care of his needs at all.

I was proud that Mattie wanted to own the responsibility, but now he had taken the message too far, and I felt terrible—terrible because it was *my* responsibility each morning to make sure he actually had everything he needed once he told me he was ready; terrible because it was enough of an ordeal for Mattie to get out of our tiny basement apartment every morning dragging two tanks of oxygen behind him while I dragged two additional ones for him from my wheelchair; terrible because I didn't have an extra two dollars to run into a convenience store and buy him another hot chocolate; terrible because the only hot drink I could offer him right then and there—my coffee—wasn't sweetened, and I thought it would taste vile to him.

I told him to take a few sips, warning him that I only used cream and no sugar so he might not like the taste, but it would help him warm up.

He took one sip, then another, then said, "This is the best stuff I've ever had in my life."

"I already had a couple of cups of coffee before we left this morning," I told him. "Have it all." I figured he loved it that day because he was so cold but also because it was cool to be drinking coffee, and that would be the end of it.

A few days later, on Saturday morning, he climbed into bed with me for a snuggle, as he did every weekend. We'd turn on the TV, watch cartoons, and read the newspaper.

This particular Saturday, a few days after that cold morning, I was about to get into my wheelchair to refill my coffee cup when Mattie jumped up and said, "I'll get it! Let me bring you coffee in bed. I know just how you like it!"

After he brought it to me, he said there was a teeny bit left in the pot and wanted to know if he could have the rest. I asked to see the pot. There was enough for half a cup, and I always made the coffee weak to save money, so I said okay.

The following Saturday, he asked again for a cup of coffee, at which point I had a chat with his doctor. The doctor said that not only would a cup a day be fine but also that it could help with Mattie's breathing because caffeine can be useful for children with respiratory difficulties or asthma. Mattie drank morning coffee from then on, even becoming a Starbucks lover eventually.

The story of Mattie and morning coffee actually reaches further back than that, though. He and I had really started sharing this morning ritual not when he was seven, but on the day I realized I was pregnant with him.

I had never been a coffee drinker before I started having children. My typical day never began with caffeine but with a two-mile run and aerobic exercises. In the spring of 1985, however, a year after I had married and shortly before I turned twenty-six, I suddenly starting craving it. A week later I found out I was pregnant with my first child, Katie, and I quickly stopped drinking coffee because of warnings in the news that caffeine wasn't good for the baby.

The same thing happened with my second pregnancy, and my third—a week before realizing I should get a pregnancy test, I began craving coffee, then went off caffeine as soon as the pregnancy was confirmed.

After my third child, Jamie, was born with the same unusual condition that took my first two, I decided I wasn't having any more biological children. Medical professionals still did not have a name for what was causing my children's demise, but it had become clear that it was not a one-time anomaly or a recessive trait, explanations that had been previously suggested.

I took many precautions not to become pregnant again. So when I craved a cup of coffee upon waking up the morning of Christmas Eve 1989, I almost started crying.

I went that day to a Catholic agency for a pregnancy test, and the attendants soon came out with the plus sign, calling out, "Congratulations!" I burst into tears. I knew that short of a miracle, I was going to bring another child into the world to suffer and die. It was devastating to have that wonderful feeling that I was carrying a baby, yet having to wonder whether I was doing this *to* another child or giving another child a chance for life.

I called my parish priest and asked to meet with him, wanting to know whether it would be worse to deliver this child or abort. The priest looked at me and said, "This baby has already been conceived—you've already given it life. That's no longer a choice. It's a gift from God." It was at that moment I decided if the baby was a boy, I'd name him Matthew, which means "gift of God." He was not an accident—he was a spirit that was meant to be.

When my pregnancy started showing, people at my church said, "I'm so sorry." My obstetrician and several of Jamie's doctors asked me when I was aborting. People looked at me as if I were a monster for conceiving again. It was one of the loneliest periods of my life. Only Sandy said to me, "Congratulations, another baby to love!"

The whole experience of feeling a baby grow and move inside of you is one of the greatest joys a mother has. There is nothing better than feeling a baby touch you from inside. Yet every time I felt Mattie, I knew that without some unforeseen medical advancement, he was going to be born to die all too soon. It filled my heart and broke it at the same time. I was crumbling with dread.

Then, on the morning of July 17, 1990, I had excruciating labor pains like I had never experienced. I was thirty-six weeks pregnant, as I had been with each of my pregnancies when I went into labor, so I knew that was not a good sign.

By lunchtime, I had not dilated at all. I did not dilate during any of my labors. I didn't know it at the time, but it was a sign that I had the same disease as my children. Dilating in labor is an autonomic response, and it never happened for me.

A couple of hours later, the doctor told me I had to deliver that day because the baby's vital signs were fluctuating. I said no, that three years ago to the day, my eldest child, my daughter Katie, had died, and that I could not deliver another on her death anniversary. It would be mixing up first breath and no breath.

By five in the evening, the doctor said if she didn't perform a Caesarean section right then, I could die and my baby could die because neither of our blood pressure readings or heart rates were where they should have been. She reminded me that I had another baby at home to raise—Jamie was still alive and running around like a typical toddler at that time, albeit on life support. So I consented to not waiting till midnight.

As soon as they pulled the baby out, I was right back where I had been with Katie—not hearing that first cry. "Make her cry," I kept screaming as soon as she was born. "Make her cry, MAKE HER CRY!"

Within ten minutes, they had whisked Katie, gray and not breathing well, out of the room and up to the Neonatal Intensive Care Unit. Within twenty minutes, she was on a ventilator, and the doctors didn't know why my five-pound infant was acting like a one-pound preemie. After forty-five minutes, they told me they had to send her to a tertiary care hospital because the hospital where I delivered her wasn't equipped to meet her critical needs. They let me reach my hand into the incubator and touch her once before they took her away. It was the first time I saw her, and it was hard to find the baby under all the tubes.

She was gorgeous—tons of dark hair with little bits of blond around her forehead, which they soon shaved to start IVs and insert needles in her head because babies don't have good veins in their arms. But she was also covered in blue and white ventilator tubing, gray wires coming from everywhere and tape all over her face just to hold everything together.

It was my sudden immersion into the next twenty years of my life. I had gone into the hospital expecting a typical, healthy baby but instead spent fourteen of the next twenty months raising my child in the ICU. Katie eventually was fitted with a tracheostomy tube connected to a ventilator because she couldn't breathe on her own. Then, after barely growing but learning to walk and talk and dance and generally delight everyone around her, she died one day when her kidneys and bladder stopped functioning as a result of a dysautonomic episode.

I was in my seventh month at the time with my second child, Stevie, who was "going to be fine," because Katie was an undiagnosed "fluke of nature," as the doctors put it, assuring me it wouldn't happen again.

Also born a month prematurely, Stevie *seemed* fine at first, weighing six pounds. He was taken to the ICU just as a precaution because of what happened with Katie. It was there they detected that Stevie was hypoglycemic and having pauses in his breathing. By the time he was three or four days old, his heart rate had fallen into the 40s—it should have been above 100—and by the time he was three months, he, too, was breathing with a ventilator through a trach. By then he weighed three pounds instead of six, deteriorating far more rapidly than Katie. Still, he was a beautiful baby, with auburn hair and bright blue eyes—a different beauty from Katie's, whose hair eventually turned blond all around and whose eyes had been a gentler blue, with flecks of gray. Stevie would smile a huge lopsided grin for me.

When he turned six months, I threw him a half-year birthday party. I needed to celebrate *something*, and some friends humored me. There was a cake shaped like a bear, and balloons filled the apartment. Two days later, twenty minutes after I videotaped him playing with leftover balloons—Stevie died, too. One of his oxygen tanks had malfunctioned due to a frozen valve, and the oxygen couldn't get through.

After I lost Stevie, I went through not just emotional counseling but also genetic counseling. They couldn't find anything wrong with my cells or with those of the children's father. At the time, I was very athletic and active. "We can't explain it," they said, "but it's a recessive gene, so with each pregnancy, you have only a one-in-four chance of giving birth to a child with the condition. You've already had two children like this, so the odds are stacked in a third child's favor." We were all optimistic that things would be okay the next time around.

Four months after Stevie died, craving coffee for the third time in my life, I took a third pregnancy test that came back positive. I gave birth to Jamie in February 1989, once again at thirty-six weeks. At one minute after birth, I had a "bouncing baby boy." At five minutes, I had a floppy newborn, and at twenty minutes, I had someone telling me, "We've put a little tube in to help him breathe." That's the gentle way you put it to a parent who has never been through this. I knew what I was in for.

The doctors suggested inserting a tracheostomy tube early on, rather than waiting until Jamie couldn't breathe on his own. He had one put in at four weeks, and by the time he was a year old, this boy with curly blond hair and hazel eyes, like mine, was growing at a fairly normal rate, knew his ABCs, and was singing and dancing. With him, this gentle joy

I nicknamed Moose, I had learned to act preventively rather than wait for a dysautonomic storm.

Still, my decision not to have any more biological children was firm—Jamie could not breathe without life support, and the doctors could not explain what was happening to my children. Then, shortly before Jamie's first birthday, I craved coffee for a fourth time. It was Christmas Eve 1989. With this pregnancy, the doctor told me that a cup of coffee a day wouldn't hurt the baby, so Mattie and I shared a morning cup from the beginning.

Mattie's gestation went like all the others, with the sonograms always showing the baby growing and gaining weight at the right pace. When my children were inside me, my body took care of them. But the moment Mattie was born, just four and a half years after Katie's birth, I found myself right back in the exact same place.

"Make him cry."

"We're doing our best."

"MAKE HIM CRY! Pinch his feet. Smack him on the butt."

"We're doing our best. You need to stay calm."

With the first three, the doctors and nurses in the room said they'd do everything they could to see the baby through to a healthy place. With Mattie, they said, "I'm sorry. Do you want him baptized before he dies?" They did not expect him to make it through the night. His hands and feet had already turned dark from not being able to oxygenate.

I insisted that before they close me up, they tie my tubes to prevent another pregnancy.

A month later, Mattie had stabilized enough to be home—as long as he was on oxygen and connected to monitors—when his heart stopped. I had just begun to drive with him to church when the alarm for low heart rate sounded. I jiggled him for stimulation, but the alarm would not stop. It was a bright August day, and I lifted my sunglasses to see that he was the same color as his blue infant car seat.

Grabbing Mattie and his equipment, I ran back to the front porch of the house, where Jamie was in a swing being tended by a nurse. Jamie was attached to one hundred pounds of medical equipment, so the nurse had to run into the house without him to call 911. In the meantime, I grabbed the cannula from Mattie's nose and put it into my mouth. I was going to perform CPR and wanted to give him as much oxygen as possible but was thinking, how much air do you breathe into a four-pound infant? At the same time, I had to begin compressions, not knowing how much pressure to apply to a tiny baby. I pressed two fingers to his chest and began.

His tongue was ice cold and slimy and getting in the way of air, so as I breathed into him, I used my own tongue to hold his down. Each time I gave him a breath or compressed his chest, the lights on the monitor came on as they should, and each time I paused, they went off. Mattie was completely gray.

After several minutes I could hear the sirens. The paramedics ran onto the porch. I stepped back and said, "Please, Mattie, please," at which point his back arched and his heart started again on its own. Still, the paramedics told me it didn't look good. Mattie's pupils were dilated and fixed—a sign that significant brain damage probably occurred while his heart stopped beating and that he might even be brain dead.

An hour later, when we arrived at the hospital, Mattie was making gurgling noises, looking around, and acting hungry. He wanted a bottle! The doctors said there was no way his heart had stopped because he wouldn't be so alert and responsive, yet the recording device in his monitor showed that the cardiac arrest lasted a full five and a half minutes.

I was told that the brain can swell after such an event, so the doctors wanted to assess his condition further. They said they could put a trach in him but didn't advise it because there was going to be brain damage. "He will probably never walk, talk, or think like a normal child," they told me. "You should consider putting him in an institution and not bonding with him." Not doing everything possible for Mattie, with whom I bonded the day I learned I was pregnant, was never even a consideration for me. His first trach was put in days later.

I spent the next couple of years in a logistical nightmare in addition to the emotional one, juggling long stays in the ICU with either Jamie, Mattie, or both. In November 1990, Jamie went into septic shock and suffered significant brain damage after a cardiac arrest, when the tube entering his heart for blood transfusions and IV medications became infected. Mattie, in the meantime, had repeated episodes of respiratory distress and infections. I felt exhausted and overwhelmed. A few months before Mattie turned two, I mentioned my fatigue to one of Mattie's doctors, thinking I had mono or Lyme disease, or was just exhausted from the stress. The doctor saw that my eyelids were drooping, a common sign of neuromuscular disease, and suggested I go for testing of my own.

I did and was soon told that there was "good news and bad news."

The "good news" was that there was now a medical explanation for why all my children were born so sick. Ninety-four percent of an essential component was missing from my mitochondria, and I handed the defect on to my children—except that their situation was worse. I developed the adult-onset form of dysautonomic mitochondrial myopathy, but the deficiency progressed further for the next generation. They were missing even more of that essential component, which is why they came into the world so unwell.

The "bad news," as it was put to me, was that "all your children are going to die. If one child is born with a mild form of this, all their siblings are, too. They generally survive without ever even having to go on life support," the doctors explained. "But if one child dies, all the siblings do. It is called 'fatal form, infant onset.'" Despite the new information, the condition remained (and still remains) poorly understood, with bizarre symptoms, and our exact genetic mutation is so rare that I and my four children are the only ones in the world who have been identified with it.

Jamie was already in organ failure as a result of the septic shock. With this new information, I made the decision that when he went into another crisis, we would no longer intervene with "heroic measures" to prolong his life.

On the other hand, Mattie, nearly two, was doing well, and I thought maybe the doctors had made a mistake about how the disease would fatally affect every sibling. He was already going hours each day without the ventilator. A week later, tests showed that it was even safe for him to begin sleeping without the ventilator at night. Soon after, with his doctors on board, I decided to have his trach removed. The trach and ventilator had seen Mattie through his unstable infancy, but the equipment could also *cause* life-threatening problems. And if he started to fare more poorly later on, there'd be something to give back to him to help him breathe better.

By this time, Mattie had shown signs of accelerated emotional and intellectual development. When he was thirteen months old, he had gone over to a little girl who was crying because her ball rolled away, given her back her ball, patted her on the head, and gave her a kiss— unprompted empathy from a baby. As he turned three, he was already reading, having unintentionally acquired "phonics" during speech therapy sessions with flash cards after the removal of his trach. By the time he was four, he was composing and writing down his own poetry.

That same year, a children's videotape finished on the TV one morning, and footage of the Oklahoma City bombing suddenly appeared on the news before I could shut off the set. I explained to Mattie that someone made a bad choice and we had to pray for the victims, but he told me no, we had to pray for the people who did this because they were the ones who had lost God. Mattie wasn't just reading and writing at such a young age; he was developing his philosophy of peace, although neither of us would have been able to articulate that then.

The doctors had clearly been right about something in giving their prognosis after Mattie survived a long cardiac arrest as a newborn. He would never think like a normal child.

I wanted him to go to our local public school even though he was so bright, and even though his health was so compromised. I felt it was imperative that he have the opportunity to socialize with other children his age. But it never really worked out quite the way I had hoped. One reason is that he had skipped a couple of grades, so that by the time he was eight, he was significantly younger than his classmates. And, due to his health, Mattie rarely was able to enjoy outdoor recess with the other children. Furthermore, school rules prevented other children from staying indoors with him. Mattie was also in the position of being everybody's pal and nobody's friend. While he was popular, he was rarely invited to play or hang out at a classmate's house after school. One mother even *uninvited* him to her child's birthday party an hour before the event because she decided it would be too difficult to look after his medical needs, even though I promised to sit right outside in the van. (I couldn't go in because the home wasn't wheelchair accessible).

Between the lack of social interaction with peers and his deteriorating health, Mattie's daily trips to school were becoming more and more untenable. His last day of public school was during the fall of 1999, when he was nine. There was to be a field trip to a science center, and he was so excited because he didn't always get to go on school outings. Either I wouldn't have the two- or three-dollar fee, or he couldn't walk the same distance as everyone else upon arriving at his destination.

By that point, however, he had already gotten his wheelchair, and I was able to put aside the money. But when we arrived at the school, we were told that he was going to have to go alone on a special bus rented for him rather than with the rest of the children, even though the bus that was outfitted for someone like Mattie had seats for plenty of other children. After much wrangling, a few of his classmates were allowed to go with him, but it was a miserable victory.

That night, I told Mattie I wanted to chat about the idea of homeschooling. He was thrilled. As much as he was an extrovert and loved being around people at school, he wasn't getting to be around them in a way that let him truly grow close to anyone. He was tired, too. His condition by that point was getting the better of him, and travel back and forth every day took a lot out of him.

In September 2000, a month and a half after that portentous conversation on the pier, we started homeschooling on the first day of the new school year, right after Labor Day. It was not only Mattie's first day of a full year of homeschooling, it was also his first year of high school. Once I took him out of school the year before, he flew through the middle school curriculum and was now more than ready for the rigors of high school courses.

Also new that September, besides the advanced coursework, was our apartment. It was in a basement, like our previous one, and this time it had no windows, but it was painted white and had a brighter feel than the other. In addition, while Mattie loved the family from whom we had rented the previous apartment, two brothers who lived upstairs in the main part of our new space were also being homeschooled, as was Mattie's friend Hope, who lived just up the road, so he had some nearby company.

Sandy's children also provided company. They took Mattie to community events like arts programs, or they'd watch him sometimes when I went to an evening class and he didn't want to come along. At that time, I was edging slowly toward a Ph.D. in early childhood special education at the University of Maryland. Mattie also enjoyed going to Mass every Wednesday to serve as Minister of the Word, reading from both the Old and New Testaments.

After Wednesday Mass, we'd always go over to Lorraine and Don Retzlaff's house—Aunt Lorraine and Uncle Don to Mattie. These two incredible friends would do everything from tending to our laundry to changing the oil in our van. They'd feed us well, too, giving Mattie a really good breakfast—pancakes with crisp bacon, French toast, always something special. And they linked us up with food handouts at our church, which allowed us to move beyond items that might be provided through less personal community sources, where people often donate items after cleaning out their kitchen cabinets—a jar of black olives, a box of stuffing mix, or cans of garbanzo beans.

The reason we depended on others' generosity was that after leaving my marriage, I lost my job when the advocacy organization I worked for closed. With the progressive decline in both Mattie's and my health, finding another job that fit with our logistical needs became a challenge. As a result, my income was limited to the small stipend I received from the university where I was pursuing my doctoral degree, and supplemented by the kindness and generosity of many friends.

The Retzlaffs were among a number of people who stepped in when they realized our financial difficulties. Their support began during Christmas season 1997, one of our most difficult years. I had paid three dollars for a nearly needleless tree that Mattie and I stuck up in a corner and decorated with ornaments. The problem was, it smelled of urine because a dog had relieved himself on it in the tree lot, and I had to hang three Christmas tree–shaped air fresheners along with the ornaments to try to neutralize the odor. Don happened to stop by during that time—which is when he started asking questions like "What are you going to have for Christmas?" and "Why don't you come over for dinner Sunday after church?" Every Christmas after that, he'd tell Mattie to find the biggest branch he could find on any evergreen on his property and Don would cut it off for us. Put up in a corner and decorated, a huge branch looked quite like a tree and gave us that part of Christmas tradition we had been missing.

Besides helping to take care of us materially, Don spent time with Mattie, which meant so much. He even taught him to drive a golf cart. "Go to the right, Mattie, go to the RIGHT!" he shouted on their first golf cart foray, as they were about to run into a bunch of lilac bushes filled with bees. But Mattie didn't. He grabbed his oxygen tank and somersaulted out of the cart, yelling, "Every man for himself!" as Don rolled, driverless, into the bushes.

Our Wednesdays with the Retzlaffs were wonderful breaks in our routine. But even on those days, we would start the morning the way we always did—with coffee and conversation, both about the day before and the day just starting. All people need a way to assess where they have been and think about what's ahead. But it was especially critical for Mattie and me to try to ground ourselves in a daily plan, because while every family's plan veers off course sometimes, for us it was more probable. Chest pains, spells during which Mattie couldn't think clearly, other complications—life threw us surprises every single day.

There was no plan to have three children born to die and another now getting worse even while relying on the best medical technology had to offer. There was no plan for me to one day find out I had the same condition as my children, which would only make it more difficult to raise the one I had left, to say nothing of the guilt engendered by the knowledge of my genetic contribution. There was no plan to care for a child who was lonely by virtue not only of his medical needs but also his almost unfathomable intellect, no plan for him to end up in a wheelchair, grow weaker, need ever more oxygen and medication, recognize at the age of ten the fragility of his own life span. You cannot plan a life that's fading even as you're considering it.

Which is exactly why it was imperative that every morning we'd make a daily schedule—no matter what. In a life where you can't truly plan or count on anything, you have to have some skeletal framework to anchor yourself, gird yourself as best as possible against the inevitability of being pushed off your footing.

We'd start, over our coffee, with whether there was anything left over from the day before that required tending, like homework that still needed going over or a feeling about something that happened that needed to be aired. Then we'd talk about such things as keeping medical appointments and checking Mattie's equipment and supplies. Fun and celebrating life always made the roster, too. I insisted on consciously inserting fun into the day because in a life as medically complicated and academically rigorous as Mattie's, it would have been all too easy to let fun slip by the wayside.

Fun could take the form of watching a movie, or seeing friends, or even adding to what we called our "Dweeb Tape." Once a month we'd put on costumes, make up goofy stories and songs, and record ourselves acting like clowns. The tape also had another role. One of us was going to go first, and the other was going to want to look back at our celebration of life together.

Once the morning coffee chat was done—it took only about fifteen to twenty minutes somewhere between six and seven A.M.—we'd put away the breakfast dishes and say a prayer to know God through the day, to feel His presence no matter what was going on, whether it was hopes being realized or our fears come to pass. Fears we called *hesitations*, a euphemism I came up with for things we dreaded. These included everything medical (medical emergencies were always Mattie's number one dread because he knew from his siblings that they could go hand in hand with sudden death); bad feelings about potential court dates because of experiences during previous proceedings that made me Mattie's sole guardian; and looming fears on Mattie's part that something would happen to me.

Finally, we'd say the Pledge of Allegiance and get to work—except on

Wednesdays, when we left for church and Mattie took his work with him to do at the Retzlaffs. In certain ways, the overall picture of our new life at home was absolutely wonderful. It allowed Mattie to pursue his academic interests with a fervor he wasn't able to let loose in the public school system. He could study poets like Maya Angelou, William Blake, Langston Hughes, and William Shakespeare and then try to emulate their style of writing as he shaped his own maturing style. Then, too, homeschooling gave our days more flexibility. I could take Mattie to the university campus more easily, where he enjoyed auditing many of the classes I was taking. And I could get him together with Hope and other homeschooled friends so that he had far more opportunities for social interactions than in public school.

Even with the flexibility, though, and a new learning protocol at home that protected him from feeling "apart" at school, Mattie's adjustment to this new kind of life had its difficulties. One thing he particularly missed was the annual Write-A-Book Festival, a countywide contest for which you had to be in public school to enter. Now he no longer had a formal outlet for sharing his work and for reminding himself, "One day I'm going to be an author."

Mattie felt something else slipping away as well. He was beginning to feel a sense of loneliness that comes with a worsening disability. Now a preteen rather than a very young child, he was losing the endearing qualities of being a little boy with a physical challenge, and that left him feeling more isolated. He was also even more aware by this point of the extent of his fragility and how much hung in the balance. He couldn't miss it; his condition wouldn't let him.

For example, the Retzlaffs had a huge tree in their backyard, and Don would sometimes push Mattie on a swing he had attached to it. But that fall, as Don was pushing him one day, Mattie turned gray when the swing came forward from high up. Lorraine and I were watching from the kitchen window. His blood pressure bottomed out and he slumped, face-first, into the dirt. I thought he had died and I started crawling with panic out the back door, trying to get to him, because the wheelchair ramp extended from the other side of the house.

"What happened?" I asked him when he came to.

"I don't know," he said. "I felt dizzy, and everything just disappeared."

The medical situation was also declining in another way. The alarm on Mattie's cardiorespiratory monitor started going off more frequently during the night, even though he was on a BiPAP machine at bedtime that should have helped him breathe better. Sometimes there'd be a leak in the seal of suction connecting the machine to his face, depending on the position he was lying in, so I'd have to reposition the mask. If the alarm kept going off every few minutes, I'd go in and sleep on the floor next to his bed so I could reach up my hand when necessary. Getting into that position took some doing. I'd have to roll down onto the floor and crawl to his bed so I could fit myself into a space too narrow for my wheelchair and then lay down for the night. Up until the time Mattie was six, I could crawl fairly well. By the time he turned eight, it was getting more difficult, and by this time, when he was ten, the crawl was like a boot camp training maneuver. While I was in better shape than Mattie autonomically at the time—meaning that my body functions like heart-beat and breathing were closer to normal—I was losing the use of my muscles faster, the condition hit us in different ways. Mattie was strong enough to help me get back in my chair in the morning. He'd be my "turtle," getting on his hands and knees underneath me then pushing me up into the chair from my bottom while I lunged forward.

By the time I was sleeping on the floor in Mattie's room on a some-what frequent basis, it was mid-October. We had been having coffee together in our new basement apartment every morning for more than a month by then. The leaves were starting to turn. The air had changed. People began leaving pumpkins on their front porches and doorsteps.

We had been so absorbed in our new routine that we were somewhat taken by surprise—the season had moved forward, and the anniversary of Mattie's grief was upon us.

Mattie with "Uncle Don" Retzlaff, spring 1999

Mattie with his best friend, Hope Wyatt, at the Pumpkin Patch, fall 1999

Mattie and Jeni working on homeschool work, September 2001

CHAPTER 3

Pumpkin Season

Mattie visiting his brothers' and sister's grave, Halloween 1997

Matties like to touch
Pumpkins and toys.
So, Matties touch them. . . .
But Matties can't touch
Jamies anymore,
Even if they want to.
So Matties touch their tears instead.[1]

" I see Mamie?"
    "No, not right now," I told Mattie. "Mamie is resting."
It was November 1992. Mattie hadn't had his trach out all that

---

1 From "Touch of Love" in *Loving Through Heartsongs*, page 16.

long—he was just two—and hadn't learned yet how to pronounce the letter *j*, so Jamie was "Mamie."

Every morning, the first thing Mattie did when he came down from the attic was to go see his brother, Jamie, in his room and talk to him. We had a tiny, two-bedroom house, and each bedroom was too small to fit both boys with all their medical equipment, which is why Mattie had a space carved out for him upstairs.

But that morning, when he came down to greet Jamie, Jamie's door was closed. Jamie had died during the night, and I wanted Mattie to go to preschool, as usual, so I could plan the logistics of the wake and funeral. I didn't want him to know yet.

I dressed each of my children for their funerals. When Katie died, the funeral home gave me a lovely room with gentle lights, her head on a flowered pillowcase, to get her ready. But when I lost Stevie, there was no space available in the funeral home to prepare him, and they put me out in the garage, next to a hearse, with Stevie on plywood held up by two sawhorses and a naked lightbulb swinging overhead.

I wasn't going to take that chance with Jamie; I decided to have his wake in the house. Three going on four, he'd be lying in his bed when people came to see him, the same way they had seen him lying there in the two years since his brain damage from septic shock.

When Mattie came home from preschool, I told him that Jamie's muscles and bones didn't work anymore but that his spirit was going to live with God. I explained that Heaven is all around us, any place there is something good, and that since Jamie is good, we'd always be able to feel his spirit nearby even though we couldn't see him or touch him. A person's spirit, I said, is what makes him special inside; it is a gift from God.

Mattie wanted to climb into bed with Jamie, but I didn't want my living child in bed with my deceased child. I explained that Jamie's spirit wasn't in his body anymore and pulled a chair up to the bed so Mattie could at least get next to Jamie. I told him he could put his yellow caterpillar to Jamie's ear as he liked to do, and sing or talk to him. But at that point Mattie became alarmed because Jamie's ventilator and monitors were disconnected. Mattie was attached to some of the very same equipment.

"Mamie's vent, Mamie's vent!" he cried out.

"Jamie doesn't need a ventilator anymore," I told him. "That was just for his muscles and bones. His spirit is fine without it."

That evening, one hundred or more people came to pay respects. There was food; there were Sandy and her three children, ages ten through sixteen at the time, who came to play with Mattie, to keep him company; and there was Jamie in his bed as usual. Yes, we had the windows open and the air conditioner running even though it was November so that Jamie's body wouldn't decay. But otherwise, it seemed like a party to Mattie, with everything as it should be. He didn't yet understand that with death, something changes.

The morning after, we went to put Jamie's body into a little white casket on the floor. Mattie was being entertained by Sandy's children in the living room, which was just outside Jamie's room. I hadn't shut the door but had pushed it closed almost all the way. Mattie was going to have to see the casket at the funeral, but I didn't want him to see his brother inside it. As a curious two-year-old, though, Mattie came and peeked his head around the corner just as Jamie was being lowered into the box.

I saw his eyes widen with concern. "Look," I said, trying to show that Jamie was comfortable. "He's got Mr. Bear, Little Blue Bunny, his moose hat, a picture of you with him."

I could tell how distressed Mattie felt. First I had disconnected Jamie's machines, and now we were putting him into a box on the floor. So I repeated to Mattie that this was where Jamie's muscles and bones were, but not his spirit. "It's sad," I told Mattie. "We're going to miss him because we're not going to see his body anymore. But his spirit is with God in Heaven. Look, he has a Jesus Cross," Mattie's phrase at that point for a crucifix.

I said all of this in as positive a manner as I could muster. It was what needed to be emphasized—that Jamie's spirit was free. It was horrible for me as a mother to know that at that point, death was the best thing for Jamie's spirit. I wanted him back. But I took comfort in his soul's passage to Heaven myself and didn't want Mattie to be afraid.

I told Mattie to go back into the living room. "Mommy will be right out."

We soon brought Jamie's little casket to the van—I had decided against a hearse—and took him to the church. I told Mattie there was going to be a celebration—Mass literally means "celebration." But Mattie had seen the "party" the night before and was now expecting a celebration in the vernacular sense, so he kept thinking that Jamie was going to jump out of the box and yell, "Surprise, I'm back!"

After the service, I was holding Mattie's hand, and just as the casket was being carried out of the church, he knocked on it. "Come out, Mamie. Say, 'Boo! All through!'" He wanted everything to return to normal.

Sandy took Mattie back to the house while the rest of us went to the cemetery for the burial. When I arrived home, he came running out the door. "Mamie?"

"No, Mattie. We buried Jamie's muscles and bones, but now we have his spirit to feel."

Just then I noticed a rotting pumpkin on the front porch. Halloween had occurred exactly a week earlier, and each year I had a little Jamie pumpkin and a little Mattie pumpkin. The Mattie pumpkin, which I decorated to look like him, had already rotted through and had been thrown out. But the Jamie pumpkin lasted a bit longer and was still there. It had a little Jamie trach with colorful shoelaces holding the vent tubing in place, just as I used to secure my children's vent tubing. By this point the pumpkin was listing and oozing, and I absentmindedly picked it up and threw it out.

On Monday, I sent Mattie back to school so he could return to his normal activities, and I also met with a school psychologist to ask how to handle Mattie's reactions to Jamie's death. I wanted Mattie to be able to get through this with as little emotional trauma as possible. I explained to the psychologist that the two brothers had been very close, particularly because they spent a lot of time at home together due to their health conditions.

The psychologist told me not to mention Jamie's name anymore, to rearrange his bedroom, put away all his toys and pictures, and, if Mattie mentioned him, to just say "Uh-huh" and move on. "Mattie will forget and grow up without the memory," he said.

I thought it was the worst advice I could have been given. Before having children, I had already been studying in a Ph.D. program, learning how to tend to people's emotional needs, so I knew something about grief and how to deal with children from an academic point of view. But I went home and did exactly as he recommended because it was coming from a professional with "emotional distance."

I couldn't actually rearrange Jamie's room because it was so tiny. But I put his pillow where his feet went and arranged the sheets from the other end of the bed. I also put all of his toys in the closet and packed away his clothes. I did keep a picture out but put it on a high shelf with photos of Katie and Stevie so Mattie wouldn't be able to see it. And I never mentioned Jamie's name. When Mattie brought him up, I'd say, "Mm-hmm, I remember. So what did you do at school today?"

This went on for two months, from November until the middle of January. In the meantime, I was suffering my own numb grief. After Katie's death, I cried incessantly. I went to her grave every day and sat there from the moment the Gate of Heaven Cemetery opened in the morning until the moment the gates closed in the evening. I talked to her, sang to her, read to her.

When Stevie died, even more suddenly than Katie while he was watching *Sesame Street* one afternoon, I couldn't cry. I was too numb with pain. I rocked myself, didn't talk to anybody, didn't do anything I didn't have to do. For weeks I was as close to a catatonic state as you could be without actually being catatonic. Each day I'd go to the cemetery and read and sing; I'd bring toys; I'd cut the grass around the family grave marker by hand. I was, in effect, trying to be a mother to dead children at their gravesites. It took time for me to be able to touch the world again.

Jamie's death I anticipated from the time he lost much of his brain function two years earlier, but I still made what one might call "the sound." It's not a cry or a wail or a moan that a mother makes when her child dies. It's a kind of noise, which for the third time came out of me.

For the next two months, I walked around numb once again—not the same numbness as with Stevie but, rather, as part of a surreal feeling, as if I were in a bubble while taking care of an active but medically compromised two-year-old.

I was pulled out of it in the middle of January, when I was getting reports from Mattie's school that my delightful boy, my gentle, nurturing, sweet, smart, loving child, was acting out. He was banging his head against the wall. He was screaming. He was tearing pages out of books. Mattie had become sullen at home, but nothing like this.

It all started after the school transferred a little boy out of Mattie's classroom. The boy looked very much like Jamie, and Mattie had kept trying to hold his hand, saying, "Mamie, my Mamie. I love you." When the boy was removed, a second "Jamie" died. Mattie didn't get to see him anymore and didn't know what had happened.

I finally received a call one day to pick Mattie up because he was too out of control to handle. Getting him home and holding him in my lap, I said, "You're so angry. What is it? I'll try to do what I can. Just tell me."

"It's wrong!" Mattie blurted out, climbing out of my lap and running into Jamie's room. He put the pillow right and tried to rearrange the sheets. He took all of Jamie's toys from the closet. Then he sat on the floor and sobbed, calling, "I want my Mamie."

I started crying also. "I want your Mamie, too," I said.

When we left the bedroom, I took sheets of paper and a pen and wrote at the top, "The Story of a Very Special Brother, as Told by Mattie Stepanek." Then I proceeded to ask Mattie a series of questions. "What is your name? How old are you? Do you have any brothers or sisters? Tell me about you and them."

From that I put together what was essentially Mattie's first book, drawing illustrations on every page. Mattie talked about Jamie's nurses, his medical equipment, how he would take out his own little doctor kit when the physician came so that he could help the doctor take care of his brother, and about when Jamie died and was tucked into his little white box.

I helped Mattie articulate his feelings, too: "Sometimes I feel sad. When I feel sad, I want to cry. I need to be rocked, and held. Sometimes I get angry. I want Jamie to come back, but he can't. I stomp my foot. Sometimes I don't know how I feel. I roll on the floor. I act silly. I giggle. Sometimes I like to pretend to *be* Jamie."

Mattie carried the book around with him for several months. If he felt sad, he opened to the page with the picture I had drawn of us on the floor, me holding him. If he was mad, he'd open to the page where there was a picture of him stomping his foot.

As the months passed, the book went on a shelf, and Mattie moved on to expressing himself in new ways. He started telling his own stories, which I would type for him. These were his beginnings as a writer, as he learned about the value of getting out onto the page what was in his heart.

Through the course of spring and summer 1993, Mattie would often work through his feelings by putting on costumes from the huge assortment in his costume chest. One was of the Wicked Witch of the West. "Who killed my brother? Was it you? Was it *you*?"

Another was Peter Pan. He doesn't grow up, but he doesn't die. Mattie weighed the choice. And there was Pinocchio: "Blue Fairy, how do you decide which boys you bring to life and which stay wooden and dead?"

One day some months later, when Mattie had already turned three, he saw me jotting down his imaginings. In preparing the speeches that I had started giving to professionals about helping families cope with loss as a part of the advocacy work I did, I would include his pretend games in my talks, urging that children be allowed to express their grief, their fears. I would explain that it was therapeutic for Mattie, that he would put his costumes away when he was done and be Mattie again and that encouraging children to bottle up their painful emotions doesn't mean the emotions have dissipated. Mattie asked me, "Why do you write down what I say when I play?"

I told him that in my work, I tried to help people who have children with disabilities be able to talk to the children and their brothers and sisters about muscles and bones not working anymore. "Do you mind if I share how you play?" I asked.

"Oh, no," he said. "I want you to share. I want you to share my Jamie stories." He even read a little out loud and said, "Mommy, these are just like the meditations and poems you read to me at night before I fall asleep." In addition to *Mother Goose*, I always looked for children's prayer poetry that helped my children cope with their feelings. I explained to

Mattie that poetry begins with the words in your stories getting shaped in a special way on the page.

From that point forward, he started "writing" furiously, either by dictating to me or talking into a tape recorder and asking me to type what he said.

> *I give my mommy*
> *'Buried treasure'*
> *Just like the little boy in Peter Pan.*
> *But I can't give my mommy*
> *'Buried Jamie.'*
> *He is in the Heaven*
> *That is the hole in the ground,*
> *Like a treasure.*

By the end of the summer that first year after Jamie died, Mattie's writings were still largely about his brother, but they were not unhappy, and he was not angry. Everybody usually lived "happily after-After," as Mattie would say. In almost every story, his grief was resolved.

But then, in late September, the anger, the negativity, was back. I couldn't figure out what was wrong. I knew it backfired the last time I tried to make the grief go away by making believe it wasn't there, and I didn't want to repeat my mistake. So I asked Mattie what was the matter.

That's when he told me about the pumpkin. I had by this time put a Mattie pumpkin on the front porch, and he was seeing pumpkins all around. Mattie explained that Jamie died during pumpkin season, and Jamie's pumpkin also died and had to be thrown out—like Jamie, in other words.

Mattie was having an anniversary reaction. Moreover, by this time he had begun using supplemental oxygen again, after a brief respite without it around the time his trach was first removed. He told me at times that his heart hurt so much it felt cold "like ice cream." His own health was starting to hang in the balance, and he was aware of the changes.

When Mattie finished explaining about the pumpkins, I pulled out his calendar, which hung on a wall in the kitchen. I wanted him to at least have the benefit of a time frame for his grief, the way I did. I turned two pages and showed him November 5 and told him that was a special day because it was the day Jamie died. I asked him if he wanted me to write it on the calendar, and he said, "Yes." I explained that he would still miss Jamie on other days—that you couldn't make grief go away just by turning a calendar page or even by switching calendars for a new year. But you could use the anniversary to focus your grief rather than feel very, very bad for a long time leading up to the day. Then, addressing what I knew was his fear, I explained that while he had the same condition as Jamie, he was stronger than Jamie, he didn't get an infection, and his doctors were taking special care of him.

But it wasn't just Jamie's death or his own health that troubled Mattie that fall. My walking by that point was quickly becoming more and more unsteady, and it's frightening for a young child to see his mother so vulnerable. Also, kids at school had started bullying him again, as they had the previous year—being short for your age and unhealthy makes you an easy target. In other words, with pumpkins came bad things.

Pumpkin Season touched Mattie every year of his life after that. Fall for him was a time of dread and loss. Always, first and foremost, in his mind, was the loss of his brother. At age five he wrote:

> I remember sitting in his bed
> And reading a book to him.
> I remember squeaking his
> Yellow caterpillar in his ear.
> But that's all.
> I remember . . . things that are
> Good for a remembering heart.
> Everything else is so, so sad.
> I remember not getting in bed
> With him after he was dead in bed.
> I remember him in his little white box.
> I remember his little white box in church.

I remember he was buried in the cemetery.
I remember the pumpkin rotting on the porch,
And we threw it away,
On the same day,
That we buried my brother.
But that's all.
That's all.

There was also fear of losing his mother, fear of losing his own life, being told that "normal boys don't need oxygen," being bullied in school. One child even stabbed him in the chest with a sharpened stick when he was in first grade. And while I left my marriage and filed for divorce early in 1997, many of the related court proceedings occurred during the next few fall seasons.

There were other Pumpkin Season losses, too.

In 2000, the year Mattie turned ten and began high school at home, his very good friend Rebecca Francis, also ten, died in November. He had known her for several years through MDA Summer Camp until she succumbed to a neuromuscular disease called spinal muscular atrophy. She was the younger sister of another friend, Racheal, who had the same neuromuscular disease as her sibling, and Mattie and Racheal discussed that Rebecca's death, like his brother Jamie's, was "a preview" of their own deaths and their own parents' grief. Racheal was the first person Mattie met who, like he, was going to die from the same disease as a brother or sister, and they considered things like: "What songs will our parents choose for our funerals? What color caskets?"

These accumulated losses darkened his outlook every year from the end of September through October and into November.

As the years moved along, we dealt with Mattie's grief and his hesitations in more mature ways, moving from costumes and reassurances that Jesus could hug him even if he didn't have any muscles and bones to conversations about coping with dark moments. We talked about peace, about the fact that if you're not at peace with yourself, you can't really be at peace with the world. We talked about not saying anything unpleasant about someone unless you had to for your safety. But what I particularly worked to impress upon Mattie as he was growing up was the importance of choosing what to emphasize in considering your life because it would affect your attitude going forward.

There was the reality of Mattie's body growing weaker and weaker across time. There was the fact of our poverty, our living in basements for much of his life, our having to accept food handouts. These were realities that couldn't be ignored. But I would literally engage Mattie in listing the blessings along with the burdens—true friends, a strong spirit, and so on—so that he could choose a brighter vision for himself and move forward without misgivings, fear, or rancor.

I could see that he was able to make use of our talks. He was very disappointed when he had to give up martial arts because it took too much out of him. He said in a speech that he gave at his final Black Belt banquet that "things have changed. They are difficult changes that are scary. But," he added:

> I can't say that they are bad changes. Changes are a part of life. . . . My body still wants to do all the physical things it used to do. . . . But . . . just like my body and mind followed my spirit, and good things happened, the time has come for my spirit to work with and follow my body and mind.

With the same view toward moving forward with inner peace, we talked about the "Our Father," particularly the line in this prayer that asks God to "forgive us our trespasses, as we forgive those who trespass against us." We talked about health and finances but also about times he had been bullied, about emotional distress that dragged on during the divorce and custody proceedings. We discussed that sometimes forgiving someone is difficult, that relationships are not always fixable or even safe, and that you may have to leave something, or some disagreement, unresolved and continue on without coming to common ground with another person and getting what you think is your due. But you still need to forgive even while you choose to move forward in peace *apart* from someone else; otherwise, you go forth with anger that will strangle your blessings as well as your opportunities to embrace new blessings, which is the same as not going forward at all.

That open, peaceful attitude I taught him also allows a person to meet his future without hesitation. If you've truly forgiven and truly feel okay with yourself inside, you can live a life not overshadowed by the darkness of anxiety, even legitimate anxiety. You can move forward in peace, rather than in fear or anger. Mattie and I talked about these concepts throughout the year, of course, but particularly during Pumpkin Season.

I wasn't alone in helping him through his dark days. Sandy's daughter, Jamie Dobbins, whom we called Jamie-D to distinguish her from Jamie Stepanek, was always there for Mattie in his season of grief, of fears, and of doubts.

Sandy and I first met the year before Mattie was born, when my Jamie was an infant. She worked on Project Assist, a University of Maryland initiative to provide support to parents of young children with disabilities. I hadn't wanted to join the group—"I'm a strong woman," I said to myself, and I was—but the truth was, I really needed some support at that point. Tending to a third child with a life-threatening condition, I was very stressed.

In addition to leading a weekly support group, Sandy was assigned to come to my home once a week to talk with me, and we immediately hit it off.

It was a few months later that Jamie-D met my Jamie. There was a potluck dinner for Project Assist, where all the families came together to mingle once the group sessions and home counseling concluded. Jamie-D came bouncing in on a pogo stick, little blond ponytails bobbing on either side of her head, and her first reaction to Jamie, a sickly infant connected to one hundred pounds of medical equipment through a tube in his neck, was, "Oh my goodness, he's so cute. What's his name?" She loved that they shared a name and spent the evening playing peek-a-boo with him and generally cooing over him.

I thought that was the end of it and that I wouldn't see Sandy after that, or Jamie-D, but some weeks later, my phone rang. It was Sandy, saying that Jamie-D's tenth birthday was coming up and that what she said she wanted for the occasion was to "please go see that little boy again." So Sandy brought her over, and she read to Jamie, blew bubbles for him, and gave him a Slinky and showed him how it worked.

From there my friendship with Sandy grew. It wasn't just that we were both studying for advanced degrees, and it wasn't just that we both had less than ideal marriages that eventually ended in complicated divorce cases. For me it was that, unlike so many other people, Sandy didn't try to swoop in and make things all better like a hero, and she didn't run when my children died.

It's extremely lonely being the mother of dying children. You can't share any of the normal milestones, the normal sense of community with other mothers. And people either want to solve the problem, which they can't, or they want to leave when the situation becomes too difficult. It's not out of callousness. It's out of pain; watching children die is hard.

But Sandy tried to neither fix nor flee; she just wanted to be my friend. And she helped in very real ways. She would bring her children over and share night shifts with me when Jamie and Mattie were both alive and on life support so I could get some actual REM sleep. She would find diapers on sale; keep me company; babysit for me while I coached Jamie-D in youth soccer, running up and down the field with the team before my disability kicked in. She grew, across time, to be a true sister.

And in parallel fashion, Jamie-D became a sister to my Jamie. When he died, all three of Sandy's children felt absolutely miserable. They each went into Jamie's room with the windows open and the air conditioner running, hats and gloves on, to spend time with him, to say good-bye to him. But it was Jamie-D who had fallen in love with him, who couldn't stop crying. And it was that night she decided she was going to be a big sister to Mattie.

"The day Mattie was born," she once told me, "I was excited that Jamie now had a little brother. He'd get to know that joy, like I did. But when Jamie died," she continued, "I knew Mattie would never really get to know what it was like to have a big sibling, as I did." (Jamie-D is the middle of Sandy's children, with older sister Heather and younger brother Chris). "I wanted to become Mattie's sibling because I knew that one day he would come to realize that he had lost his. I wanted him to know he wouldn't go through life alone, without a playmate."

Jamie-D made this clear to Mattie when they were children, often telling him, "I'm your sister from another mother." She meant it. When Mattie was an infant and toddler and communicated through American Sign Language because his trach limited vocalizations, Jamie-D learned it as well so she could understand what he was saying. Later, she learned to read his signs of medical distress: "His color's not right. Is he cold? Is something wrong with the oxygen tank?"

Her feelings were never lost on Mattie. In first grade he wrote in an essay:

> Jamie-D is like a sibling to me, and she helps me find happiness . . . when I am sad or scared. . . . We are alike in many ways; we are both very ebullient, and we love each other very much.

In talking about Jamie-D's helping him to feel happy when he wasn't, Mattie was in large part referring to the fact that she helped him cope with Pumpkin Season every year, and also tended to his emotional needs in general. It was true, and it meant a great deal. While I could hold Mattie and comfort him, there's just something about another child— one who's old enough to help yet still young enough to play—that brings a dimension a parent can't.

The October after Jamie died and Jamie-D was twelve, she helped move Mattie through his still-raw grief by playing with him. Across the years, she helped him with lingering grief, whether it was related to his brother, his friends, or other things. They had both a spoken and unspoken connection. And she tried to help him with the same philosophy I did, which was never to deny reality but to put the spotlight as much as possible on what was good about life rather than troubling.

"I couldn't change the reality he was living," she later told me. "I couldn't keep him from feeling sad. But I could at least make his time manageable and give him other things to focus on. We'd go to the park, to the zoo, to my house"—anything to diffuse the dark feelings. "We would play; we would laugh. I would crawl into the play space at Mc-Donald's with him and in that way move forward with him. And by at least creating some happy moments, I could reconnect him to his Heartsong."

Mattie with his brother Jamie, Halloween 1992

Mattie and Jamie-D enjoying a tender moment together, summer 1993

CHAPTER 4

Shaping Heartsongs

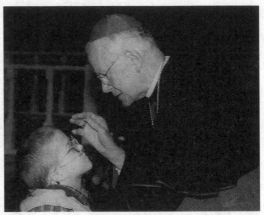

Mattie with his first five homemade volumes of "Heartsongs" poetry, spring 1999

Mattie with Cardinal James A. Hickey, summer 2000

> . . . *The job of the poet*
> *Is to leave stains of the storms*
> *Yet echo laughter of the light*
> *That is seen from the soul.* . . .
> *The job of the poet*
> *Is to . . . capture*
> *And to spirit and to script*
> *The pulse of life.*[1]

Mattie was in the middle of playing, perhaps with Legos or plastic dinosaurs—I don't remember which—when he suddenly dropped

---

1 From "Duties as Designed" in *Reflections of a Peacemaker: A Portrait Through Heartsongs*, page 5.

to his knees and lifted his eyes upward. About ten minutes later, after he rose to his feet, he asked me to please record what he was about to say.

It was a poem about a church turning into a carnival ride that rises to a place where the passengers *"see light all around, and Angels singing 'Alleluia!'"*—then goes where it will become *"windy and dark, and the Light of the Angels will disappear"* while the laughter turns sinister. At the end of the ride, when the church lands back on earth, all the passengers have to *"go through the doors, to make our choice."*[2] Mattie was four years old.

This wasn't the first time he recited a poem after assuming a prayer-like pose. He had starting doing so months earlier, telling me each time he rose to his feet that he had "a story to tell from God."

"God puts messages into my heart," he'd say. "My job is to shape those messages with words so that I can share with other people what God wants them to know." He even wrote a poem about it some time earlier, called "Private Revelations," also after a meditative interlude:

See now, and listen to me . . .
God speaks into my heart,
Then I choose the words
To shape the message, so you
May understand and know
What God wants us
To understand and know.
See now, and listen to me . . .
Do you hear my voice
Shaping with words
What the Voice in Heaven
Puts into my heart?
You will hear it now and
You will hear it again
When you come into Heaven.

---

2 From "The Church Ride" in *Reflections of a Peacemaker: A Portrait Through Heartsongs*, page 152.

See now, and listen to me . . .
I say to you,
Follow your heart.
This is what
My voice, and
The voices of Heaven
Now say to you . . .
See now, and listen . . .
These are the words I choose
To shape the message from God.
Follow your heart . . .
Please,
Just follow your heart . . .

I never allowed this poem to be published before now because I didn't want people to judge Mattie—or laugh at him. I quite frankly wasn't certain how to react myself. I told him that the idea of his being God's messenger was a wonderful one but that it was something we should talk about only at home. I didn't want people thinking my son had delusions of grandeur. I even put the concern to him myself.

"Tell me about your conversations with God," I said to him after he recited the poem about the church ride. "Do you *hear* God? What does God sound like? Is it a man's voice? A woman's?"

Mattie looked at me as though I were nuts. "It's not like two people *talking*," he said, putting his hands near each other and moving his fingers to make the signal for yakety yak. "It's not a conversation like that. The message goes into my heart, and then I put it into words."

That relieved me, but I still brought up the issue to a priest in our parish at the time. "There's this wonderful poetry on the one hand," I said, "and these absolutely beautiful messages that are coming through his heart from God, but it's so different from other things he has created—first the grief poetry about his brother, then little poems about trees and rainbows that you'd hang on your refrigerator."

The priest told me it made perfect sense. "Mattie's living on the edge," he said. "His mortality and his spirituality are closer together, more intertwined, than other people's. Is this something you shout from the mountaintop? No. Is it something you write down, allow to be nurtured? Absolutely."

That allowed me to move forward in comfort. I wouldn't have been able to articulate it at the time, but what the priest was saying was that Mattie's spontaneously uttered poems were expressions from his thin space—that place where body and spirit interact more closely than ever, and more palpably than ever in God's presence. Living on the verge of his mortality, as he did, left Mattie *always* in the vicinity of his thin space.

The poetry took yet another twist after he turned five. He had written a poem one night and wanted to read it to me the next day. He explained that it was special because he had deliberately woven together a story of his own with God's message. That is, he hadn't simply "translated" into words something that flowed through him from elsewhere. He was now consciously putting God's message into his own poetry, into his expressions of joy, grief, wonder, or other emotions.

"I have to share a message of goodness from God," he explained, "and I have poetry to write, so I put God's message in there whether I hear from Him or not."

It wasn't anywhere near Christmas, but he was wearing a holiday sweatshirt with a little music maker right over his heart that played "Silent Night" when pressed. As he leaned across the table to explain excitedly to me about this new kind of poetry, the shirt pushed into the edge of the table, and the mechanism went into action.

"Listen, Mommy!" he said. "It's the song from my heart!"

That song always had special meaning for him because he used to sign it for Jamie at Christmastime. *Sleep in heavenly peace* wasn't just about the baby Jesus in the manger; it was also about Jamie at peace in Heaven. Now it had added meaning because it started playing as he was describing his self-expression through poetry. "When I take God's message and combine it with my own," he explained, "that's my reason for being—my *Heartsong*."

It was the first time he used the term, saying that because he was good with words, and because what he wanted most was happiness and love, he would offer messages through his poetry that helped others find happiness and love, and from those emotions, hope and peace. "That'll make me feel good," he said. "I'll be really happy; I'll feel the love." It was the essence of what the word "Heartsong" meant to him throughout his life—that the only way you can get what your heart wants more than anything is by offering that very thing to others.

He said it himself years later in a journal entry:

> *Whatever it is that a person needs or wants, they understand why that matters, and that is the unfolding of their Heartsong. When a person offers that—what they need and want most—to others, that is the next part of their Heartsong. . . . And as we learn in almost every religion or philosophy of goodness, it is in giving that we receive. In sharing our Heartsong with others, it goes out into the world, and somehow, circles back to us.*

In that same journal entry, he explained that different people share their Heartsongs in different ways:

> *Some people have talents in sports or humor or academics. Other people have talents in service or patience or nurturing. Still others have the gift of using words to shape a message. . . . That is how I share my Heartsongs—through words.*

He went on to say:

> *. . . if a person cannot hear their own Heartsong because life has been too loud or dark or difficult for their spirit, then we should offer to let them borrow our Heartsong until their own is reawakened.*

♥

But back when he was five, immediately after "Silent Night" sounded and the word "Heartsong" shaped itself around the concept as he sat at the table, Mattie composed his poem titled "Heartsongs":

> *I have a song, deep in my heart . . .*
> *If you believe in magical, musical hearts,*
> *And if you believe you can be happy,*
> *Then you, too, will hear your song.*[3]

Soon after, each time he wrote a poem, he would offer it to someone. He saw his expressions of Heartsongs as gifts, literally. This was the beginning of Mattie's mission as a poet.

He soon had an opportunity to share his Heartsongs in a big way. He was in kindergarten, and it was the occasion of his first Write-A-Book Festival. Any student in the county's public schools could participate.

Initially, his school librarian said the poems and illustrations he put together as a book couldn't be entered into the contest because they contained the word *God*. It was a separation-of-church-and-state issue, she said. When Mattie came home and told me, I advised him to take out *God* and substitute words like *Creator* instead. But Mattie stood firm. "It's poetry," he said. "I'm not telling people what to believe."

The librarian still said no the next day, but after some chatting, during which Mattie reminded her that it says "In God We Trust" on a dollar bill and that it's an expression in common use, she begrudgingly accepted his entry.

He came in first place in our county. He even ended up at the center of a media blitz, including an article in *The Washington Post*, because he had stood his ground. And a woman from PBS came to the house to conduct an interview with him.

---

3 From "Heartsongs" in *Heartsongs*, page 25.

I left the room during the interview because I didn't want him looking at me for reassurance. Also, I figured it was his fifteen minutes of fame; I didn't want to use up seven and a half of them with "the mom's story." I didn't deserve to, anyway. I was the rule follower who told him to delete the word *God*. He was the one with clarity.

Toward the end of the interview, the woman asked Mattie, "Do you have a personal philosophy for life?" From around the corner, I was wondering whether he even knew what a *philosophy for life* was.

"Yes, ma'am, I do," Mattie responded. "Remember to play after every storm. Storms aren't necessarily clouds with rain. They're things that darken your day."

I sat there awestruck. Mattie had never said that to me. I was struck, too, by Mattie's comfort level with this perfect stranger. He had been very shy as a toddler and preschooler, never striking up conversations with people. Now that was changing.

By the time Mattie was four, I had started traveling around the U.S. and Canada, giving speeches to health professionals, counselors, educators, and others who work with families in which there is disability or loss. The aim was to give caregivers tools so they could better help families with children who had life-threatening conditions. I talked about the idea of a family's having a child who was in kindergarten now but would probably not live to graduate from high school. How do you celebrate life in the middle of that uncertainty?

Mattie never heard any of my speeches—I didn't think it was appropriate for him to listen to my stories about grief—but he did hear people saying afterward that when they got back to work, what I said was going to make a difference, that they could help families celebrate life in the middle of life-threatening illness.

He also would go into the exhibit halls at the convention centers where I spoke, trolling from booth to booth for free pads and pens, candy, and other freebies. He called it trick-or-treating and would take a bag with him to haul his "loot." At the same time, he'd give out little slips of paper about the size of those in fortune cookies with Heartsong expressions he had handwritten: "You can always find something good buried deep inside the heart"; "One of the greatest gifts of all is to be a gift to other people."

With these frequent social interactions, Mattie, by the time he turned six, had gone from being a bashful little boy to a confirmed extrovert. I used to joke that if you went one floor with Mattie in an elevator, you would exchange names; two floors and you'd understand what mattered most to each other in life.

It's not that Mattie was precocious. He would walk around these professional meetings carrying Mr. Bunny in one hand and pushing a stroller containing his oxygen tank with the other. Inside the stroller, too, was his "Honey-Baby" Cabbage Patch doll, replete with nasal cannula. In other words, Mattie was not simply a bright kid trying to show how smart he was. He was a child who just had something to say, and that's what made people fall in love with him.

At one of these conferences, Mattie was invited with me to a breakfast at which there was going to be a speaker. I generally skipped such breakfasts or secured a babysitter because I didn't want Mattie exposed to adult-oriented discussions. But that day, I was told, "He's delightful, he's so well-mannered. Let him come with you." So I relented, giving Mattie his headphones and a book to read in case he didn't want to listen to the speech, which was about getting along with coworkers even when things get tough in the workspace.

The speaker gave a very powerful talk, and Mattie listened to every word. When it was over, an open-mike session was announced for anyone who wanted to come up and share reactions with the audience. Mattie raised his hand. I told the speaker he was only six and didn't have anything to say, but Mattie piped in, saying, "Yes, ma'am, I do." We went back and forth for a minute, and I finally relented because it would have caused more of a scene for me to stand my ground. I was afraid people would laugh at him, consider him adorable when he was trying to be serious.

Off the cuff, in front of thousands of people, he shared that his classmates were his "coworkers" and that life was very hard because he was sometimes bullied by them, on top of having lost his brothers and sister.

He talked about the difficulties of being a child whose parents were divorcing, and about financial concerns. He ended by sharing his new "philosophy for life," the one that he shared with the PBS reporter about playing after every storm.

The talk went on for about five minutes, at the end of which, Mattie said, "Thank you, ma'am," and handed back the microphone. People's jaws dropped; they sat there in tears. From that point on, whenever I was asked to give a speech, the organizers of the event would request that Mattie say a few words before I did. It was the beginning of his public speaking.

Until Mattie turned eleven, he gave three kinds of speeches. One was for the Muscular Dystrophy Association, both to raise funds and to thank the volunteers who worked on the organization's behalf. MDA learned about Mattie's speaking abilities from his years of going to MDA Summer Camp. When a person is diagnosed with a neuromuscular disease, MDA offers a variety of support services, ranging from clinic visits to wheelchair repairs to disease-specific research. But Mattie's favorite MDA activity was spending a week at their local summer camp, and he wanted to "give back" to the organization.

During those speeches, Mattie would tell his audience that in addition to raising money for research toward a cure, MDA raised hope for being able to have a good life, even if it was a short one. Among attendees in those audiences were Harley-Davidson motorcycle riders and different divisions of the International Association of Fire Fighters, both huge supporters of MDA's efforts. In that way, Mattie's friendship with firefighters like Bubba from New York and J.J. from Canada—both of whom he met at a softball fund-raiser when he was seven—took off. They'd call him between tournaments to chat and see how he was doing and visit him when he was in the hospital.

The second kind of talk Mattie gave was for Children's Hospice International. When people think of hospice care, they tend to think of the last six months of a person's life, when there is no hope for curing what the person will die from and little hope that his or her health will turn around. The care during the hospice period is primarily to relieve pain, not to treat the condition or prolong life with CPR or other methods.

Once you receive hospice services, you give up your right to try to pursue living.

But children, Mattie would explain in his speeches, are not little adults. They are resilient, sometimes able to live on the edge for a decade and then bounce back. They can easily "almost die" for six months before going on much, much longer.

Mattie first shared these thoughts when he was seven, during interviews for a televised documentary on hospice entitled *Final Blessing*. But he went on to make the same points to people who would then lobby senators and members of the House of Representatives, so they could help our legislators understand why hospice rules needed to be changed for children.

These speeches on behalf of hospice for children were sometimes hard for Mattie. It was difficult for him to talk about death; he had already been written off once. But he was asked to do so by Children's Hospice International after they had interacted with him for a few years at an annual event called the Christmas Fantasy Flight, and he appreciated opportunities to make a difference.

The Fantasy Flight is something various organizations put on at air ports across the country every December. Children with life-threatening conditions are taken on an airplane (in our case, a United Airlines jet at Dulles International) and "flown" on the Secret Reindeer Route for a party at Santa's home. The airplane never actually leaves the ground. But the shades are pulled because "nobody can know the secret route," and the plane taxis around, at one point speeding up until it "lands" at the North Pole.

Mattie's very first year on Santa's lap during a Fantasy Flight, when he was five, he didn't say what he wanted for Christmas. He said, "Your home is at the North Pole. That's so close to Heaven. Would you please tell Jamie, and Katie and Stevie, 'Merry Christmas' from their little brother?" Santa, a man named Tommy Kianka, cried when he relayed the interaction to me.

Mattie saw the same Santa every December. He never knew who it was, but Tommy couldn't forget Mattie. When Mattie was six, he asked to become one of Santa's elves because he wanted to "help make toys for other children." When he was seven, Santa had an elf outfit waiting for him. The year he was eight, Santa named him Head Elf. By that point, Mattie had begun making toys year-round out of empty egg cartons and such and would bring them to the North Pole each December in a huge plastic bag. Before we left the airport, Tommy would give one toy to me and tell me to put it under the tree. Mattie loved waking up on Christmas morning and seeing that Santa was so pleased with his creations that he made it a point to give one back.

By the time 2000 rolled around and Mattie had turned ten, he had been seeing Tommy as Santa each Christmas for the better part of a decade and had been making speeches for Children's Hospice International for several years. One morning that fall, a month or two before Christmas, he made a presentation to members of Congress on Capitol Hill, and I could tell by the time he finished that he found it particularly draining emotionally and that it would be good to get him home. But someone from the organization came up to him with a surprise, which was that even though he was an unpublished author, the Library of Congress would be accepting a book of his poetry, and he'd be getting a tour of the library that very day. The person also said there was going to be a gathering that evening with even more people and asked Mattie if he'd give the exact speech he had just given. Mattie replied that of course he would.

But when he and I went to have lunch and were sitting just by ourselves, he started crying. "It's sad to be missing Jamie so much," he said, "and I want to see him, but I'm afraid I'm going to be seeing him too soon." It was Pumpkin Season again.

I said, "Honey, you do not need to give that speech tonight. We can say you're tired, or whatever you want me to say. I'll tell them *I'm* feeling tired."

He said no, that he had to do this. "But I just need God to give me some message that what I'm doing is going to make a difference, and that Jamie is happy—that I'm not just telling sad stories."

He gave the speech to a huge crowd that evening. It was particularly moving, and afterward, Virginia Congressman Jim Moran told Mattie that "hospice laws for children *will* be changed because of you."

Then a man in a business suit came over, knelt down next to Mattie, and asked, "Do you know who I am?"

It was Tommy, and Mattie recognized him right away as "Santa."

"I heard you were going to speak," Tommy said, "and I came with a very special gift. I don't know why it's special, but my belief is that it means something to you. Think of it as being from Santa Claus, who lives so close to Heaven." At that point, Tommy took a pin off his lapel and attached it to Mattie's collar. It was a moose pin. Mattie burst into tears. "Moose" was our nickname for Jamie.

The third type of speech Mattie gave was to educators. He would talk at conferences and at universities, about what it was like to be a student with a disability, which means a student with an IEP, or Individualized Education Plan, because there are always accommodations that need to be made for people with challenges. For instance, Mattie's handwriting was poor and slow as a result of his difficulties with fine motor skills, but he couldn't be penalized for that by virtue of his IEP.

These talks were entitled "Student Self-Representation in the IEP Process." They made the point that just because a child has a disability and receives certain supports, it can't be presumed he doesn't want a say in his education. Mattie would explain, "If I were allowed to be present during my own IEP meetings, I would ask to tell my classmates about my condition *myself* so that it would make them less afraid and more willing to interact with me; I would ask for a keyboard so I could keep up with the other students when they wrote in longhand and not lose out because of my difficulties with fine motor skills."

All of Mattie's speeches, no matter what group he was talking to and no matter what the purpose, always included a poem, a Heartsong. His speeches were affecting, too—for what they made people forget as well as for what they urged them to keep in mind. That is, he was chosen as a speaker because he was a boy in a wheelchair connected to equipment, but he was able to make people stop thinking about that part of him even as they knew his condition was the reason he was there. He would talk about his hobbies, things he did for fun, authors he liked, and so on, and in that way humanized himself and others on whose behalf he was trying to make a point. Once a person with a disability is seen as "just like me," it's easier to make the leap to understanding why what he is saying is important, why by helping him with what he needs you're respecting yourself as well.

Mattie was beguiling, too, because he remained a boy even while talking about very adult subjects. He never tried to be something he wasn't. Once, when he was giving a lecture for the National Education Association at around the age of eight, his head started to go lower and lower behind the table in front of him on the stage. He kept talking, never missing a beat, even when his entire body finally slipped behind the dais and he couldn't be seen for a minute while he spoke. People were nervous that he was having some kind of episode. Afterward, when he took questions, someone in the audience asked him whether something medical had been going on, and he replied, "No. I don't tie my shoes very well, and one of them had fallen off, and I thought it was unprofessional for me to be speaking with one shoe off, so I went to put it back on while I was talking." The crowd sighed with relief—and pleasure.

Even for all that, however, his speeches to various groups were a world apart from his spiritual teachings to students enrolled in CCD (Confraternity of Christian Doctrine, a Catholic Sunday school program). Why Mattie was teaching CCD by the fall of 2000, at the age of ten, when most Catholics are not even confirmed until they are fourteen, goes back to when Mattie first met Cardinal James A. Hickey in 1998.

A week after Mattie received his First Holy Communion at age seven, as is the custom, Cardinal Hickey came to our church to administer the sacrament of Confirmation to the teenagers and adults who had spent a year preparing for it. Part of the process involves the cardinal asking questions of the confirmandi: What are the gifts of the Holy Spirit? What are the Holy Days of Obligation? Who can define Paraclete?

Mattie was off to the side, next to me in my spot as a choir member. But every time the cardinal spoke, Mattie's hand shot up. "Mattie," I whispered, "this is not your Confirmation. Please put your hand down." By the last few questions, Mattie was so anxious to answer that he was squirming.

At the reception afterward, Cardinal Hickey went up to speak with

Mattie, telling him that he saw him raising his hand and wanting to know whether he had any questions.

"Oh, no, sir," Mattie answered. "I knew the answers. I wanted to share them." After listening to Mattie's responses to several of the questions, the cardinal talked a while with our parish priest, Father Isidore Dixon. Afterward, he came over to me and said, "When somebody has a condition that may result in death before the age of Confirmation, we can confirm early with the parent's consent. I'd like to confirm your son today."

I responded that Mattie had just received his First Holy Communion only a week earlier and that if he were confirmed that day, he might know some of the answers but he wouldn't understand that this sacrament is a gift of the Holy Spirit, a sign of God's grace. Cardinal Hickey made a suggestion. Mattie would study for Confirmation for a year, at which point he would come back and personally confirm Mattie himself.

He started to walk away after we made the arrangement but turned around to say, "Do you recognize what your son is?"

"Excuse me?" I answered, confused.

"Do you know who your son is?" he asked. "Your son is a messenger."

"I am so sorry," I responded. "He has been saying that since he was four years old. I told him he's free to *be* a messenger but not free to go around telling that to people."

"He did not say it to me," the cardinal replied. "*I'm* saying it."

Mattie was confirmed a year later at the age of eight (he chose the confirmation name Thaddeus because Jude Thaddeus is the patron saint of hopeless situations), and during the summer of 2000, he asked Father Dixon if he could assist in teaching a CCD class that fall. "I'm confirmed," he said. "I'm no longer *in* CCD."

A teacher of second graders agreed to let Mattie help her, even allowing him to plan and teach the whole hour on baptism one evening. She prepared a lesson plan of her own, just in case his didn't work out. After all, many of the children in second grade were already taller than Mattie, and here he was in a wheelchair with two tanks of oxygen. Would he really be able to command the attention of a bunch of wiggly six- to eight-year-olds?

The extra lesson plan turned out never to be needed. "The class was mesmerized," the teacher told me. "It was like watching Jesus with the children around His feet. They hung on Mattie's every word."

Mattie loved being able to focus directly on giving a spiritual message, doing God's work in such a straightforward way. Still, in the midst of many blessings, his health continued to decline. It was getting harder and harder for him even to play. He was now connected to his BiPAP machine almost all the time, even during waking hours, which kept him tethered to a wall because it had to be plugged in; there were no batteries or charger.

The increasing reliance on the BiPAP was due to the fact that the nasal cannula simply wasn't delivering enough oxygen to his body. Also, he was not getting deep enough breaths on his own. Even the oxygen mask Mattie switched to from the cannula was not doing the trick. He had begun having gray spells during speeches, passing out during activities. "I can't breathe," he would say. To eat, he'd switch from the BiPAP, which was sealed to his face, to the oxygen mask to let the food reach his mouth. But he'd have to take a break in the middle of his meals to go back on the BiPAP, which would push deeper breaths and more oxygen into him.

In the weeks after New Year's Day 2001, he became too weak even to play at his best friend Hope's house. He'd sit on the floor, playing next to his bed, or roll the BiPAP into the living room and plug it in there so he could watch TV. He'd stay quiet. His body was, literally, hypoxic—lacking oxygen. The skin on his fingers, his toes, his lips was rough, even peeling a bit, from too little oxygenation, although I didn't realize the reason at the time.

During January, in the middle of this decline, Mattie went to tour a brand-new research laboratory at Children's National Medical Center devoted entirely to finding cures for muscular dystrophy and related diseases. He was physically miserable. He couldn't wear his glasses because he had the oxygen mask on, and he felt like he was suffocating, anyway.

Afterward, sitting in the atrium entryway to the hospital, he said to me, "Mom, I can't see because I don't have my glasses. My fingers are so dry. . . ."

"It's winter, Mattie," I interrupted. "Maybe they're chapped. Maybe some lotion . . ."

"Mom, I'm having a hard time breathing. I can't eat, and I can't talk with the BiPAP. I could scream for you and you wouldn't be able to hear me under that thing. This is not living. This is just passing time while my body's getting worse."

I wasn't sure how to answer. I was scared and at a loss. But Mattie wasn't.

"I think," he said, looking straight at me, "it's time to put my trach back in."

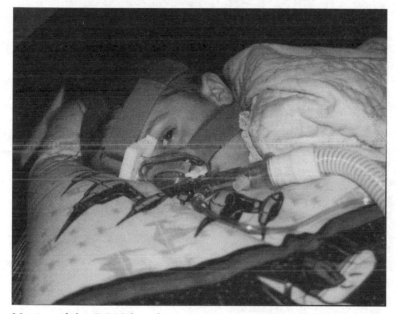

Mattie with his BiPAP breathing equipment, spring 2000

CHAPTER 5

Awakening After a Close Call

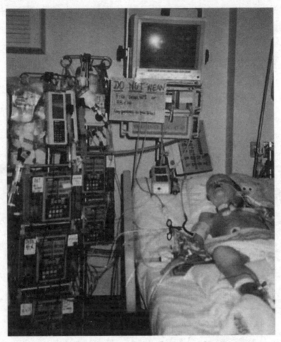

Mattie in a coma as a result of severe dysautonomia,
spring 2001

Don't believe the Christmas Trees. . . .
The Angels are more than
Just males and females with wings,
They glow with the Light
Of Every-color!
One color at a time,
Or all at once, or none at all.
But there is no darkness.
There is no darkness in Heaven. . . . [1]

---

1   From "Awakening After a Close Call" in *Loving Through Heartsongs*, page 53.

A child's saying he wants a tracheostomy tube is not what a mother wants to hear. What Mattie was communicating with that statement was that he needed a machine to be alive. All his other equipment—the nasal cannula, the oxygen mask, the BiPAP machine—were for respiratory support. This was a request for *life* support. He was talking about a ventilator attached to a trach tube inserted through his neck that would take over the job of his lungs, breathing for him twenty-four hours a day.

I told Mattie that we'd walk right then from the hospital atrium to the doctor's office to make an appointment and get his opinion.

I was miserable. All four of my children, Mattie included, had had trachs and ventilators, and the machinery didn't save the lives of my first three.

I wondered aloud to Sandy afterward whether I was about to "ride the roller coaster" again. "I don't want to get on that ride," I told her. "Please tell me I'm in a line for a different ride."

I sincerely hoped I might be. I had been thinking for a while, even with Mattie's health declining, that maybe he had beaten the odds. Children with his disease always die in utero, or as infants or toddlers, and here he was ten years old, having made his way deep into uncharted waters. Furthermore, this was an infinitesimally rare disorder with many unknowns, largely because only four children in the world—Mattie and his three siblings—ever had this exact permutation of dysautonomic mitochondrial myopathy, which was a further mutation of my own unique condition. Maybe, I thought, he'll get better with time.

My thinking was buoyed by a conversation I had had with his doctor a few months earlier, a pulmonologist named Robert Fink. He had been Katie and Stevie's doctor, but I switched hospitals after they died. I switched back when a physician at the other facility asked me why I'd take heroic measures to save Mattie only to prolong the end point. Mattie's condition was shifting for the worse then, and that doctor told me, "You're just dragging out the inevitable." I feared that if Mattie crashed, the medical staff was going to think he wasn't worth fighting to keep alive. Dr. Fink's facility, Children's National Medical Center, never took that position. No matter how sick my children were, their aim was to save them if that was what I wanted. Dr. Fink never criticized my medical decisions, accepting my wanting to make the call about when to keep going and when to say "enough." "Come on back," he had said when I phoned him and asked for Mattie to be returned to his care.

He was so happy to see a Stepanek child talking and growing up, so happy for Mattie to have become old enough to be able to show us who he was on the inside. All Dr. Fink had seen before was my children dying as infants or toddlers. And in that conversation some months before we went in to discuss the trach tube, he offered hope even while remaining frank.

"Where Mattie is now," he had said, "is on a narrow median strip in the middle of a highway. High-speed traffic is coming in both directions. The strip is going to get narrower and narrower as puberty comes on. As his hormones kick in, his body's not going to know what to do. The growth spurt will cause a major crisis. It's going to be the storm of his life.

"If we can keep him standing still—medically stable—we'll be able to wait for a break in the traffic so he can get off the highway. I don't ever foresee him not having his disease, not needing help with his breathing. But I do see him becoming stable with medical support if he can ride out puberty. These seven children he always talks about having could be his."

It was those words I held on to while waiting for our next appointment. In the intervening weeks, I decided to make sure Mattie had a light schedule and plenty of rest. By the time we saw Dr. Fink in mid-February, I figured, we'd still talk to him about a trach, but it wouldn't be anything he'd think we needed to tend to right then.

When the appointment rolled around, Mattie told Dr. Fink, "I always feel like I'm not getting enough air. Sometimes I can't think clearly. And my fingers are beginning to burn."

His already dry fingers had progressed to a bit of splitting and bleeding around the nails. But even then I was still thinking his chapped hands were about winter, about a need for different soaps and lotions rather than too little oxygen reaching his extremities. And while his breathing was stressed, and his speaking was more fragmented with the need to take extra breaths, he couldn't be said to be in respiratory distress. He wasn't gasping for air.

Dr. Fink said he thought a trach was a reasonable consideration and asked Mattie whether he remembered what having one was like. "No," Mattie answered, "but I do remember seeing my brother with it, and I've seen pictures of myself with it, and I was smiling in them, so I was definitely happier than I am now."

In private, after Mattie excused himself to go to the bathroom, I reminded Dr. Fink of Mattie's prediction that March 30 would be a dark day for him. This had come up in a visit with Dr. Fink back in the fall.

"I remember," he said, "but I don't think Mattie is saying he needs a trach based on that prophecy. He knows his body.

"The trick with most kids," he went on, "is to stay one step ahead medically. With Mattie, it's two steps, or you're one step behind. Right now we're only a single step ahead, and we're losing ground. It's a quick operation—he'll be home a week later."

He told me to call him if there was a crisis, but that in the meantime he'd notify the Pediatric Intensive Care Unit, or PICU, to put aside a bed for Mattie when one was available. It was a small unit, and the tracheostomy was considered nonemergency, elective surgery, so Mattie would not go for his operation until there was room.

A week later, I called Dr. Fink to say that Mattie's breathing seemed about the same but that his fingers and toes were getting worse. He wasn't sure there was a connection between these symptoms and his respiratory status but told me he would let the PICU know that Mattie needed to be moved up in priority for his procedure.

By mid-March I was calling Dr. Fink every day. I didn't understand what was happening. I was still thinking his fingers were chapped rather than lacking oxygen, but nonetheless I was feeling anxious that the surgery had not yet been scheduled.

In the meantime, I took Mattie to see the community pediatrician. Was the extreme chapping the result of an allergy? An infection on his fingers? Was it some kind of skin disease?

As soon as the nurse in the pediatrician's office took one look at him, she called out, "Oh my God, this child's cyanotic," meaning he was blue as a result of oxygen deprivation. "We need to call 9-1-1."

"Before you call 9-1-1," I said, alarmed, "you need to call Dr. Fink. My son is on a waiting list for a trach."

The nurse called Dr. Fink, who told her that Mattie was a kid who sometimes turned blue or dusky. She told him no, that what she was seeing went beyond a mild respiratory malfunction. I hadn't quite seen it myself because the change occurred so gradually across the course of months. Also, I hadn't wanted to sound alarmist because a parent runs the risk of being ignored if her concern turns out to be an overreaction—I was always walking that tightrope.

Mattie was admitted to the PICU the very next morning—March 21, 2001. He packed his backpack for a weeklong stay, and I packed one, too, knowing I'd be sleeping on a bench in the waiting area outside his unit. That was fine, as long as I could be near him.

But there was trouble as soon as we arrived. I was told I had to wait outside while Mattie was admitted because the doctors in the PICU were "on rounds." I looked around and saw that most of the children were sedated or unconscious. Mattie, on the other hand, knew everything that was going on; he was an alert ten-year-old about to be forced to weather this on his own.

When I was allowed back in, several hours later, Mattie said to me, "Mom, there are children in here who are dying. I'm listening to the sounds of sadness the whole time." There were sixteen beds in the unit—six along Mattie's wall, six along the opposite wall, and four along a wall at a right angle to the other two. Those were isolation rooms. The rest of the beds were separated only by curtains, so what you couldn't see, you could hear all too well.

The curtains had an underwater theme, the irony of which was not lost on Mattie. "Everybody in here is already underwater," he said. "We're struggling to breathe. Who would choose an underwater theme for people who are suffocating?"

When Dr. Fink saw Mattie, the first thing he did was ask me why I hadn't told him the situation had gotten so bad.

"I tried to," I said.

"But you sounded so calm. His fingers look like they've been scalded. He's not circulating oxygen." The calmness was part of the tightrope walk—sounding in control when the situation seemed completely out of control so that I would be taken seriously. It was a catch-22.

Two days later, on March 23, Mattie went to the OR for his trach surgery. We were all nervous because the anesthesia required for surgery could wreak havoc on the autonomic system of someone with Mattie's condition—everything in the body has to "wake up" again as a patient regains consciousness, and Mattie's autonomic system wasn't always "awake" even without being dampened by anesthesia. But he appeared to come through with no complications.

When they wheeled him back to the PICU, still sleeping, I looked at my son and hated seeing his neck with the hole and the trach tube. I had allowed him to be mutilated. At the same time, for the first time since he was two, I was able to see his face without anything on it—no cannula, no mask. *Wow, he's beautiful,* I thought. And he was breathing so comfortably, with his skin already looking pink instead of grayish. Still, I felt indescribably sad and kept weighing whether I had made the right call. What if he still declines? Even worse, there was a big sign above Mattie's bed that said DO NOT WEAN. The goal for children in the PICU is to ultimately get them off oxygen and lower the vent settings delivering life support. For Mattie, the goal was just the opposite. There was no respite from the worry—no good decision versus bad decision. It was all a severe compromise.

As soon as Mattie woke up an hour later, he whispered, "Hi, Mom, I love you." They had warned me that some people can't talk with a trach. I prayed and thanked God.

The next morning, March 24, I stayed with Mattie from about five thirty in the morning till seven, the usual time I was forced to leave while the doctors made their rounds. When I was allowed back a few hours later, he was sitting up and smiling. The PICU staff notified us that they'd call the equipment company within a couple of days to have the necessary ventilator apparatus for home care delivered. Mattie would be home inside of a week, they said. I was glad, but March 30 was getting awfully close, and it was gnawing at me.

That evening, by around seven or eight, Mattie started to say he wasn't comfortable. "I don't know what's wrong," he told me, "but my whole body hurts. I can't isolate the pain." I thought it must be the ICU bed. They're hard in case the staff has to perform CPR.

By ten P.M., Mattie said he needed to urinate but couldn't. "I feel like I'm going to explode," he told me. Immediately, my mind shot to Katie, who stopped urinating and died three days later. The general consensus was that as a result of the anesthesia, certain parts of Mattie's body were having a hard time readjusting themselves. Around midnight they catheterized him, and he felt great relief. The next day, he began to urinate on his own again.

The day after that—we were up to March 26—the plan was to send him home in three days. But sometime that afternoon, he woke from a nap irritable, not himself. He didn't want to eat, didn't want to know what was going on in the news, didn't want to listen to music, and kept saying he was in pain.

As the twenty-sixth moved into the twenty-seventh, Mattie entered a semidelirious state, waking just long enough to say he didn't feel well, then falling back to sleep. On Wednesday the twenty-eighth, Dr. Fink pulled me away from the bed to ask me whether Mattie had any sense of what date it was. I told him not since March 25, and he then instructed everyone in the unit not to mention the date around Mattie. He didn't want what Mattie had said the previous summer to become a self-fulfilling prophecy.

By Thursday, Mattie was really out of it—he obviously could not be released, as had been planned. Then on Friday, March 30, just before I was made to leave for morning rounds, Mattie opened his eyes and said, "It's so dark, it's so dark. I can't see."

When I was allowed back in, he had a nurse assigned to sit there and watch just him—the sign of a crisis. And he had numerous IV fluids going into him that were not there when I had left him earlier. The nurse explained that they couldn't rouse him and that his blood pressure was falling and that all the liquids were to try to stabilize it.

A couple of hours later, one of the PICU doctors asked, "We're losing him. Would you like to have a priest come in and anoint him in case he doesn't make it?"

"What do you mean, in case he doesn't make it?" I responded.

"He's dying," the doctor said. "His body is not working."

They put me at the nurses' station to call whoever I needed to come. I phoned Sandy and our church.

By the time the Retzlaffs came with Father Dixon, Mattie had slipped into a coma. Father Dixon began to anoint him. I bowed my head, begging God to save him.

"In the name of the Father, and of the Son . . ." I heard Father Dixon say, and then there was a pause. The priest had started crying. I thought my son had died, and I looked up. But that's not why Father Dixon was crying. With all of the tubes in him and by now completely unresponsive, even to the pain that came with being poked and prodded with needles, Mattie was moving his arm and making the Sign of the Cross.

"And of the Holy Spirit," the priest continued. "Amen."

At seven that evening, a shift change forced me away from Mattie's side once again and into the waiting room. The night shift nurse was told, "This child is going to die on your shift tonight. There's nothing we can do. Not only will he die, but this is the mother's fourth and only surviving child—you're going to have to tell her."

The night nurse looked up and saw the last name. "Oh, no!" she said. "I took care of his sister and brother. Not on my shift is he going to die."

Midnight came and Mattie was still alive. He made it to March 31. "Please, God," I prayed. "Let that be a sign."

But Mattie's entire system was shutting down. His glucose had shot up to 800, causing temporary blindness (which was why he couldn't see—March 30 was, literally, a dark day for him, as he had predicted the summer before). He was having hypoxic seizures, meaning his body was reacting negatively to a lack of oxygen. He soon developed pneumonia from all the fluid he was receiving to keep his blood pressure from bottoming out. His lungs were so filled with liquid that the doctors couldn't even see his heart on a chest X-ray.

For the next two or three weeks, until past the middle of April, Mattie's situation was up and down, touch and go. There were days we thought he was doing better, and days we thought, "This is it." I was told that even if he came out of his coma, no guarantees could be made for his brain function.

I had already prayed three times across the years, desperately, for God to save a dying child. Here I was doing it a fourth. But this time the prayer changed a little. "My son says You chose him," I said, "that his reason for being is to be a messenger. If he's done, okay, I'll be broken-hearted. But if he's not done yet, You have to give him more time. You've got to perform a miracle."

Around that very point in time, John Paul II sent a Papal Blessing to Mattie. To this day, I don't know how the pope learned of him.

Soon after, one of the PICU doctors decided to draw blood simultaneously from one of Mattie's arteries and one of his veins. The monitor kept indicating his oxygen saturation was anywhere from 98 to 100 percent, yet the seizures he started having suggested he was oxygen deprived. It didn't make sense, and an analysis of the blood from an artery and a vein might explain why.

It turned out that the amount of oxygen in his veins was, at times, almost identical to that in his arteries—a life-threatening problem. When oxygen-rich blood leaves the heart and travels to all the body's organs through the arteries, it's supposed to drop off the oxygen to those organs; thus, the blood making the trip back to the heart through the veins should be very low in oxygen. But Mattie's tissues were not extracting the oxygen from the blood in his arteries—it was an autonomic response that had stopped working. He was suffocating in every tissue of his body, and that is why he had fallen into a coma.

Until that point, the doctors had been keeping his supplemental oxygen at 60 percent. That's such a high level it's considered a borderline toxic concentration—room air is 21 percent oxygen. To try to force more oxygen out of his arteries and into all his body's tissues, they upped his oxygen even more, to 100 percent. You can't survive long at that level. All that oxygen is corrosive to the body. But we were out of options.

Fortunately, Mattie soon began stabilizing. He was weaned to 80 percent oxygen, then back to 60 percent. Soon the doctors were able to start withdrawing his blood pressure medication. His lungs began clearing. But he remained comatose; there was still the question of whether he would ever wake up. And if he did, was it going to be Mattie who awoke, or just Mattie's body as a result of brain damage?

At this point we were into late April. I had not left the hospital for more than a month. Had it not been for Sandy, I don't know what I would have done. She worked two jobs and still had two teenagers at home, yet came to visit at least three times a week. She brought me changes of clothes. She would literally pick me up and drag me to the shower, since the parent shower room was not wheelchair accessible. She helped with Mattie's baths, too, and would bring two dozen hot Krispy Kreme donuts at a time to the PICU staff.

Sandy would stay till three in the morning if Mattie was stable, six if he wasn't. She'd let me get some sleep on the bench in the waiting room. I was so tired that one night at two A.M., twenty-five feet from the PICU, I fell asleep with my hand on the joystick of my wheelchair and rammed into a wall after being called in for one of Mattie's emergencies.

For my own part, I kept Mattie's stuffed animal puppet Mr. Bunny right by his head, along with Grey Hero. It was a gray-colored wolf that had always sat in the office of Mattie's social worker from the time he was six, and she brought it because she knew it symbolized strength to him.

I also kept a tape recorder with soft music by his ear. I didn't want him incorporating cries like "Crash cart! Clear the unit!" into his comatose mind. Some of the tapes I played included music that had been a comfort to Mattie as a baby—Handel's *Water Music Suite*, Bach's harpsichord concertos, hammered dulcimer Christmas music. Maybe, I thought, this music would suggest to him that all was going to be okay.

Then, one day, Mattie started opening his eyes. It wasn't like with Jamie, whose eyes *fell* open. You could see a sense of, "Where am I?"

"Hey, Buddy," I said. "How you doing?" I wasn't sure whether he'd know me, or know anything.

"I'm tired," he responded in a little, squeaky whisper of a voice.

"I love you," I told him.

"Love you," he whispered back.

It was clear he knew who I was, but I still wasn't sure whether he had retained the better part of his brain function. Then he looked over my shoulder and said, "That's just wrong."

I looked behind me to see what he was referring to. Hanging from the ceiling at the nurses' station was a giant banner with balloons that read, "Welcome to the PICU—LAURA, ROBERT, and IAN!!!"

"Who would celebrate children coming to a place like this?" Mattie asked. The sign was for new nurses, but Mattie didn't know that. What *I* now knew was that Mattie recognized me, could read, and still had his same personality. I started praying and saying, "Thank You." Mattie's reason for being was not yet completed.

It took time for Mattie to learn to swallow again. We knew he was in for a long, slow, arduous recovery, that his body had been through the mill and he might not be able to give speeches anymore, hold a pen, move his body. But technology could fill in where his body left off. Cognitively, spiritually, emotionally, it was still Mattie. He had his life, and I was profoundly grateful. We were talking again about getting him home once more, about getting the ventilator equipment to the apartment.

But then one day in early May, I was suctioning secretions from Mattie's trach (a routine procedure) when I noticed that they were pink. I brought it up to the PICU staff, who told me it was nothing to worry about, that if you suction deeply, you can get a little blood mixed in with the normal secretions.

But across the course of a week, the color went from pink to red. When Mattie was breathing, I was able to see blood coming into the trach and the ventilator tube.

On Mother's Day, the staff decided that we needed to find out what was going on and did an emergency surgery, a bronchoscopy, to explore his lungs and trachea with a camera. Afterward, the doctors asked to talk to me in private. That's never good news, when they bring you away from the bedside to give results.

Not only were there several doctors in the meeting room when I arrived but also a social worker. They put a box of tissues on the table.

"His airway is completely denuded," the surgeon began.

"What does that mean?" I asked.

"There's nothing left but bare cartilage," she said. "His trachea, and even into his lungs—it's gone. It's bare cartilage and pulp."

"What does that mean?" I asked again.

"He's going to die."

You may as well have taken a cinder block and thrown it at my head. Mattie had just survived the dysautonomic storm of his life. He was in rehab—out of crisis.

"What's going to happen," the doctor continued, "is that he's going to cough, laugh, sneeze, say a word, and his trachea is going to split and perforate. There's nothing to protect it. He'll suffer in an excruciating manner, and he'll be dead within twenty minutes."

"When will this happen?" I wanted to know.

"Three days, maybe three weeks. We can sedate him when it happens. Do you want him to wake up again so you can tell him? Or do you want us to just keep him sedated?"

I was in shock. "Can you do a tracheal transplant?" I said. "This is the twenty-first century!"

"There's nothing we can do."

At that point I went into action. "He needs moist air, and not warm air but lukewarm to cool," I said, "with high humidity." It was the opposite of everything you do in the ICU, but I wanted to keep his trachea as bathed in moisture as possible.

"And absolutely he needs to wake up," I continued. "I've always promised him that I would tell him the truth. You need to let *me* tell him what is happening. I can tell him without scaring him more than necessary."

When Mattie woke up, before I could start to tell him what the doctors had found, the anesthesiologist from the surgery walked by to check on another patient. "Oh, so you decided to let him wake up after all," he said. "After that surgery, we thought you might choose not to let him."

Mattie started crying. Staff came over and pulled the anesthesiologist away, and I managed to calm Mattie down. I explained the situation and told him it was very serious but that we were going to do everything we could. He asked me if he was going to die in days, weeks, or months, and I said nobody knew, because they didn't. "There are no guarantees for anybody, Mattie," I said. "We're just going to move ahead."

He asked me what he was going to do while he waited, and I said Sandy was going to bring in his schoolwork so that he wouldn't be behind come September. I wanted him to know that I was still planning for his future. I also told him I'd make sure he had a TV so he could watch all the videos he wanted, and whatever toys he wanted, too. "We go on living, Mattie," I said. "Are you okay with that?"

"If you have enough breath to complain about anything," he answered, "you have more than enough reason to give thanks about something."

Across the next two weeks, we set up living, rather than dying, in the PICU. Sandy brought in *What About Bob?*, *Yellow Submarine*, and other videos. She brought in his schoolbooks. The staff let Hope and some other friends visit a few times, even though technically they were too young.

It was hard to approximate living there. The lights never go out, the noises never change. Day becomes night, night becomes day, and crises surround you: "We need a crash cart at Bedspace J"; "We need a doctor in Isolation 1." But I tried as hard as I could to create normalcy. On school nights, Mattie at least had to have the light above his bed out by ten P.M., with no movies or games and no unnecessary procedures or interruptions until six the next morning—no bathing, weighing, bandage changes, or other routine care that could wait. On weekends he could stay up until eleven.

Of course, the rhythm I tried to impose was always jarred. One day a typical call came: "CLEAR THE UNIT! ALL PARENTS OUT!" Mattie started crying. Because parents had to leave during a crisis, he had now been seeing children die all around him for almost two months, excluding the weeks he was in a coma. I had always dutifully left the room.

"I can't listen alone to another child die," Mattie said. The nurse looked at me.

"I can't leave my son," I said.

The nurse put his finger to his lips and pulled the curtain around Mattie's bed so I wouldn't be noticed. I was so appreciative. While the PICU at Children's National Medical Center was the best you could ask for medically, and while the staff treated Mattie wonderfully, the arcane rules for parental visitation during his years there had a hugely damaging effect on him. He could not bear to witness drama after life-and-death drama by himself without me there to comfort him. He did not want to be alone watching people die, or almost die, just a few feet from him.

"It's A.J., Mom," Mattie told me when the nurse walked away. A.J. was a teenager who had been in and out of the PICU many times. I don't know how Mattie knew it was A.J. who was about to die; you couldn't see through the curtain, and A.J.'s bed was three spaces to Mattie's left.

I held his hand. "Do you want to talk?" I asked.

"No," he said. "We need to pray—for A.J. and his family. They love him very much."

Suddenly, about an hour later, he whispered to me, "Bow your head."

"Why?" I asked.

"A.J.'s about to pass by. Say a prayer."

Through an opening in the curtain, I saw a utility cart. "But, Mattie, it's just a laundry cart."

"No, Mom," he told me. "It's a practice casket." At that point, the cart caught on the curtain at the foot of Mattie's bed. The curtain opened in a kind of slow motion as it moved along, so I was able to get a good look. There was a blanket spread across the top.

"Mattie, that was a utility cart," I said.

"No, Mom. It was a practice casket. They don't want people to know in the hallway."

When the nurse came back, Mattie said to him, "Would you tell my Mom?"

"Tell her what, Mattie?"

"I do know. I know that was not a utility cart. I know shrouds never seem to be available in the right size. I know which doctors and nurses cry when a child dies and which just move on to the next bedside. I know the names of the code drugs, the amount you give depending on the child's weight." He rattled off some.

"You're right, Mattie," the nurse said. "That was A.J. I'm sorry."

More time passed. The Retzlaffs, who were lay ministers in our church, would bring Communion, and a chocolate malt. Sandy and her kids would come by. Nell came, too, wearing a duck tied to her head with one of the same shoelaces we had used to tie them to our heads the summer before. She wore it the whole time she visited as if nothing in the world were unusual. That authentically made Mattie laugh, and he thanked her.

A day or two after Nell's visit, I was about to be made to leave the PICU before doctors' rounds when Mattie said he wished I didn't have to leave that day.

"I wish so, too, Mattie," I said.

"Mom, I think I might die today," he continued. "There's something different about my breathing."

"I'll tell your doctor," I said.

"I already did," he told me. "They think I'm just anxious. But I'm telling you, I think I'm dying."

I went to the doctors' and nurses' station, and they said they thought Mattie had PICU-*itis*, that he was just getting a little morbid and a little anxious but that he was medically stable.

I went back over to Mattie to tell him what they said, and he asked me if I was going to believe them or him. "I'm telling you," he said, sounding hurt, "I think I'm going to die."

I cried when I was banished from the PICU then. When I was allowed back in five hours later, there was a sign at the edge of Mattie's bed in his own shaky handwriting: *SEDATION NOW!* Underneath, in smaller lettering, he had written, *Wake me up on my birthday, then don't wake me up again until I'm HEALED*. He also told the staff, "I can't handle the waiting anymore. Please sedate me. Wake me up on July seventeenth to celebrate, though."

Later that day, Mattie was having a harder time breathing. Sometime in the late afternoon, he looked at me all of a sudden and said, "This is it! I can't breathe!" He lips started turning blue.

His nurse was with another patient. She glanced at his monitor from the other patient's bedside and saw that Mattie's oxygen saturation was 100 percent. "You're fine," she called out. "I'll be there in a minute."

Knowing that monitor readings on Mattie often gave a false sense of security, I rolled my wheelchair into the middle of the PICU and called out, "I NEED HELP! I NEED HELP!!" A doctor ran over to Mattie, took one look at him, and grabbed a resuscitation bag to force air into his lungs. He was gasping for breath.

"I think a shred of skin has fallen from his trachea and covered the opening to his lungs," she said. She explained that her only choice was to push it into his lungs, even with the risk of infection. "We'll grab it out later," she called out.

Mattie went limp and said, "I see an angel."

"No, Mattie, it's just me, your doctor," she told him. She was cradling him, still trying to force in air, but Mattie fell unconscious. Finally, she succeeded in getting the piece of skin far enough in. Mattie immediately started ventilating better, and an emergency bronchoscopy was performed to surgically remove from Mattie's lungs whatever foreign material the doctor couldn't retrieve.

The next day, I was sitting by Mattie's bed when his eyes finally opened. "Don't believe the Christmas trees," he said. It was early June. I assumed there was brain damage. Then he added, "Everything is so much more beautiful and wonderful and glorious than we can imagine or compare or create, especially the light and the angels. The angels are nothing like what you put on a Christmas tree."

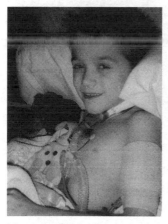

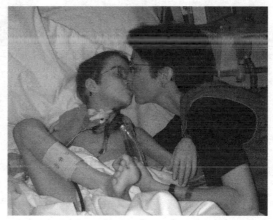

Mattie with Mr. Bunny and Little Bear in the Pediatric Intensive Care Unit, spring 2001

Mattie and Jeni sharing a close moment, spring 2001

CHAPTER 6

Three Wishes

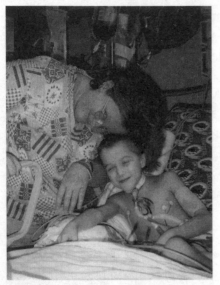

Mattie and his "Very Favorite Adult Best Friend" Sandy, summer 2001

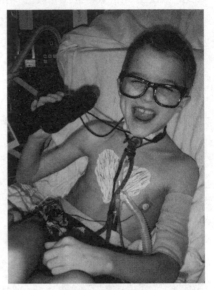

Mattie "PICU Stud-Muffin" (inspired by Austin Powers), summer 2001

> *I need a hope . . . a new hope.*
> *A hope that reaches for the stars. . . .*
> *A hope that inspires me to live, and*
> *To make all these things happen,*
> *So that the whole world can have*
> *A new hope, too.*[1]

*P*sh, *psh*. Whipped cream was flying. Mattie had finished out the school year, and we were engaging in our annual ritual to celebrate the end

---

1 From "A New Hope" in *Journey Through Heartsongs*, page 61.

of the academic calendar—squirting whipped cream into each other's mouths, eating it straight from our hands, and, in general, making a mess.

By this point, Mattie had been in the PICU for three months. I tried to keep him happy with games and action figures. Sandy introduced him to Brit wit; she'd come in every Saturday night and put on comedies shown on the PBS channel, one of the few stations available on the PICU television. The two of them would laugh like crazy at the English humor.

Mattie always had a stack of books on his hospital tray, too, surpassed only by his stack of papers. He was continually writing—a poem for the family of each person who died, journal entries, thoughts about peace.

But even all these activities did not take up enough of Mattie's days. No matter what, he couldn't escape PICU tedium, the desire to be away from there.

One evening, when Sandy was visiting, she was helping him get ready for bed just after they watched Robin Williams's *Hook* on the VCR. The movie had resonance for Mattie because he had often referred to *Peter Pan* to cope when Jamie died. In this film version of the story, Peter Pan has grown up but has lost his "happy thought," regaining it only when he touches a little Teddy bear that he had as a child. Mattie told Sandy that he had lost his happy thought, too, his Heartsong, and needed *that* bear to get it back.

Amazingly enough, Sandy had an uncannily similar-looking bear in her car. It had been left at her office's lost-and-found, and no one had claimed it. She brought it upstairs, and Mattie began making the stuffed animal a kind of proxy for himself. When he went through trach suctioning, so did Little Bear; when he was fitted with ankle braces, so was Little Bear.

One evening, Little Bear said he had had enough. "He's done," Mattie told Sandy. "He just wants to run away."

"I think I can help with that," Sandy answered. I looked at her like she was crazy, but she ignored me. "I come to this hospital several nights a week," she said to Mattie. "I could draw a map—from the PICU to the elevator, to the main floor, to outside. Freedom!"

Little Bear escaped the hospital that very night. Sandy brought him back the next evening, along with some new toys for Mattie and some

delicious take-out food. "He slept in a real bed with big, comfortable pillows," she told Mattie. "I gave him a great big breakfast. Now that he has
broken out, he says he thinks he can handle being back."

"I can handle it, too," Mattie said. I could never thank Sandy enough
for her ingenuity, for her love for my son during trying times.

Mattie had been coping with a lot. Having his trach tube changed
every week—as was medical protocol—was painful because his trachea
was eroding, essentially having turned into a mass of blood and pulp.
Trach changes were scary, too, because they always came with the risk of
a life-threatening crisis. Removing Mattie's trach meant removing his airway. For fifteen seconds, if all went smoothly, his life was literally in the
hands of the people taking out the old tube and inserting the new one.

And it didn't always go smoothly. You had to go in at a curve, and if you
missed it, there'd be blood and the trachea would be hard to see. Mattie
would spasm with anxiety, taking a breath even though he wasn't supposed
to, and the stoma, or hole in his neck, would constrict, changing the shape
of the entryway, and you'd have to pause, losing valuable seconds.

Sandy helped me with this procedure every single week; it was part
of my "normalization" of Mattie's life in the PICU—to have people he
knew tend to as many of his medical needs as possible. She'd take the
old trach out, and I'd put the new one in, or vice versa, to make it go
faster—four hands instead of two.

Sandy would bring Mattie a chocolate shake from McDonald's every
week for when we finished the procedure, telling him to let us get it done
quickly so he could drink the shake before it melted. "Okay, let's get this
over with," he'd say. We called it his weekly McTrach change.

The ankle braces were difficult for Mattie to adjust to also, as was all
the physical therapy to strengthen his body after waking from a coma
and spending so long in a hospital bed. Some doctors and nurses asked
me why he needed to be able to stand again since he was going to die,
anyway.

"Because he's alive today," I said.

There was no denying that Mattie's reacclimation to life was incom-
patible with waiting for his trachea to perforate and kill him. Mattie

recognized this himself. But while he was still here, I was going to make sure he lived rather than just lay there.

By June, the hospital was on board with my approach of normalizing, even celebrating, life in the PICU. Typically, the hospital staff did not send entertainment to the PICU, because children there are so often sedated or too ill to enjoy such distractions. Since Mattie was living and dying at the same time, however, they broke the mold for him. The "Clown Care Unit" now passed through, along with puppet shows, music shows, railroad setups that allowed the children to be conductors.

They even managed to bring in Olympic Gold Medal soccer players Mia Hamm and Brandi Chastain. Although athletes often travel around to hospitals, they don't typically visit the PICU. When it was explained to them what it was like in that unit, the two young women answered that if Mattie had to handle it all day every single day, they could handle it for fifteen minutes.

Mattie was a huge soccer fan and recognized them immediately. He wrote Mia a poem while she was there and explained about people's Heartsongs. Mia was so taken with him that she came back on her own the next day.

"You talked about leaving a lasting impression," she told Mattie, "about passing things on, so I thought you might like to have a video camera to help pass on what's important to you. I want you to have this gift as a thank-you for teaching me the lesson of Heartsongs." She handed him a tiny, lightweight video camera that she had gone out and bought for him.

Mattie therein started the *PICU-Cam*, interviewing nurses and doctors: "What's it like to work here?" "What's the hardest part?" "What's the best part?" "What's it like to have *me* as a patient?" "What are your hopes?" "How do you unwind after working in a place like this?"

Mattie also had some other wonderful distractions.

One of them came in the form of child life specialist Terry Spearman. Usually child life specialists are there for children in other units, talking to them about coping, growing, moving on. But Terry, a social worker for adolescent patients, was assigned to Mattie after he put up his SEDA-

TION NOW sign. Terry made sure he had UNO cards, access to the one working TV in the PICU with a VCR machine so he could watch movies, other diversions. "He can't tune it all out with a book," she said.

By this point, Mattie was more than a patient to the PICU staff. He had become a friend. They'd bring him coffee from Starbucks so he wouldn't have to drink the standard brew from the hospital cafeteria. They'd bring him movies, treats, a new book to read, photos from their vacations. They were, in effect, bringing him the world in his little area—Bedspace H.

Mattie also got to "attend" MDA Summer Camp from that bed. MDA Summer Camp is without doubt the highlight of the year for children who have a neuromuscular disease. It is the week they are like all the other children, the week they are "normal." Mattie once wrote, "*Children mark the passing of each year more by that experience than by Christmas or their birthdays.*"

MDA had approached a new doctor in the research lab, Devin Dressman, and said to him, "You're in the hospital every day. There is the coolest kid in the world sitting in the PICU. Could you give him five minutes to an hour every day for a week?" Devin gave Mattie much, much more.

The theme for MDA camp that summer was Outer Space. The first day, when Devin came in and told Mattie he was going to be his camp counselor, he brought along a calculator because he thought Mattie would like to see how much his mother weighed on other planets—especially Jupiter, where everybody weighs more than twice as much as they do on Earth. Mattie loved that.

It turned out Devin, like Mattie, was a Weird Al Yankovic fan, so the two of them could often be heard singing Weird Al parodies.

Devin also helped Mattie perfect tricks with his remote control fart machine, taping one half to the underside of a chair at the doctors' station. A doctor or respiratory therapist would sit down to work at the computer, and Mattie would trigger the sound from his bed. The person would look around, knowing he or she had nothing to do with it but feeling embarrassed, anyway.

Devin helped the PICU staff relax even more with Mattie than they had before, showing them that it was okay to go outside protocol and bond with this child, have fun with him, even though he was going to die. They'd play a round of poker with him if they had a short break, sit with him and just talk with him. They even introduced him to the movie *Austin Powers: International Man of Mystery*, which had enough innuendo that I never would have allowed him to see it at home. That is, they gave him the mischievous taste of preteen life that his mother couldn't.

At the end of camp week, Devin brought in balloons and asked Mattie to tie his wishes to them, just the way it's always done at traditional MDA Summer Camp. Mattie tied three wishes to three balloons, and Devin went outside the hospital to release them into the air.

Around that time, one of the PICU attending doctors, Christi Corriveau, came up to me and said, "You know, there are all these organizations that grant wishes for dying children. Have you tried any?"

"We have looked into that," I told her, "but his *real* wishes don't meet their requirements. They want a fantasy, like meeting a movie star, or they want a necessity, like an air conditioner."

"What *are* his wishes?" she asked.

"Ask him," I suggested.

So she did. And he told her the same three wishes that he had articulated to me on the pier a year earlier.

One, he wanted to publish at least one book of his poetry to share his message of hope and peace.

Two, he wanted to talk about peace with his hero, Jimmy Carter, for fifteen minutes, to make sure he was approaching peace from a truly productive perspective. Mattie first learned about Jimmy Carter several years earlier when he read an article about a peace agreement being proclaimed as a result of the former president's mediation, with a quote from Carter along the lines of, "Look what these people have chosen for their country. They've chosen peace." What impressed Mattie was not only the mediation by this man but also that he gave credit to the people choosing peace. Mattie began studying more about his new role model and wrote in one essay,

> When I grow up, I want to be a peacemaker, like Jimmy Carter.
> I would like to be "an ambassador of humanity" and travel to

many places, teaching and inspiring people to choose to live together in harmony. I will encourage people to love their neighbors that live around the block from them, and their neighbors that live around the world from them.

And three, he wanted Oprah Winfrey to share his message of Heartsongs on her show:

. . . or however she felt it was most powerful. People turn to Oprah Winfrey for inspiration, and for lessons about things that really matter. . . . I told my Mom when I was six years old that God put Oprah and me on earth at the same time for a reason. She is part of God's plan for me.

Wishing was not frivolous for Mattie. He had written in the same essay that:

. . . wishing is very important. It helps to build an imagination, new ideas, and a vivid mind brimming with life. . . . Wishing brings optimism and hope to life, through creativity and determined focus.

All three of Mattie's wishes were based on his Heartsongs, not just the one pertaining to Oprah. His books of poetry were the communication of his Heartsongs, and his ultimate Heartsong was, at bottom, a call for peace. Living so without peace, from the death of his brother to the dissolution of his parents' marriage, the war his condition waged on his body, the bullying and ostracizing he had experienced, and his vulnerability as a boy with a disabled mother and few material resources, he knew better than most the full meaning of what peace meant and how important it was that it become available to all. He wrote:

My Heartsongs will become the echo and silhouette of my life, after my spirit moves from my body. Some people call this a eulogy or epitaph. I prefer to think of my lasting essence, and my legacy, in more poetic terms, because the gift God gave me to share with the world is the gift of shaping words into inspirational messages. . . . If my Heartsongs grow big enough, if I can share them powerfully enough, maybe they will spread around the world and become like the seeds of peace. And even if my spirit has moved on from my body, other people around the world can nurture these seeds, and grow my message of hope and peace into a powerful reality. Then, my three wishes can become a powerful legacy. . . .

"Anything else, Mattie?" Dr. Corriveau asked after he articulated his three Heartsong wishes, assuming it would probably be impossible to make even one of them come true.

"Yes," he told her. "I want to meet my other real-life heroes, Maya Angelou and Jerry Lewis." Mattie had five role models, one of whom was me. He said I taught him how to celebrate life. Jimmy Carter was his role model for peacemaking, and Oprah Winfrey, for humanitarianism.

But Maya Angelou, Mattie always said, was his role model for writing. *"She has a gift of shaping words for others,"* was the way he wrote it once, *"and teaching powerful lessons that take even the most oppressed past into a positive future, filled with opportunity."*

Jerry Lewis was his role model for advocacy—he didn't have a child with muscular dystrophy, so it wasn't for what he could get personally out of standing behind MDA. Mattie admired that the actor put himself out for the organization simply because it mattered, selflessly using his celebrity for the cause.

"Is there any *kid* thing you want, Mattie?" she asked.

"Like what?" he wanted to know.

"Like Disney World or a shopping spree."

"Dr. Christi," he responded, "I'm sitting in the ICU. How are they going to send me to Disney World? And what am I going to do with a roomful of toys from a shopping spree when I die?"

"Mattie, I want to be able to do something for you," she replied. "Is there at least a movie you'd like to see?"

"Oh, I want to see *Shrek* so bad," Mattie said. "But it's not going to be out on video in time." It had only just been released in theaters.

Dr. Corriveau went straight to the public relations office of the hospital and told them, "There's this child in the PICU. He has changed the PICU, made it a brighter place. He has these dying wishes, and I don't know how to get them granted. Try to make any one of them come true. At least make Oprah Winfrey and Jimmy Carter aware of this child. And I don't care how you do it, but figure out how to get *Shrek* to the hospital."

The next thing Mattie and I knew, a woman who worked directly for Steven Spielberg showed up at the hospital with a briefcase that was literally chained and locked shut. It contained the director's personal copy of the film that he kept at his home. The PICU staff popped a bag of popcorn, poured sodas, and set up the VCR. The woman then put in the tape, looked at her watch, and pressed PLAY. "I'll come back when the credits start rolling," she said.

"But I like to watch the credits," Mattie said. He did, wanting to know who everybody was, down to the key grip.

"Okay," the woman answered, "but you can't watch the movie a second time. I have to catch my plane back to California."

With that she left Mattie's bedside so he and I could laugh and thoroughly enjoy ourselves for the next hour and a half.

When the woman came back and was rewinding the tape, Mattie penned a poem for her to take to Steven Spielberg.

Within days, he and Mike Myers, the actor who played both Shrek and Austin Powers, made separate phone calls to Mattie. Spielberg told him what a cool kid he was, and Myers did Shrek and Austin Powers imitations. He and Mattie went back and forth with the Austin Powers routine. Both men also sent him boxes of goodies: Spielberg, Shrek memorabilia, and Myers, Austin Powers souvenirs.

What the attention from Spielberg and Myers did for Mattie's emotional state I cannot describe.

Soon after, a PR rep from the hospital came in and said we needed to get a phone to Mattie's bed *immediately* because President Carter was going to be calling in exactly ten minutes. Mattie could not believe one of his three wishes was truly going to be granted, and I could not remember the last time I had felt such joy myself.

Jimmy Carter thought he was going to get the "typical" questions: What was it like to be president? What was it like to be a peanut farmer? Instead, Mattie spent his fifteen minutes talking to the former president as a peacemaker. "What are the challenges?" he asked. "The joys? Do you ever get frustrated? How do you go ahead and try to make peace at times that you don't feel at peace in your own heart? We both teach Sunday school—How do you talk peace with people who don't want to use the word *God*?"

President Carter said later that what impressed him was the fact that Mattie's desire to talk with him hadn't been a dying wish; it was a living wish.

He continued to call Mattie after that. They'd talk baseball, compare practical jokes. They'd laugh together and pray together over the phone. And they always talked about peace. "I want to mentor this boy," the president said.

Mattie was beyond thrilled. Passion means literally "suffering," and Mattie had a passion for peace—he ached for it: peace for people within themselves and peace between people, peace for the future. Peace wasn't a hobby for Mattie. It was a passion woven into his entire being.

In the meantime, the ground had been laid to grant another of Mattie's three wishes, in a manner of speaking. A local publishing company offered to have a mock book signing at the hospital, a simulation of the real event that you see in bookstore chains. The company decided to make two hundred photocopies of Mattie's first book, *Heartsongs*, with poems he wrote from ages three through five, and staple them together. This was the book he had won first prize with in kindergarten, the same one that received press attention because he refused to remove the word *God*.

The book signing took place in one of the hospital atriums. The staff thought maybe fifty people would come. They hadn't known Mattie outside the context of his being a PICU patient. They didn't know he had been making speeches for years and was already someone who had achieved a certain level of renown.

Hundreds of people showed up. The atrium and the balconies above it were overflowing. Firefighters, Harley-Davidson riders, hospital and MDA staff, friends and other supporters were there. Virginia congressman Jim Moran and International Association of Fire Fighters president Harold Schaitberger both came. *The Washington Post* showed up to cover the event, as did CNN. Perhaps the most surprising guest was four-star general Richard Myers, who would soon be named chairman of the Joint Chiefs of Staff. Mattie had met him the previous fall through his work as a local MDA ambassador and had been thrilled for the honor. Although Mattie was propeace, he was not antimilitary. He knew that peace had to be planned, that it didn't just happen, and that you couldn't plan it without an understanding of self-defense, of civil rights, and of other cultures. As Mattie rolled into the atrium, the general pinned his star bar on Mattie's collar. "*You* are our hero," he said.

Mattie was able to stay at the event for only about twenty minutes. The doctor, respiratory therapist, and two critical care nurses who had escorted him from the PICU to the atrium saw that he couldn't physically handle any more than that. But the publishing company had a genuine surprise for him. They told him his poetry really had something to offer, and they were going to be giving him a real book contract. They asked him to select poems for inclusion in a longer book, to be entitled *Journey Through Heartsongs*. Mattie was over the moon with joy.

The hospital spent the next day fielding phone calls. Everyone wanted footage of "The Heartsong Kid." CNN wanted an expanded interview; CSPAN wanted a show of Mattie reading his poetry.

Mattie and Terry Spearman, his child life specialist, playfully began planning the movie of his life, recording overly dramatized scenes on his new video camera, and creating a list of all the actors who would star in various roles. "It's Haley Joel Osment for you," Terry said. "You've both got that slim build and blond hair, and he's about your age."

"And for you, Terry," Mattie responded, "Whoopi Goldberg! She *definitely* will have to play you. You two have the same hair, and humor!"

The flurry of publicity began to die down by the middle of July, at which point the PICU staff surprised Mattie with a huge birthday party with about one hundred people. They planned it for the day before his birthday because they didn't want him to catch wind of it.

There were special tests they needed to run in a room off the cafeteria, they said, to check his nutrition status. Mattie was extremely worried about what they would find—only to be wheeled in to see Sandy, Devin Dressman, friends from home, a clown troupe, and many other wonderful people. The PICU had really come through. Nobody thought Mattie would ever see his eleventh birthday, and by that point he looked very fragile, with his clothes hanging off him, but what those who planned and attended the party showed him was that, for every moment he was still here, he mattered.

The rest of July passed without much activity, all the while Mattie continuing to bleed profusely from his trachea. Still, he had managed to gain back a bit of the fifteen pounds he had lost, was able to use his arms better, and had also regained much of the strength of his voice. With ankle braces, he began bearing weight on his legs again. And his swallowing kept improving, too.

Finally, toward the very end of July, he said to me, "I think I need to finish this out at home."

"What do you mean?" I asked. Those kinds of statements from him always made me nervous.

"I'm here so that when my trachea perforates," Mattie said, "they can sedate me and I won't suffer during my final twenty minutes. That could take another day, or another month. I have so much of my life I feel is not done yet, and I can't do it from this bed. I am afraid of the pain of dying, but I have things God wants me to do. I can't do them from here. I want to go home and finish living."

We started talking with the doctors about getting all of Mattie's home care equipment in place. "This means he will probably die at home," they told me, "and there's nothing you'll be able to do to ease the agony as death occurs."

"I understand," I said. But I also understood what Mattie said: "I want to go home and live until I die rather than sit here and exist until death happens to my body."

A couple of days before we left the hospital, Don Retzlaff put gas in our van, changed the oil, and made sure the battery still worked. I hadn't driven it in months. He also told me I needed four new tires. "They're all bald," he said. "Not safe to drive the hour to your apartment."

"Don, I can pay for *one*," I told him. "Just change the worst." I hadn't even been able to afford the hospital cafeteria food. I'd eat Mattie's leftovers between care packages from Sandy.

When he returned the van, I asked him, "Which tire did you change?"

"All four," he answered. "One from Aunt Lorraine, one from me, one from Clifton Oden [a really good friend from church], and one from you. We're all helping Mattie roll forward."

As bad as things were, that was the story of our life. There were always people around to help. "Imagine if the whole world were like that," Sandy had once posited to Mattie, "if everybody helped their neighbor." That was Sandy's lesson to him once when he asked her why she did so much for us. "In the Bible," she told him, "it says, 'Love your neighbor as yourself.' Someone asked Jesus who one's neighbor was, and He answered, 'Whoever God puts in the path of your life.'"

Leaving the hospital proved extremely nerve-racking. The PICU staff was afraid Mattie wasn't going to survive the trip. "How will you deal with the lack of humidity in the van?" they worried.

Mattie was aware of how delicate the situation was. A few days earlier, a friend had brought him a relic of André Bessette—someone who had been very weak as a child, was not expected to live, and then grew up to become a priest, inspiring people to believe in hope and miraculous events.

Bessette was not yet a saint. For that, you need to have interceded to help bring about two miracles after your death, and Bessette had so far interceded with one, leading him to be beatified, the last step before sainthood.

The day before Mattie was to head for home, he picked up the relic and said, "Blessed Brother André, *you* need a miracle to become a saint, and *I* need a miracle to finish my reason for being." He then put the relic to his trachea and offered up a private prayer.

I had to leave at that point for morning rounds. When I was allowed back in, Mattie said, "Mom, my trachea has stopped bleeding." I was not happy. Whenever Mattie's trachea stopped bleeding, it meant it was drying out and that blood was adhering to his dying skin. As soon as the skin sloughed off, the bleeding would begin again, worse. So while Mattie was thinking he was the recipient of a miracle, I was thinking we were in for another emergency bronchoscopy.

I went to the PICU staff. "We know," they said. "We assume he's due for another crisis. His breathing will probably be more difficult this afternoon."

But that's not what happened. Mattie kept saying he felt better and better. By the next morning, he felt better still. "There's nothing we can do," the staff said. "You can take him home—that wouldn't be wrong. But do you want to stay here for this one crisis?"

I answered that Mattie was absolutely determined it was time to go home and that I agreed. "He looks better today," I said, "than he has looked for a year."

There was no lingering at the exit of the PICU. Hugs and kisses, and we were off.

Mattie left two boxes for the staff on his bed. One contained about three hundred of his one-liner "Fortunes, Prayers, and Quotes." The other had a brand-new remote control fart machine, rubber vomit, Mad Libs, bubbles, and an Austin Powers button that said, "Yeah, Baby." He was reminding the people who had taken care of him all those months to play after the storm.

Once outside, Mattie was lifted into a paramedic truck, while I followed in the van. The plan was to stop only if there was some kind of emergency.

About ten minutes from home, the paramedic driver put on the left turn signal. Our apartment was to the right. I panicked.

They turned into the parking lot of a Burger King. Tears began to burn in my eyes. "Why did I do this?" I said to myself. One of the paramedics jumped out of the back of the truck and *ran* into the Burger King. I began transferring myself into my wheelchair while trying to operate the lift that would let me out.

A second paramedic then ran out of the truck and toward me.

"He had a craving," he said. "We're getting him a Whopper and onion rings. Want anything?" It turned out Mattie was doing great, playing UNO in the back with his firefighter buddies. They were having a party.

When we finally arrived home, I suggested to Mattie that he rest a bit.

"In a minute," he said. He then picked up the phone and called Katie McGuire, who supervised his activities as state ambassador for MDA. "Okay, Katie, I'm home," I heard him saying. "Where do you need me?"

She told him about two golf tournaments, the firefighter softball tournament, and the MDA telethon coming up. "Put me down for all four of them," he said.

A day or two later, the phone rang. It was Oprah Winfrey. Rumor had it that people had kept putting *The Washington Post* article about the June book signing event in front of her, that they kept telling her about this kid who already had two of his three wishes granted.

She asked Mattie how he was feeling. She told him she'd like him to come on her show to share his message of Heartsongs and hope and peace.

He acted calm while speaking with her, but when he hung up, he was whooping for joy. "Mom," he said, "her people didn't call you. *She* called *me*. She didn't even have her secretary call and say, 'Oprah Winfrey for Mattie Stepanek.' People always tell me I'm 'real,' Mom. But guess what? Oprah's real, too!"

Oprah wanted him to come on her show the first week of the new season, in early September. But it became clear that we could not travel safely by van that distance. And we could not find a commercial airline that could accommodate Mattie's medical needs. Oprah then said she'd send her own private plane or an air ambulance. After more thought, she called us back.

"I'd really like to have him opening week," she told me, "but we can't take any risks. I have to make that call. I want to carefully orchestrate how to get him to Chicago, not just for the show but to give him the time of his life while he's here. It'll be mid-October. It'll be in a safe way, and once he gets here, we'll make it a bigger trip."

Mattie was beyond excited—and extremely happy—and not just because his third wish was coming true. That summer, along with doing the two MDA golf tournaments, he did the local Baltimore piece of the MDA telethon, as he had done in the past. But that year there was a change. MDA decided they also wanted to close the *national* telethon with Mattie through a live satellite feed from Los Angeles to Baltimore. So there was Jerry Lewis on one end and Mattie on the other.

MDA offered Mattie the option of a script, but he declined, ad-libbing it with Jerry Lewis for a full fifteen minutes. "My life is filled with storms and challenges, like so many people who have neuromuscular disease," Mattie said. "But as hard as life is, I'm so proud to be one of *your* kids." Jerry Lewis cried.

The week after the telethon, which is the culmination of the year for MDA, a new year of fund-raising kicked off, as usual, with a weekend-long firefighters' softball tournament at Watkins Regional Park, Maryland. The firefighters are major supporters of MDA, and Mattie had become close friends with many of them, from the president of the International Association of Fire Fighters to local crew members, and had grown especially close to Bubba and J.J. across the years. Mattie loved that tournament, raising funds selling his one-liner "Luck for Buck" quotes, liberally using his squirt gun, and cheering on the teams—regardless of the score.

That year, one of the teams from New York City won. On Sunday evening, Mattie went out on the field as the MDA Maryland state ambassador to congratulate them, and a New York firefighter who had spent several days playing ball and interacting with the children handed him the trophy he had just been given, saying, "I'm not the champion. I can run the bases with my feet. You're the champion. You run the bases with your heart."

The next morning, many of those who participated—players, staff members, and Mattie—had a final breakfast together, and then we all went our separate ways. It was September 10, 2001.

Mattie with Child Life Specialist Terry Spearman in the PICU at Children's National Medical Center, June 2001

Mattie with IAFF Firefighter buddies Bert "Bubba" Mentrassi and Jim "J.J." Jackson, September 2002

CHAPTER 7

Mosaic of Gifts

Mattie in his bedroom, fall 2001

> . . . *We have, we are, a mosaic of gifts*
> *To nurture, to offer, to accept.*
> *We need to be.*
> *Just be.*
> *Be for a moment . . .*
> *Kind and gentle, innocent and trusting,*
> *Like children and lambs.*
> *Never judging or vengeful*
> *Like the judging and vengeful. . . .*
> *Before there is no earth, no life,*
> *No chance for peace.*[1]

"Turn on the TV, quick!" One of the boys from upstairs had opened the door to our apartment and shouted down.

---

1 From "For Our World" in *Hope Through Heartsongs*, page 49.

"What channel?" I called out.

"Any channel!"

Mattie, who had been working on an essay in his bed, climbed into his wheelchair, working as fast as he could to unplug his equipment from the wall and switch to battery power so he could get himself out into the living room.

We sat there, as the rest of the country did, in disbelief. Tears started streaming down Mattie's face without a sound. "Where's Bubba?" he asked when the newscaster mentioned New York's Bravest. "Where's Tommy, Billy, Jimmy, Big Al, Doc?" All of these firefighters, including the one who had given him the trophy, had been with him throughout the long weekend for the softball tournament. They were from New York City, and from nearby Yonkers and Greenburgh, New York. Mattie knew that after having a few days off, they'd be on duty that day. He knew that the lives of several of them were going up in ashes as the World Trade Center towers collapsed.

There wasn't just sadness. There was fear. We lived just three miles from Andrews Air Force Base. We heard jets scrambling, taking off in all different directions. "They're coming to DC, Mom!" Mattie cried out. "They're coming to DC!"

We didn't know whether bombs were going to be dropped, whether they'd hit the Capitol, the White House. All we knew was that we were underneath fighter jets responding to the emergency.

When we found out about the plane hitting the Pentagon, Mattie cried out, "Where's General Myers? How many more friends am I going to lose in one day?" This wasn't just a national tragedy for Mattie. It was a personal one.

He wrote a number of verses that day addressing the attack, the fear it engendered, and his worry that the response would be one of revenge rather than rapprochement.

By evening, we finally managed to get through to some people despite the jammed phone lines, learning that Bubba was okay and that J.J. was safely in Canada. But there was no word on firefighters from New York City itself, the ones who had won the softball tournament.

Mattie couldn't sleep, and neither could I. We curled up together on the couch.

"What do we pray for, Mattie?" I asked. We prayed every night, but that night I was at a loss. "How can we pick up these pieces? I don't even know where to start." Cries for vengeance were all over the TV screen. Retaliation, anger, fear were on people's minds.

"We need to see all the pieces," Mattie responded, "every fleck of ash, as a gift in the mosaic of life. Rather than seek revenge, we have to begin to rebuild the mosaic. If we keep seeking to retaliate, it's never going to end. Why can't people see that? Fear begets fear. Revenge begets more revenge. We need to stop. Just stop." He pulled out his journal and wrote "For Our World," his third poem following the tragedy, which implored people to "just be."

After that, we dozed off and on through the night, the blue light of the television flickering as it lit the apartment.

Weeks passed, and there was a distinct shift in Mattie's speeches. No matter who the audience, he angled his talk toward the topic of peace. For a pediatric nursing conference in Philadelphia, for instance, a speech that started out being about children participating in their own medical care became a call for people to listen to other people, to see what it was they needed.

Soon we were into October, and *The Oprah Winfrey Show* was fast approaching. Mattie wanted to talk about peacemaking there, too, and though he was told that might get a mention, the theme of the episode was to be "How Does That Feel?" as in how does it feel to be blind, to be supertall, to be dying of a disease similar to muscular dystrophy? Mattie was supposed to open the show with a five- to ten-minute segment.

Oprah decided to tape the show on October 16, and it would air on the nineteenth. A field producer for *Oprah* named Shelly Heesacker came to record footage of Mattie and me in preparation for the airing. Shelly creates video segments that viewers see in the background as Oprah introduces a guest or tells a story. Her aim that day was to capture Mattie living his everyday life on tape and to have him talk about his wishes and about "how it felt" to have a neuromuscular disease. She was going to be there twelve hours—and it was going to be a grueling process, especially in a cramped, poorly lit basement apartment with no windows and two people in wheelchairs.

But the game plan quickly changed for what Shelly wanted to capture. Not twelve minutes into the first tape, she knew Mattie's segment could not be simply about his condition. He had already started talking about how the world needed to figure out a way to be at peace, finding his way back to the topic every time she asked a question, until she just went "off assignment" and asked him, "Why is peace so important to you at eleven years old?"

"We are fighting over our differences," Mattie responded, "and our differences are our true beauty." He certainly knew about being different and about paying an unfair price for it. The *value* of people's differences came naturally to him given his experiences.

Mattie didn't spend the long day with Shelly only sharing his philosophy. There was a lot of fun, too, along with the serious topics. At one point, Shelly asked me to "do something domestic," like cook, so she could tape it. Mattie started laughing hysterically because I don't cook and never did; it has nothing to do with my disability. To me, if you have to do more than "punch holes with a fork and rotate halfway through heating," it's too much. Shelly loved that Mattie and I had this dynamic of playing and praying while doing whatever it was we needed to do. It was another part of our "celebrate life" approach.

When Shelly brought the tapes to Chicago, she managed to convince *The Oprah Winfrey Show* staff that Mattie's segment needed to be more than how his disability felt. She told them she had been struck by how an eleven-year-old placed a higher priority on becoming a father someday and on relationships than on guns, cars, or the typical fantasies of a young boy. She said that she went to our apartment to get "What is it like to suffer, to have your dying wishes granted?" and came back with "What is it like to be a peacemaker?"

Soon after, Mattie, Sandy, and I were flying to Chicago on an air ambulance with a respiratory therapist, critical care nurse, and air paramedic on board, all courtesy of Oprah. The hotel room she put us up in was larger than both of the apartments we had lived in combined, with two bedrooms, two kitchens, a dining room, and a living room; we were told it was the unit Bill Cosby stayed in when he was on Oprah's show. Mattie said lying down in the bed was like resting in a pile of marshmallows. He loved sitting on the toilet in the bathroom and phoning us in the living room to say, "Guess where I am?" We had not known luxury like that in our entire lives.

The next morning, the day of the taping, Mattie woke at six A.M. and said that even though he was happy, he was "kind of scared."

"What are you scared of?" I asked.

"First, now that my three wishes will be granted, I hope God doesn't think it's okay for me to go." I had thought about that, too, but didn't dare say it.

"Second, these will be the most important minutes of my life. Oprah's giving me a window to the world. What if I get it wrong?"

"Mattie," I said, "you can never share the truth of a Heartsong wrong."

"You're right," he said, managing to lose his nervousness even while he held on to a great feeling of excitement.

I thought about the nickel that had gotten Mattie to this moment—the nickel that was about to touch millions of lives.

When Mattie was six years old, he found a nickel on the ground right outside the thrift shop where we bought most of our clothes and just about all of our household items—mugs, pots, a table—during all the years of our significant financial struggles. I told him he could keep it, but Mattie insisted we go to the store manager and ask if someone had come looking for money that had been lost. The manager said no but that he would hold on to the money Mattie had found in case someone came seeking it. With that, Mattie put the nickel on the counter. The man waited for the rest, and when he realized the total was five cents, he looked at Mattie and asked, "What can you get nowadays for a nickel?"

"A gift," Mattie answered.

"Son," the man responded, "take this nickel as your gift, then, and go buy yourself whatever you can get for it, which isn't going to be much, even in this store."

Mattie loved Legos, and stuffed animals (especially tigers), and paper, markers, pens, and pencils. But books—they were almost sacred in their worth to him. So he went straight to the book section of the thrift shop, only to find that most of the books for a nickel were for very young children and could be read while he was standing right there. Then he alighted upon *Meet Oprah Winfrey: A Self Made Woman of Many Talents.* On the back cover it said that "a determined little girl made her dreams come true." On the front it asked, "How did Oprah rise up out of poverty?" and "What is Oprah doing today to help women and children?" Inside the front cover the price was handwritten: 5 *cents.*

Mattie was hooked. He wanted to know everything he could about this woman who had struggled as a child but then grew up to be able to help others. When he finished reading it at home, he looked at me and said, "Mommy, I want to meet Oprah Winfrey. I really need to talk with her. She understands challenges, abuse, fear, criticism, and doubt. She knows what it means to live beyond an expectation. She understands that hope is real. She is the one who needs to share my message of Heartsongs with the world. God said into my spirit that she would listen, and that she is a part of this. There is a reason God created Oprah Winfrey and Mattie Stepanek to live some of our years at the same time."

He sat down and wrote the first of many letters to Oprah that night. Across the years, he penned several more, one of which included:

> *You understand about rising up and out of and beyond what tries to root us in the sadness of the past rather than the potential of the future. . . . You are a messenger, and I have a message for you to share.*

Now here we were, some five years later, with that nickel having propelled us so far forward.

In the green room, the staff prepared Mattie for some of the questions he might be asked: What does it feel like to have muscular dystrophy? How does it feel to have all three of your wishes granted?

But when he and Oprah were sitting opposite each other, she soon put down the little blue cards on which the stock questions were printed. The two of them really *conversed.*

After about ten minutes, the show cut to the first commercial. Oprah looked at me—I was sitting with Sandy in the front row—and asked, "Can he stay up here? Is he okay?"

"He needs to be plugged into electricity," I answered.

"Can we bring up a power cord?" Oprah called out to her staff. Mattie was going to be on longer than anticipated. He remained onstage with her for more than half the show.

"People now are fighting over how our Heartsongs are different," he said to Oprah, to the world. "But they don't need to be the same. That's the beauty. We are a mosaic of gifts. Each of us has our inner beauty."

He talked, too, about his near-death experience the previous spring, saying that the beauty of Heaven he glimpsed before life grabbed him back was "beyond imagination and description." And he read some of his poetry:

> *When I die . . .*
> *I will ask God if I can*
> *Help the people in purgatory . . .*
> *So they can see the face of God,*
> *So soon. , , , [2]*

People in the audience were wiping tears from their eyes. The firefighters Bubba and J.J., who had each traveled more than a thousand miles and successfully pleaded for tickets to the show, were shown on tape stifling sobs. The world was hungry for a message in those weeks just after 9/11, and Mattie supplied it. He had touched the world with a message of hope and peace, burnished in his heart by God, just as he had begun to hope he would so many years earlier. "Everybody who's heard you today has just felt a little sigh of peace," Oprah said.

Right after the show, Oprah came back to the green room to chat with Mattie some more. I thought it was pro forma but learned later that she had done that with only two other guests, Nelson Mandela and Maya Angelou.

---

2 From "When I Die (Part II)" in *Journey Through Heartsongs*, page 54

Oprah wrapped Mattie in her arms and held him, telling him, "You are so real. Thank you." It was a pure Heartsong moment for Mattie, or a "full circle moment," as Oprah called it. Mattie's comment about Oprah on the day she first phoned him was coming right back to him straight from her. She then told Mattie that she was going to make sure he had her phone number and e-mail address. "This is just the beginning of our friendship," she said.

Across the next couple of days, Oprah arranged an incredible sight-seeing tour of Chicago. We saw museums and Lake Michigan. We went to landmarks all over the city. We ate at Bubba Gump Shrimp.

Toward the end of our visit, we were given a private tour of Chicago's Field Museum. It finished near the main entrance, where there is the skeleton of a *Tyrannosaurus rex* named Sue, the largest ever found. Because it was a weekday, there weren't many people around, and a woman with a golden retriever caught Mattie's eye. "You know, he looks very well behaved," Mattie said to the dog's owner, "but aren't you concerned he might say to himself, 'I can't take it anymore,' and run off with one of Sue's toe bones?"

"No, I'm not concerned," the woman answered, smiling. "This is one of the dogs that helps me *find* the dinosaur bones." It turned out the woman was Sue Hendrickson, the archeologist who had discovered the dinosaur, which was named for her.

She and Mattie chatted by themselves for about twenty minutes while Sandy and I went to take a second look at another exhibit. When we came back, Mattie started telling Sandy everything Sue had just told him, and Sue walked up to me and said, "I understand he's looking for a golden retriever service dog."

"Yes, but it's not going to happen," I replied.

"Why not?" she asked. "You won't allow it?"

"No, I would allow it," I told her. "But you have to go on a waiting list. And it takes two or three years—they might not want to give him one because of his life expectancy."

"What if someone gave him a service dog without his having to wait in line?" Sue wanted to know.

"Sure," I told her. "But it would have to be a real service dog."

"I breed them," Sue said. "The next time one of my dogs drops a litter of puppies, I'll call you. He wants a male, and he's going to name him Micah, right?"

"Yes," I answered. Mattie had been talking about getting a dog named Micah for a couple of years already. The name is that of a prophet, a young peacemaker, in the Old Testament.

"I'll give him the pick of the litter," Sue promised.

I answered, "Thank you," but figured I'd never hear from her, that she was just being nice that day.

We flew home Thursday afternoon and watched the show from our apartment the next day, from four to five P.M. I told Mattie how proud of him I was. But I was more than proud.

In Chicago, during the taping, I kept pinching myself, so to speak, to make sure it was really happening. But at home, I felt myself in awe. This was a child who at age four said that God put messages in his heart, and I hesitated. This was a child who in kindergarten challenged a decision not to allow the word *God* in his poetry, and I hesitated. This was a child who at six said that he and Oprah Winfrey were put on earth at the same time for a reason, and I hesitated. I hesitated, too, all through his letter-writing campaign to Oprah and to Jimmy Carter, all the way through the summer that had just passed, when he said a miracle had been bestowed on him and that his trachea had stopped bleeding and I thought he was just heading into another emergency.

Where I was full of hesitation, Mattie was always full of hope. Even when he believed he was going to die, in the middle of all that medical reality, my son was able to hold on to something that mattered more than the moment at hand, and that's why my heart was so full. Instead of falling into my pattern of hesitation, he always remained steadfast in hope, to what he believed confidently was his reason for being and his singularity of purpose allowed him to accomplish his goal.

The phone rang at exactly 4:59 P.M., as the *Oprah Show* was ending. I figured it was Sandy, or perhaps my Ph.D. advisor from the university, Paula Beckman.

"Hello," I answered.

"Am I the first?" the voice on the other end said.

"The first what?" I asked.

"Any person with a beating heart inside their chest is running for the phone right now. We're five, six weeks out from September 11. How can you watch that and not let go of the anger, even the pain and the grief? How can you not pause and say, 'This kid's right. There *is* hope.' Everybody is going to want Mattie. We all need Mattie *right now*." It was Brian O'Keefe, a producer from ABC's *Good Morning America*.

That moment was, literally, the beginning of the rest of Mattie's life. CBS, NBC, Paula Zahn, National Public Radio, *USA Today*, *The New York Times*, the *Los Angeles Times*, *Time*, *Newsweek*, Larry King—*everybody* started calling.

Mattie was on ABC more than a half dozen times that fall—three times on the *Oprah Show*, three times on *Good Morning America*, and once on *Primetime Thursday* for a longer segment called "The Magic of Mattie." *Good Morning America* and ABC correspondent Chris Cuomo ultimately won an Emmy for Mattie's segments.

Chris had actually wanted Mattie on as early as June, when he learned about the mock book signing at the hospital. *Good Morning America* had been preparing a series of "Survivor Stories." But the higher-ups said Mattie was dying, not surviving, even though Chris later told me he tried to explain that "Mattie's quest to live and make a difference while living is what made him a survivor."

He truly respected Mattie, saying that "he was the right messenger, with the right message, at the right time." He told me that Mattie "was not a character, not a subject to be interviewed and reported on" but someone who needed to be listened to. "He made us believe again," Chris said, "in the things that matter. He was never outspoken, yet never hesitant to speak his heart. That made him radical."

Chris also said, "Mattie's body was a reminder of the fragility of life, his youth was a reminder of future generations, even his suffering gave us hope—I recognized that he was a tribute to and a celebration of human potential. He made my life better."

Others apparently felt the same way.

Fan mail started showing up at the apartment. Within days of Mattie's appearance on *Oprah*, the post office began delivering two big crates a day.

Life seemed good. By mid-November, Mattie started doing book signings—Oprah had recommended his *Journey Through Heartsongs* on her show, and people were flocking to stores to buy it. Mattie's friend Hope loved going with him—she would open the books for him so he didn't have to do any physical work other than writing his name. For his own part, Mattie loved interacting with every single person who came through the line, sometimes a thousand at a time.

He enjoyed his budding friendship with Oprah, too. She was calling him more often by that point, and the e-mails between them were flying pretty fast and furious. Some were about weighty topics, such as rejection by dint of being different or fear of death, but many were light— about meteor showers and Thanksgiving plans—about how both Mattie and I were going to wear purple for Thanksgiving that year because Oprah had given him *The Color Purple*, and purple had now become Mattie's color for hope.

"YOU are my new Heartsong," Oprah wrote to Mattie. *"I think about you every day."*

But for all the wonderful things that were happening, medical reality intruded. When Mattie was admitted to the hospital the previous March, he began to develop a sore on the back of his head. You could see the bandage covering it on Oprah's show. By November, the skin on Mattie's head had eroded so badly that his skull started to show right through. No one knew what to do.

A PICU doctor suggested I wean him from 60 percent oxygen to 40 percent, thinking that maybe all that oxygen was just too toxic to allow the sore to heal. I went along with it largely because by mid-November, Mattie was standing up again with ankle braces and gaining back weight. Overall, he was looking well.

Every couple of days I went down on his oxygen 2 percent at a time. He still looked fantastic—his color remained good—but he began to wake up cranky, irritable. He actually cursed one morning, which we never did in our home, and was talking sarcastically. This little peacemaker who was touching the world was suddenly acting hurtful. Later that day he began saying things that made no sense, asking why there were boats outside our door, even though we lived nowhere near the water.

I thought that perhaps it was an exaggerated reaction to Pumpkin Season. After all, Mattie watched friends' lives go up in smoke in the burning towers just two months earlier. There was plenty to grieve despite his recent good fortune. But when Jamie-D came to visit one day, she said to me after playing with him for a while, "This is not about Pumpkin Season. This is something medical. His pupils look different."

I called Dr. Fink and explained that Mattie's manner had been worsening for about a week and that he was now starting not to make sense.

"Turn his oxygen up to eighty percent," Dr. Fink said.

"To eighty? Why would I double it?"

"What do you mean double it?" Dr. Fink wanted to know. "He's on sixty, right?"

"No, he has been down to forty for at least a week."

"Too many doctors," Dr. Fink said, frustrated. "Turn him up to eighty, then wean him back down to sixty—and leave it there!"

Within ten minutes of my turning up the oxygen concentration, Mattie's affect changed. He even apologized for his behavior, although he did not remember much of what he had said during the previous week. For the rest of his life, he was never weaned below 60, and for the rest of his life, he never had a spell like that again.

But that was the easy fix. We had another medical complication looming—the festering sore. How to deal with it still wasn't clear.

Worried as I was, I had the rare luxury of some professional medical support in the home that fall. Laura Becker-Gultekin, a nurse from the Pediatric Intensive Care Unit, started coming to the apartment once a week for an eight-hour shift. I had had some home care nurses when Mattie and Jamie were babies but no help since then; most home care health providers aren't equipped to deal with medical conditions as complex as Mattie's, and it was better to go without than to watch a nurse make mistakes with my child. The one agency I did try sent a nurse who smoked in the bathroom, then tried to blame the cigarette smoke on eleven-year-old Mattie because "kids experiment at that age." Never mind that he was on life support and had just come home from five months in the hospital and understood all too well that his whole life was about making sure he could breathe.

But Laura, a PICU staffer who knew her way around Mattie's ventilator and all his other equipment, was a godsend. Eight hours a week might not seem like much, but it allowed me to take a shower without worrying as much, to go to the university where I was pursuing my Ph.D. and not have to take Mattie. One night, Laura even kicked me out of the house just to go and take a break. It had been more than a year since I had been able to do anything like that.

I was going to go to a movie with Sandy, but there was nothing playing that captured our interest. We ended up having pie and coffee at Applebee's, then driving to a grocery store to buy broccoli because Sandy was going to make broccoli salad for Thanksgiving.

Uneventful as the evening was, we were absolutely giddy with our few hours of freedom, laughing in Sam's Club like a couple of schoolgirls. Sandy, too, was exhausted, from her two jobs, from taking courses for her own doctoral program, from helping me take care of Mattie along with her own children.

Thanksgiving's arrival was a particular blessing that year—in Mattie's vision on the pier, it was the one occasion after March 30 for which he could sense he might be here.

The night before the holiday, Mattie slept at Sandy's, where the meal was going to be. I hadn't cooked a turkey in years. When Mattie was seven, our church had given the two of us a Thanksgiving turkey that was almost too big for our tiny kitchen. To baste it, I had to open the oven door fully—it wasn't one of those oven doors that opened partway— and, from my wheelchair, lean over. With the hot oven door on my knees, which I covered with towels to keep from getting burned, and the roasting pan pulled toward me and partly straddling the door and the oven rack, I would periodically squirt the juices over the bird with a bast-

ing bulb. About two-thirds of the way through, I opened the oven door
for one more basting, then flinched from the heat because I hadn't put
enough towels on my knees. That somehow moved the pan in such a way
that the bird went flying off.

I couldn't see where it went, and my wheelchair wouldn't move for
me to look. "Mattie," I called out, "I need you."

"I'm watching TV," he called back.

"But I can't find the turkey."

"Mom, the turkey's in the oven," he said.

"No, it's not," I answered.

When Mattie came in, he told me, "Uh, Mom, it's behind you."

The mystery of why I couldn't move the wheelchair was solved, but
the bird still needed to be dealt with.

"Can you get two pot holders," I asked Mattie, "and try to pick up the
turkey so I can put it back in the oven? It's not done yet."

Mattie tried, but he couldn't lift it, so I asked him to kick it around to
my feet. But we couldn't even lift it together—it was as though the turkey
was fighting us. So Mattie had to fill a portable oxygen tank and go ask
neighbors for help. We ate that bird down to the carcass, using the bones
for soup.

Mattie's sleeping at Sandy's the night before the holiday allowed me
to get a little extra sleep. Whoever was watching him had to wake every
hour or two to empty the humidity that collected in his vent tubing, or
else water would go into his lungs.

On Thanksgiving morning, the phone rang about an hour after I woke
up. It was Mattie. "Mom, guess what? I cracked an egg! I cracked it and
put it into a bowl!" The boy now had not one but two books on the *New
York Times* bestseller list and was regularly e-mailing with Oprah Winfrey, but between our disabilities and my own lack of domesticity, some
of the basics had gone by the wayside.

Mattie led Grace that day, and we all gave thanks for so many things,
not least of all the fact that he was there. Two weeks later, he received
the surprise of his life on one of his *Good Morning America* appearances.
Jimmy Carter came out during the interview and introduced himself to
Mattie in person for the first time.

Mattie literally gasped as his hero walked toward him. It was probably the only time in his life that I saw him speechless.

When the show went to commercial break, Mattie asked the former president, "Can I touch you?" They had only shaken hands for the cameras.

"Of course" was the reply, and the two embraced.

"You're really here!" Mattie said. He had been afraid at first that they sent an impersonator to make a little kid happy. He then gave the president a copy of the video he had made about the man's life, along with the report he had written about our thirty-ninth president when Mattie was eight and first began learning about him. I had brought the items along because I was let in on the secret beforehand.

The next day, December 5, Mattie served as First Lady Laura Bush's escort for her Christmas visit to Children's National Medical Center. While we were there, we went for a visit with Dr. Martin Eichelberger, who was now overseeing the situation with the sore on the back of Mattie's head. By that point, there was a puslike material oozing from the hole.

"I want you to look at it carefully when I shine a light on it," he said to me. "You can absolutely see the skull through it. It's paper thin. You cannot have a situation develop where the membrane opens and his skull is exposed. We're going to have to do a skin graft surgery."

My heart sank. How many storms could this child survive? We could never sit back and go, "Wow, we made it," not even after *Oprah*, after *Good Morning America*, after all the other interviews and media attention, the success of the books, because there was always something else.

"This is scary," I said to Dr. Eichelberger.

"I know," he replied. "It's so scary that we'll wait till after Christmas so he can get through the holidays. This is anesthesia—real, heavy anesthesia, not light. I'm not sure he'll survive it."

The next day, Oprah called. "Christmas is coming," she said to Mattie. "You're my guy. I want to give you the best gift in the world. What would you like?"

Mattie thought for a moment but didn't say anything.

"You just name it," she continued. "Whatever you want, I'll make it happen."

Another moment passed before Mattie finally spoke. "What I really need," he told his new friend, pausing even while saying it, "is prayer."

Mattie with Oprah Winfrey, during his first appearance on her television show, October 2001

CHAPTER 8

Embracing Each Moment

Mattie meeting Jimmy Carter for the first time on *Good Morning America*, December 2001

"Head Elf" Mattie with "Santa" Tommy Kianka, December 2001

Let this truly be
The celebration of
A New Year. . . .
Let us remember
The past, yet
Not dwell in it.
Let us fully use
The present, yet
Not waste it.
Let us live for
The future, yet
Not count on it. [1]

---

1 From "Resolution Invocation" in *Celebrate Through Heartsongs*, page 41.

"I'm praying for you right now," Oprah e-mailed Mattie soon after their phone conversation. "And I will start a small prayer circle at Harpo and together we will pray for you."

But Oprah's gift of prayer ultimately went much beyond a prayer circle she started within her own company. She had a much bigger gift in mind and within days sent the following e-mail:

Mattie,

This is a note to me, from someone on my staff who works the online website.

12/12/01 3:31 pm Subject: Prayer for Mattie

Here's how we plan to keep the prayer alive for the next 30 days online:

We will promote it on the home page every day, with the text of your message, and the streamed video of what you said in the show.

We will start an e-mail program, encouraging people to e-mail their friends (a good version of an online chain letter) multiplying the number of people praying for Mattie.

We will have people "sign" a message board, so thousands of names will be up on oprah.com, all the people who are praying for him and wishing him health.

We will ask people to post messages on a special message board, their personal prayers for Mattie, which will be shared by everyone who is praying for him.

```
We'll remind people in our newsletter every week.

We're looking into creating a special program where
people could sign up to get a daily reminder, every day
at noon. We will send them an e-mail to stop and say a
prayer for Mattie. We can write some different prayers
for him, or use any prayers you would like us to pass
along to people.

Will also put Mattie's poetry up, people can listen to
him reading it himself every day, so people can really
feel the connection.
```

Oprah announced the thirty days of prayer for Mattie on her show in mid-December. She talked about "my guy," as she called Mattie, facing a surgery that he had less of a chance of surviving than he did of surviving the sore on his head. She talked about "The Power of Prayer," sending a message to her millions of viewers worldwide to please pray for Mattie.

Mattie wrote back the next day:

```
Wow!!! I don't know what else to say. I asked for prayer
for Christmas, and I'm getting a whole world full of
it . . . a mosaic of gifts. Thank you, thank you, thank
you to everybody. I will heal. I will.

I love you and you love me,

Mattie
```

People had started logging on as the credits began to roll. We saw e-mails from around the globe saying things such as, "Our entire company pauses at noon to pray for Mattie." Oprah wrote to Mattie about it:

Have you checked out our website and all the MATTIE
PRAYERS people have left for you? Thousands of them . . .
you should just browse through and see some of them.

Wish you were here [at my home in California]. You would
love the purple and pink and orange sunsets. And feeling
the wind through the palm trees. There is a hammock on
the patio. . . .

LOVE TO YOU.

Mattie loved that people were pausing each day at noon to embrace a moment for a common cause. "This is for me," he said, "but imagine if we could all do this for each other every single day—pause together for the common good, for healing ourselves. If we could all unite in the common goal of stopping to think every day of what our neighbors are going through, if we got to *know* our neighbors, we *could* achieve peace."

In the meantime, he and I worked ourselves to live consciously in every single moment, not to let time go by casually, or solely in worry about the next step. Time was too precious to waste, so we went forward living life as fully as possible, which, since it was December, meant getting ready for Christmas. Not that there weren't bumps in the road.

One of our traditions was the annual Fantasy Flight to the North Pole, put on by Children's Hospice International. United Airlines couldn't use an actual airplane that year because of stepped-up security post-9/11, so they had the children go down a "magic hallway."

Of course, by the time most children are eleven, they already don't believe in Santa Claus and the North Pole, but I had kept encouraging Mattie to continue the enchantment through the years because so much of the magic of childhood had been stolen from him. That year, however, as we rolled down the hall in our wheelchairs, he looked at me with the most hurt expression.

"What's wrong?" I asked him.

"We'll talk later," he said.

Once we arrived at the "North Pole," he went through the motions, serving cookies to all the guests in the role of head elf he had assumed a few years earlier, and talking to all the youngest children. And as usual, he went last to talk to Santa—Tommy Kianka, the same Santa who had been at every Fantasy Flight. But for Tommy, too, Mattie had hurt in his eyes.

When we arrived home later that day, he was clearly feeling very sad.

"What's *wrong*, Mattie?" I asked him again.

"I don't know what's real anymore," he answered. "Mom, I didn't go to the North Pole. I've *never* been to the North Pole. You made that up."

"Yes, that's true," I answered. "It's part of childhood."

"What else have you not been honest with me about?" he wanted to know. "What have you not been honest about concerning my health?"

I picked up Mattie's favorite stuffed animal, a tiger he named Tad, short for Thaddeus. Tad was always with Mattie, either hanging off his wheelchair or in his arms and wearing wire-rimmed glasses of his own.

"Let's pretend this is your Tad, your son, who was born to you," I said to Mattie. "He's now three, four years old. He's old enough to get that a man in a red suit brings toys to children. Are you going to say that because you don't want your child not to trust you on anything that matters, you won't let him have the magic of childhood? Your son is going to be seeing Santa Claus in malls, in books, on TV, and in preschool. He's going to learn that Santa puts gifts in stockings, leaves stuff under trees. Do you want to make sure that for the sake of his never losing trust in you, you will tell it one hundred percent exactly as it is?"

"But what happens when Tad turns eleven and his daddy has been his hero, his role model, and Tad realizes that there's no Santa, that I made it all up?"

"And why would you have made it up?" I asked.

"Because I love him," Mattie said. I could see the shift in understanding come into his eyes.

"Right," I told him. "And then, the only thing that changes for the child is that he comes to understand the *real* spirit of Christmas. Think of all the things people do for children so they can feel good on Christ mas Day. That's the point. Little kids don't get the birth of the Savior. But they do get opening a gift under the tree, and then later they start to learn about giving gifts, and about the gift to the world from God that Christmas represents."

Mattie got out of his wheelchair and climbed into my lap. "Promise you'll never be dishonest with me about things that matter, like my health," he said.

"I promise," I told him. "People have told me I was wrong to let you know how bad it was with your trachea, that you could have died. But I told you the truth."

There was a pause. "We've had a really hard time financially," Mattie said. I nodded. "But every year, I got something under the tree."

"That's how parents feel about their children," I responded. "They'll do whatever they can."

"But when I opened my gift on Christmas morning, you were always so excited, as if you were seeing it for the first time."

"I *was* seeing it for the first time—I was seeing you receive it from Santa for the first time."

"But you could have taken the credit," Mattie said.

"I had the joy of seeing you happy," I told him. "I didn't need the credit."

After we finished our conversation, he went and wrote a poem that he then handed to me on Christmas morning:

> . . . *This year I have been skeptical*
> *If Santa Claus is real,*
> *But now I know the spirit is*
> *And the red suit's for appeal. . . .*
> *The greatest Kringle of them all,*
> *My mom's my best Christmas present.*
> *She makes my life a special gift,*
> *Each daily celebration pleasant. . . .* [2]

---

2   From "Ms. Santa Claus" in *Reflections of a Peacemaker: A Portrait Through Heartsongs*, page 79.

♥

Not his deepest meditation in verse, perhaps, but I treasured the gift.

Mattie went through the rest of the month with a freer heart after that talk. As in years prior, as the holiday season began, he read his "December Prayer" live on MIX 107.3's *The Jack Diamond Morning Show*, a local radio program:

> *. . . There are so many ways*
> *To celebrate faiths,*
> *There are so many faiths*
> *To celebrate life.*
> *No matter who,*
> *No matter what,*
> *No matter how . . .*
> *You pray.*
> *Let's say a prayer*
> *This season,*
> *Together, for peace.*[3]

Another December morning, Mattie put a little blue marble by my bed with a note taped to it that said: *"To Mommy, Love Mattie. Hint: A sky of our love."* That marble remains by my bedside to this day.

Every day, no matter what else was going on, I had to clean out Mattie's sore. And every couple of days we had to go to the hospital to have the sore cleaned more thoroughly and rebandaged. What we saw was always the same—no change in the level of pus oozing or the size of the hole. Still, we kept enjoying the season, despite the fear of what lay ahead.

One afternoon we went to the university. I had meetings to attend plus an evening course, and Mattie had a plan. He wrapped a Nerf ball in foil and put plastic around the foil, calling the creation his *crystal ball*.

---

3   From "December Prayer" in *Journey Through Heartsongs*, page 58.

He said to each person on the staff, "For a dime, I'll tell you your fortune; for a dollar, I'll tell you eleven things, and I'm sure you'll like at least one of them." He needed money to buy crafts supplies to make Christmas gifts, and this was his way of raising the needed cash.

One of the people to whom he presented his crystal ball to raise money for buying gifts was my dissertation advisor, Paula Beckman. She handed him a dollar when he showed her the crystal ball, and he told her ten things. "What about the eleventh, my bonus fortune?" she asked.

"Well, it's special," Mattie explained. "I can see that you're going to have a date with a handsome young man. He has blond hair and blue eyes, and his mother has a three-hour class tonight that he's not interested in at all."

Paula then took Mattie for dinner at the Student Union building and afterward to the university bookstore. She frequently brought him there to pick out a book. It had started when he was five. She had taken him to the children's section, and he just looked at all the kiddie books and asked to go to the science fiction section, since he was making his way through the Star Wars series.

"Mattie," she said when he picked up a hefty-size Star Wars book, "I don't think you'd be able to read that."

"I've read almost all of them, Paula," he said. "But I haven't read this one yet."

"Okay, if you can open it and read me the first sentence without any hesitation," Paula told him, "I'll buy it for you."

"It was a time of uncertainty in the Galaxy," the five-year-old Mattie intoned. "After the end of the brutal Sith War, the galaxy again began the long road of rebuilding. . . ."

A store clerk leaned around the aisle. "Sounds like he gets the book, lady," he said.

With his crystal ball strategy, Mattie made about thirty dollars. From the crafts store, he bought kits to make lamps, clocks, and soaps. For Sandy he produced a lampshade with characters from *Yellow Submarine* on it, since she had introduced him to that Beatles movie at the hospital earlier in the year. Jimmy Carter and Oprah each received a lamp decorated with little Heartsongs. The clocks said "Be prayerful," "Be playful," or "Be peaceful" next to each number. The soaps were a disaster—they didn't come out looking nearly as good as on the package and cost more to make than they would have cost to buy. But Mattie did like putting little plastic mice and spiders in the bars of soap that he made for our friend Diane Tresca, who would soon be visiting, because she was afraid of things like that. Despite his many health limitations, Mattie still had the inclinations of a little boy in him.

He loved giving gifts much, much more than receiving them. No doubt that was a large part of the reason he was terrific about the modest spread of goodies that awaited him most years under our tree, about the fact that I couldn't get him whatever was the hottest item for kids each Christmas. That year, what he would have loved was a set of the *Harry Potter* Legos that had just come out. Mattie was a huge *Harry Potter* book fan. The first *Harry Potter* movie had just been released weeks earlier, and everything *Harry Potter* was the rage.

I felt bad that I couldn't give him what he most wanted, but money we were expecting from book sales had not come through yet. And when it did, the proceeds would be going into a medical trust fund designated for health needs. Granted, once that was set up, my small stipend from the university could be stretched further, covering other expenses. But even if I had had money, I absolutely could not have gotten him the gift that was selling out instantly. I bought him a small box of regular Legos instead.

Christmas Eve arrived just a couple of days after Mattie finished crafting his presents. He and I were getting ready to go to midnight Mass, where he would sign "Silent Night" in honor of his brother Jamie. Around nine P.M., shortly before we left for church, there was a knock at the door. It was a delivery company bringing a box to Mattie from Harpo Productions. Shelly Heesacker had packed it with gifts from Oprah, the staff, and herself.

That box was the first thing Mattie opened on Christmas morning. Inside was another huge box, with a tag that said it was from Santa. It was the *Harry Potter* Legos. Shelly had no idea how important they'd be to Mattie. She had been in a toy store, shopping for someone else, and a woman was returning them after finding out that the child she had bought them for was going to get them from someone else. Shelly knew

Mattie was a big *Harry Potter* fan, so on a hunch that Mattie would like them, she bought the set from the woman right there, before she even had a chance to return it.

In retrospect, Shelly's kindness that Christmas is not surprising. "I meet a lot of people as a TV producer," she once told me, "and I would say without hesitation, Mattie is one of the . . . most important people I've ever met in my life. . . . He inspires you to be your best self."

Oprah's gifts from the big box included a book about peace, a camera, and cash, part of which Mattie used to buy a television set, a VCR, and twenty videotapes for the hospital PICU—everything from Barney and Disney movies for the younger patients to *X-Men* and *Ferris Bueller's Day Off* for the teens.

As we opened our other gifts under the branch cut from Don Retzlaff's property, *A Christmas Story* played on TBS in the background. Our mood was light. Then the phone rang while we were having our coffee.

It was Jimmy Carter. "The twenty-two members of our family are sitting here," he told Mattie, "and our Christmas gift this morning was the video you made of my life. We are laughing and crying with joy. You gotta work on my Georgia accent. Where did you find out all that information?" Mattie had even included that Miss Lillian told her son to get his feet off her bed right after he informed her that he was going to run for president.

Mattie, eight years old when he made that video, acted a number of parts: Jimmy as a boy in overalls and a straw hat, stirring peanuts in a pot; Carter as president (Mattie had forgotten to put his shoes back on and was mortified for the president's family to see him playing with his toes in that scene); and then, as a peacemaker, building a Habitat for Humanity house with a hammer and saw in his hand.

At the end of the video was some footage of Mattie, still age eight, going through his martial arts moves. "It's hard to imagine the amazing things your body did as a Black Belt," the president told Mattie. "And now that you're in a wheelchair and not angry—that you still find hope in our world, seeing what you lost—I'm even more in awe seeing what you left behind, that you didn't miss a beat in bringing happiness to the world despite what you have gone through."

Rosalynn got on the phone to wish Mattie a Merry Christmas, too, capping off the call. When we hung up, Mattie just looked at me and said, "Wow, can it get any better than that?"

The answer came almost immediately, when the phone rang yet again. It was Oprah. "Merry Christmas, my guy!" she said to him. The two chatted about anything and everything—about what he was going to do with the money she sent, about how Shelly had sent the *Harry Potter* Legos, about signing "Silent Night," about how he now understood about Santa Claus. She told Mattie that she printed out and framed one of his poems, "Awakening After a Close Call," and hung it from her tree. "Now I have a real angel on my tree," she told him.

We went to the hospital twice between Christmas and New Year's. Everything was essentially status quo. The green pus was still coming, and the sore was as big as ever. We knew we were soon going to have to make an impossible decision. Mattie couldn't risk a brain infection resulting from an exposed skull, and he couldn't risk the surgery.

Fortunately, we were buoyed that week with lots of visits. Friends from the hospital came, doctors, nurses, social workers. Sandy's kids came, Hope and her parents, Susan and Ron, came. Flora and Paul Beaudet came, too. They were the people from whom we rented our first basement apartment, and Mattie adored "Auntie Flora and Uncle Paw." Mattie met them when he was very young, before he could pronounce the letter *l* well, and Paul always wrapped him in a bear hug, so "Paw" seemed apt, and stuck.

By the day of New Year's Eve itself, the visiting really crescendoed, and it felt as though the whole world had descended on our basement apartment. People wanted to say, "Wow, you made it," and also to express concern about what came next, to tell Mattie they loved him. Sandy was among those there that day, as was Nell (with the duck on her head), Nell's husband, Larry, and the Tresca family, who was staying with us.

We met Diane Tresca, her husband, Sal, and their daughters, Laura and Annie, through Flora and Paul, back in 1994. The Trescas were from Rhode Island, and Flora and Paul had a little beach house across the street from Diane's family there. Diane, Sal, and the girls were so much fun, and shared Mattie's and my penchant for the goofy. Sal's first memory of meeting Mattie was Mattie's coming to the door in a cowboy hat and boots and saying, "Howdy, pardner." He was hooked that moment.

When the family visited, which they did several times a year, we'd have Dr. Seuss Day—everyone had to speak in rhyming couplets. We'd have Opera Day—everything had to be sung. We'd start laughing at three in the morning over bathroom humor. At Christmas, the kids would set up a manger with sheep, oxen, and camels—and a tiger and dinosaurs and *101 Dalmatians* that all came to worship the Newborn King, with Santa's sleigh on the roof.

Mattie, Laura, and Annie would also put on plays (Laura was Mattie's age, Annie three years younger). One of the most memorable was *The Tired Princess,* which Mattie penned to accommodate Laura's not wanting to memorize any lines one day. Laura lay there, a princess in a deep sleep, while Mattie played the part of the prince (he was as in love with her as a little boy could be), and Annie had to act the parts of twelve other characters. She was four or five at the time, and at one point she became so confused, she came out wearing bits of three different costumes.

This year, with the hole in Mattie's head deepening and widening, we reminisced—about the Christmas Laura felt left out and made a *101 Dalmatians* figure bite the baby Jesus on the leg in the crèche (when asked why she did so, she replied, "Maybe he thought he wasn't getting enough *attention*"); about the year Mattie and I had gone to roast marshmallows on the National Yule Log; about the year we had a Wear-Your-Clothes-Backwards Day.

As the day wore into evening, Sandy and I went over the resolutions we had written down, ranging from silly to serious, and as evening wore into night, Mattie went through his annual New Year's Eve lists. He wrote those lists because, he said, "As important as resolving what you want to change is capturing what you need to take forward with you." His lists, which he had been making from the time he was four, included everything from favorite songs to traumatic memories. "Let go of the hurt, but move forthward with the lesson," he would say. He'd also recite a list of victories from the past year to take with him into the new year and build on.

Finally, we all counted down to midnight, and at the stroke of January first, I gave Mattie the first kiss of the year, as always, and told him, as I always did, "That's for you to grow on." Then we cheered, "Hap, Hap Hap-py New Year," which we had been doing since he was two.

Right then Mattie just looked at me—it felt like a moment in slow motion—and then yelled, "I made it! *We* made it!" He ripped off his shirt, started dancing, and drank straight from a bottle of sparkling cider. He cried tears of joy. "I made it! I made it," he kept repeating. "I'm in 2002! Look at this, Mom. We made it, after this whole year. We have a whole other year to start now, a whole new set of moments!" He held that particular moment in his hand as if he could study it. He threw it in the air and let it come down as confetti. He embraced it, almost literally.

When he finally calmed down, he went and wrote the following poem, a series of haiku, really:

Haiku for the Bubbly

i

Midnight ticks closer,
Anticipation grows, swells,
Heart rate quickens pace.

ii

Marking, counting time,
Each moment more palpable,
I, hear, time, Pass'ing.

iii

Memories edge near,
Reflect on lessons to keep,
Observe, move forth-with.

iv

Mom's New Year rite lands:
My first kiss of tomorrow,
To grow through each day

v

Five. . . Four. . . Three. Two, One
Future now touches the past—
I celebrate 'Now!'

Two days later, Mattie went to the hospital for one of his twice-weekly visits. What happened he put in an e-mail to Oprah:

GUESS WHAT??? They told my mom, "Whatever you are doing, keep doing it because it's making a difference." If you never saw the hole in the back of my head, you would look at it and say, "Oh, that looks horrible and gross." But if you had seen it for the last 10 months, and especially during the last two months, you would say, "Wow! It looks so much better." So I still need the prayers to keep it healing, but it is actually healing, and it never would before. It would begin to heal a little, but then a few weeks later it would be worse again. Now it looks better than it's looked since last July!

You see any whales [during your visit to Hawaii]?

I love you and you love me,

Mattie

Oprah wrote back:

This is the best news yet!

Didn't see any yesterday, but the last time I was here, I saw and heard two baby whales with their mothers. The boat captain put a microphone with an amplifier in the water, and you could hear them "talking" to each other.

Within very short order the surgery was canceled—taken off the table. Mattie was right—the sore still looked awful. His bandage wouldn't be able to come off for another year. But slowly, surely, his skin was growing back, forming healthy scar tissue over the lesion and safely covering his skull. The pus was gone. Dr. Eichelberger was as shocked as any of us— his eyes actually opened wide as he pulled away the bandage right after New Year's.

On January 14, Oprah re-aired the "How Does That Feel?" episode, and Mattie's *Journey Through Heartsongs* immediately became number 1 on the *New York Times* bestseller list, while *Heartsongs* shot up to number 3.

On January 15, Oprah aired a show for which she had interviewed Dr. Eichelberger, during which he explained that everything the doctors had been doing for nearly a year hadn't made a bit of difference. "I guess I need to say 'thank you' to Oprah's viewers for helping us," he said.

Mattie was then cleared by both Dr. Eichelberger and Dr. Fink to move forward and give more speeches, to resume his role as the messenger he felt he needed to be. "Don't stop praying," Dr. Eichelberger reminded everyone.

Dr. Fink also urged me to use some of the proceeds that would be going into Mattie's medical trust to purchase a house. "It's your money," he said. "But I think Mattie needs a real home. That's a medical need—a safe environment with windows, without worry that the family renting to you will move out, leaving you to find another basement. I would be willing to go to court and explain why a home is a medical need that would satisfy the criteria for taking money from the trust to pay for it."

Mattie and I immediately started talking with Sandy. She lived in the same neighborhood as we did, but she decided to sell her townhouse so the two of us could buy condos next door to each other.

Mattie, meanwhile, had told Oprah that he could start giving speeches again but would only be traveling locally because our van wasn't set up to supply the humidity he needed for his trachea.

"What if I gave you a van that had the proper setup?" she then asked me.

"No, that's too generous," I told her. "We couldn't accept that."

But the next day, three men showed up at our door from a place that builds vans to the specifications of people with disabilities, wanting to know my needs for such a van as well as Mattie's. I tried to send them away, but they said they were told to stay there until I broke down and let them in.

After a long while, I finally did let them in and called Oprah to thank her. I couldn't deny Mattie the opportunity to be the messenger he wanted to be. He was going to have a piece of equipment in the van—a high-power electricity inverter—that would supply all the humidity he needed. And I was going to be able to shift gears electronically rather than push a gear shift, which by that point was becoming impossible due to the progressive weakness of my muscles.

It was now mid-February. *"Hello my Valentine guy,"* Oprah wrote to Mattie in big red letters on the fourteenth. *"Am sending you even more love today than usual."*

It was a gift even I couldn't argue with.

Mattie on the phone with Oprah Winfrey, sharing the good news that the "Power of Prayer" has helped him heal, January 2002

CHAPTER 9

Breath of Hope

Mattie with his stuffed tiger "Tad" on a road trip, spring 2002

Mattie shares his message of hope and peace during one of his many appearances with Larry King, summer 2002

We are growing up.
We are many colors of skin.
We are many languages.
We are many ages and sizes.
We are many countries . . .
But we are one earth. . . .
We are growing up, together,
So we must each join our
Hearts and lives together
And live as one family.[1]

---

1 From "On Growing Up (Part V)" in *Journey Through Heartsongs*, page 41.

"What are we fighting over? Land, money. They don't really matter. We're also fighting over religion. But with religion, there's always one basic ideal—we're trying to become better people—and also the belief that there is something greater than us, greater than the here and now. There are many names for that. . . . It doesn't matter how we try to become a better person."

Mattie was being interviewed on *Larry King Live* about his views regarding global aggression post-9/11. The van that Oprah was having built for us wasn't ready and we couldn't travel long distances yet, so Larry King interviewed Mattie in CNN's Washington studio.

Mattie also continued to do local book signings in metro DC, Maryland, and Northern Virginia, as well as give speeches and conduct interviews for every U.S. media venue imaginable. But now international media, children's publications, and television shows were seeking his thoughts, too. Democrats, Republicans, news-oriented, faith-oriented, young, old—every demographic was touched by Mattie's message.

The tenor of Mattie's talks had again taken on a new tone. He still spoke for MDA, having by that point become the organization's 2002 National Goodwill Ambassador rather than just the Maryland state representative, and he still advocated for Children's Hospice International. But he widened his themes to talk in much broader strokes about peace, and about hope, in a world that was still reeling from the terrorist attacks. He began to speak directly about religion, too.

Regardless of how you pray, he said, regardless of the name you choose or are raised with to call the "supreme being," what matters most is using prayerfulness to become a good person, a better person. Most people end up in the religion they were born into, he would say. It's what they're surrounded with and what they become comfortable with. The Roman Catholicism he was born into and embraced was right for him, he said, and helped his spirit both in times of great joy and in times of great pain and suffering. But, he explained, just because someone's religion might be a different kind of Christianity or did not embrace Jesus as the Savior, in no way did he think that it meant he or she was loved any less by God.

Being a good person, he said, was what mattered most. That was also true, Mattie believed, for people who didn't embrace religion or spirituality. The way he saw it, God doesn't fault you for that when you die if you've lived a life of goodness.

But while Mattie was not preachy and his agenda was not to convert people to Catholicism, he *was* passionate about turning people toward something greater than themselves. To be your best self, he said, you had to recognize consciously that you were part of something that went beyond you. You could not be your best self in isolation because achieving that goal required reaching out to, encouraging, and supporting your neighbor to be *his* best self. It was, to Mattie's mind, a collaboration that required learning about one's neighbor—his preferences, strengths, and needs—and then working with that person to meet *everyone's* needs, involving the whole world in the effort. When basic needs are met—food, water, safety, shelter, medical care, education, hope, and happiness— peace follows, Mattie said. He was, in effect, working to encourage people to leave the best legacy they possibly could, to recognize their purpose here on earth and follow through by understanding that it connects with everyone else's.

Apparently, he was getting through. Priests wrote, rabbis wrote, ministers and imams and atheists wrote. Mattie received letters from people who told him, "I never prayed a day in my life. I don't know that I'm praying now, but I'm trying to connect with something beyond me. Is that prayer?"

At book signings, at speeches Mattie gave in schools, retirement homes, conferences, he was getting the message from people that he had put hope back into their lives, their futures, at a time when optimism felt most elusive and the argument for war in the wake of 9/11 was growing stronger.

One family came to a book signing and shared the story of how their adult son with mental illness had been in a near-catatonic state for years until his parents put one of Mattie's poems in front of him. From there the young man started to talk again, "to touch the world again," as his father put it, and moved to a group home where he went on to live a productive life.

"We're using your poetry in a bar mitzvah," people would tell him. "We're using your poetry in our mosque. I go to a Muslim school," one child wrote, "and we're talking about you as a peacemaker."

People also shared stories of redemption. One woman wrote to tell Mattie that when her granddaughter was born, she wanted to raise the girl to hate her father, who had walked out on the woman's daughter. "But I see your book on the table," she said, "so I want to raise her to love what she has." Inmates wrote from Death Row to say they never felt remorse about what they had done before they heard Mattie speak or read his poetry but now they did; they understood why their actions were wrong.

Larry King's producer, Michael Watts, saw the effect for himself at a book signing in Baltimore when he was gathering footage of Mattie. Hundreds of people were there, hanging over the store's balcony, sitting on the floor, getting in line to shake Mattie's hand and have a few moments with him after he finished sharing thoughts and answering questions.

"Watching the crowd, they're mesmerized," Michael told me. "Little children, old ladies, priests, and rabbis are all in the audience. It's the mosaic of life that Mattie talks about. It tells you something about who he is reaching out to. *Everybody* is represented. *Everybody* is getting something out of his message."

The same thing then happened on *Larry King Live* as on Oprah's show. Mattie was supposed to be the show opener for the first fifteen or twenty minutes, but Larry kept him there for all but the brief closing segment, when a clip aired of country singing star Billy Gilman performing his hit "My Time on Earth." That episode with Mattie was one of only three shows for which Larry King was ever nominated for an Emmy. The other two were with Paul McCartney and Karla Faye Tucker (for which he won an Emmy). Larry himself said, "This is one of the five best interviews I have ever done in my life, and will probably ever do in my life." As soon as he boarded the plane to fly back to his home in California, he called his wife and started reading Mattie's poetry to her.

Ironically, Mattie's impact was at odds with his halting cadences. Because of his ventilator, his breaths came at intervals that made it difficult to speak without interruptions. But they were, literally, breaths of hope. Mattie's words made people feel there was a future to look forward to.

Father Dixon, our parish priest, believed it had to do with Mattie's conviction, citing the Gospel of Mark, chapter 1, verse 22, in which the Bible talks about how Jesus spoke with authority. Mattie conveyed that same assurance of knowledge, Father Dixon said, that same sense of "I know this because God has communicated it to me, not because I learned it."

Mattie's message was further spurred on by the publication of his third book of poetry, *Hope Through Heartsongs*, which instantly arrived on the *New York Times* bestseller list. It was very much a post-9/11 work, incorporating the themes of hope for within, for each other, and for our world. *Good Morning America* had Mattie on to promote the book's release, and while we were in New York City, he visited Ground Zero. Afterward, sitting nearby at the headquarters of the Uniformed Firefighters' Association, he talked with a firefighter named Jack Ginty, who had actually been in one of the towers when it collapsed. "You climbed out of a burning building hours after it fell," Mattie said to him. "There was death all around you. You should be angry, hateful. But I encourage you to move forward with peace, with hope."

Jack started crying and asked where the key to his locker was. When he opened it, he took out a pile of folded material and handed it to Mattie. "Here are the clothes I was wearing when I crawled out," Jack said to him. "I want you to have them. And I *will* move forward in hope and peace."

Around this time, Mattie was also invited to be the keynote speaker at a Verizon conference in Baltimore. The company, with more than one thousand employees attending, wanted someone who was very inspirational. It was a clear indicator of the shift happening for Mattie. He was not being asked to speak as a boy with a disability, but as someone with a message for how to approach life in general.

Mattie's talk for Verizon was partly about respecting other people's desire to express their purpose in life and partly about courage, which to him was having strength when there was something to fear. In the end, Mattie believed, courage looked like peace; it looked like hope—because moving forward with courage meant gliding into the future with an attitude that things were going to work out, not with your back up, looking to defend or retaliate.

While waiting backstage to give his speech, Mattie chatted with the conference coordinator, Jeff Bouchard, who told him that when his kids found out he was there with Mattie Stepanek, they were "going to go crazy. They're going to wish they had come on this trip with me." Jeff's family lived near Detroit.

"Why don't you call them on your cell?" Mattie suggested. "I have a half hour before I go out. I could talk with them." Mattie then got on the phone with Jeff's two younger sons, Kyle and Travis, and two new friendships were launched. Jeff gave us his home number and said that if we ever had reason to come to Michigan, he would make sure we had a good time. We didn't know it then, but Jeff is a huge name in entertainment. He has written songs with Kenny Loggins, is good friends with Christopher Cross, and knows many other celebrities.

The speech went over beautifully. Mattie was even given Verizon's Courage Award.

Mattie also began giving larger and larger talks on behalf of MDA in his new role as National Ambassador, which he started in 2002. Speaking to thousands of Harley-Davidson riders at MDA's annual Ride for Life event, he explained that MDA wasn't just about raising funds for research but also about hope and peace. "Peace begins with meeting basic needs, which allows someone to be okay with who they are as a person," he said. "And because MDA recognizes that people with neuromuscular diseases are not simply waiting to die but need to have fun, go to summer camp, participate in life, the organization is helping to meet the needs of living, and therefore creating a more hopeful, peaceful world."

He gave a similar speech to the Senate Spouses' Luncheon at the Capitol, where he was invited by Laura Bush to talk to the wives and husbands of our nation's one hundred senators, and to do a poetry reading. On another occasion, Mattie was given the Children's Hope Medal of Honor by Senator Barbara Mikulski of Maryland. The medal is bestowed on young people who have shown "valiant effort and courage in facing life's daily challenges. If anyone deserved it," Senator Mikulski said, "Mattie did."

Soon after he received the medal, Mattie watched Maya Angelou on the *Oprah Winfrey Show*. Dr. Angelou explained to Oprah that if some-

one came up to her and said, "I'm a dancer, I'm a singer, I'm a writer," and
she responded by requesting that the person "dance me a few steps, sing
me a few lines, recite me something you've written," and the person hung
her or his head in false modesty and said, "Oh, no, I couldn't," that wasn't
real. If you have a gift, Dr. Angelou said, you hold your head up and share
that gift with the world.

Right then and there, Mattie resolved to memorize some of his poetry.
"In case I ever meet Maya Angelou, I'm going to be ready," he said.

By coincidence, the very next day I saw that Dr. Angelou was going to
be coming to a bookstore just off the University of Maryland campus to
do a signing. Mattie could not contain his excitement.

The book signing was to start at seven in the evening, but Mattie and
I got there at five, anticipating very long lines. It was a bit chilly outside—
too cold for Mattie to sit and wait for two hours because of his body's
difficulty adjusting to even slight temperature dips. The store was closed
in preparation for the event, but I knocked on the door.

"We're not trying to cut in the line," I explained (we were about three
hundred people back, with another thousand or so behind us), "but my
son needs to have warmth, and needs to have his equipment plugged into
a wall for proper humidity. Can we wait inside and, before she comes,
we'll go back out?" They graciously allowed us to come inside.

When Dr. Angelou arrived, I started unplugging Mattie and getting
ready to leave. But before we had a chance to exit, she walked over to us
and said, "Why, Mattie Stepanek!"

"Maya Angelou!" Mattie gleefully said back.

"Let me hug you," Dr. Angelou responded.

It suddenly dawned on the bookstore owners who Mattie was. His
books with photos of him were being sold there, but until that moment
they hadn't made the connection.

"What are you doing here?" Dr. Angelou asked Mattie.

"I came to see you. You're my role model for being a poet."

With that, Dr. Angelou asked for some extra space to be cleared for
Mattie to sit by her side during the signing. "I would like to talk with him
between people coming up to see me," she said.

As people came to the front of the line, their attention was split between Dr. Angelou and Mattie. Many knew who Mattie was and were shocked to see him there.

"Mattie is the future of poetry," Dr. Angelou would say to attendees as she signed their books. To those people who did not know who he was, she said, "I'd like to introduce you to my friend, Mattie Stepanek. He is a fellow poet." This renowned poet who had spoken at presidential inaugurations and was beloved by millions was shining her own light onto Mattie as brightly as she could. It was one of the most wonderful moments of his life.

"I could recite some of my poetry for you, if you would like," Mattie said, having taken her words from the *Oprah Winfrey Show* to heart.

"That would be lovely," she replied. So Mattie spoke lines from his poems, and that sealed their bond.

"What's next for you?" Dr. Angelou asked. Mattie told her about some of his upcoming speeches and about some of the traveling he would be doing once the van Oprah had commissioned for us was ready. "I'll also have another book coming out this summer and one after that next year," Mattie told her.

"When you get your thoughts organized about the new books," she said, "will you send them to me? I'd like to write something."

"Do you mean like a Foreword?" Mattie asked enthusiastically.

"I would be honored to write the Foreword to one of your books," she said.

Mattie was amazed beyond words, and amazed at Dr. Angelou's way of interacting with the public, too. "People are coming to see her," he told Oprah, "but she's watching *them*. She knows who's coming just to look at fame and who's really coming to meet *her*."

With all of these exciting events going on, Mattie was still a child trying to live a child's life. Homeschooling and homework happened every day. Hope, who never let Mattie's worsening physical shape across the years interfere with their friendship, would come to play.

Mattie always tried to have fun, too. This came into particular relief on the *Larry King Live* episode.

In the middle of all of Larry King's very serious questions—"Why don't you think hope is an illusion?" "What about your life expectancy?"

"How old were your siblings when they died?" "Have you ever lost your faith in God?"—he also asked, "Do you play? Are you like a normal kid?" The screen immediately went to footage Michael Watts had taken of Mattie entertaining himself while I had a meeting at the university one day. There was Mattie putting his plastic dinosaurs on an overhead projector, throwing large images of them onto the walls and intoning in the accent of a British paleontologist, "And here we have the tibia of the *Tyrannosaurus rex.* . . ." There was Mattie sitting with his watch in front of him because I told him he had to do *x* many minutes of homework, counting down the last several seconds until he could close his books— "Five, four, three, two, one, I'm free!" There was Mattie talking about how much he liked *Harry Potter* and *Lord of the Rings,* and pretending to frighten the camera crew with his *Monty Python* "Killer Bunny" stuffed toy.

Mixed in with the fun, always, were twice-monthly visits to the hospital for checkups and once-a-month blood transfusions. Mattie's health was as stable as we could ever hope for by that point. He felt good and he looked good—but this was still a boy on life support. The sore on his head still needed to be cleaned daily. The transfusions were necessary to optimize his oxygenation. There was always the lingering concern that his trachea could start to erode again. We never knew how long a period of relative stability was going to last, when the "what next" would come.

That's why, even when the van from Oprah arrived and Mattie was able to take his inspiration on the road, every trip that required going away overnight required careful planning. We needed to pack a backup ventilator and supplies. We needed to know the hospitals en route. We needed to try to schedule trips in between blood transfusions and other medical routines.

One of our first trips away from home in our new van was to Richmond, Virginia, for a speech to a hospice group called Noah's Children. Mattie talked there about his message of hope, which was well received, but what made that trip particularly special was that we had the opportunity to stay with my first cousin, Jo Ann Stoddard, who sat on the Noah's

Children board of directors. I had not seen her in years, and Mattie had never met her. It was a wonderful time, and very emotionally gratifying for Mattie, as well as for me, to be able to connect with extended family. Jo Ann, her husband, Harry, and their daughter, Jo Beth, who was a couple of years older than Mattie, treated us so well. And it was great to be able to do an event away from home and not be in a hotel but, rather, in the home of loved ones, particularly because Mattie had a bad headache on the day of the speech and a hard time breathing. It would have been much more difficult for him to deal with those health issues in a hotel room than in his cousins' house.

A few more one- or two-nighters followed Richmond, and then Mattie and I were off on a three-week trip of speechmaking and book publicity through the Midwest. Our first stop was Independence, Missouri. Mattie was invited to talk to five thousand students and their chaperones at that city's Children's Peace Pavilion, a museum dedicated to peace. Jane Goodall had been the invited speaker the year before.

Mattie wrote an outline for his speech just before we left home but decided to rewrite it in the van, once we were traveling. His original plan was to talk in general terms about how one's Heartsong leads to peace, but he changed it to focus on the more specific need to come up with a *plan* for peace.

"Peace doesn't just happen," Mattie decided to say. "There are many areas of gray that need to be examined. It's not a simple black-and-white issue." He noted ideas in his journal:

> We have to make plans for peace the way we make plans for war. . . . It's not simply about people of two races or cultures or religions getting along in some moment. Our world is multi-colored, multi-hued, and multi-issued. We have to join together and celebrate all races and religions and become a festive fabric of humanity. We must dab our collective fingers into the waters of change and come together as a family in the human race. It's about completely moving beyond these walls that divide us, about uniting beyond them.

Mattie articulated three steps for the plan:

We need to make peace an attitude—want it, be a peace seeker.
We need to make peace a habit—live it, be a peace maker.
*We need to make peace a reality—share it, with people around
the block and around the world, even people we disagree
with. That's being a* peace bringer.

I loved it and thought he was all set. Then, right before he went out on stage, Mattie came up with yet another change. I was nervous for him to be making so many alterations so close to giving such an important talk. But what he said to me was that it was not right to tell people these were three *steps*. "I'm going to call them *choices*," he said. "Steps are optional, detached. A choice, you have to own. If it's a choice," Mattie told me, "you would have to say to yourself, 'I'm *not* choosing peace.'" The responsibility for *no* peace would lie squarely on your shoulders.

Mattie was well received, with the audience cheering him as he came out and also during his speech. Then, at the end, he said, "All right, everybody on your feet!" Five thousand people were screaming and jumping up and down and chanting the "Three Choices for Peace." The refinements he made to his talk had made it that much more powerful.

Once the audience quieted down, Mattie took questions. "What's it like to know you're going to die?" someone asked. "Are you afraid?"

"I'm not looking forward to missing all the wonderful things that happen during life," Mattie answered. "Life is wonderful even with all the challenges that I have. And I have to be honest, I'm afraid of the pain that comes with the process of dying. But I'm not afraid of being in Heaven. It only gets better, and this is already fantastic."

"What are your feelings when you see other kids running and playing?" someone else asked.

"I feel blessed that I had the opportunity to run and play earlier in my life. Some people who are born with a disability never know the joy of bodysurfing an ocean wave, or climbing a tree, or rolling down a grassy hill, as I have. And I do miss being active. But I thank God every day that I have the memory of such wonders. I thank God, too, for being lucky enough to live in this country, where I can have a wheelchair and life support, and where there are laws that protect me and guidelines that support my ability to be a member of my community."

Mattie was asked tough questions wherever we went. But he never was thrown off balance. And his candid answers always provided lessons as well as information.

"If you've lived a rotten life," some people asked him, "is it ever too late to change?"

"Never," Mattie said. "And if you fall back into old ways," he told them, "it's never too late to change again. God never stops loving you. It's your decision to be open to God's love."

"Can you bless my baby?" some asked. "Can you touch my belly and bless my unborn child?"

"God is the one who gives blessings," Mattie told those people, "but I would be honored if I could share my love with your baby."

From Missouri, Mattie and I drove to Minneapolis, where he did a book signing at the Mall of America for a huge crowd. The bookstore ran out of books, even though they had stocked 3,500 copies in preparation for the event. Mattie was pleased about that, but just as pleased that the mall had a store devoted entirely to Legos.

After visiting Minneapolis, we headed for Wisconsin. Harley-Davidson has its headquarters in Milwaukee, and Mattie was asked to give a speech on behalf of MDA.

In every city we visited, Mattie did local television, radio, and print media interviews, leaving him exhausted but happy that he had so many opportunities to get out his message of hope and peace.

Mattie particularly enjoyed our stop in Chicago, where in addition to speeches and book signings, we visited with Oprah. He loved seeing her privately as opposed to just on her show. He played with her dogs, and they had a great time talking. She even went down to the garage to get a look at the van she had given us, checking out the tons of buttons for computerized control. "Did you have to get a pilot's license to drive this thing?" she asked me. I was glad she was able to see the medical security she had provided us, not to mention the luxury—the van had a DVD player and lots of other "goodies" that made travel so much fun. We didn't even have a DVD player at home.

From Chicago we drove on to Indianapolis. It hadn't been on our itinerary, but we received a call from Children's National Medical Center in Washington that a family by the name of Hemelgarn, who lived in Michigan but owned a car that raced in the Indy 500 every year, had invited Mattie to be their guest for the upcoming race.

We arrived at the hotel in Indianapolis very late on a Friday night. Mattie woke up at seven the next morning, found out what room the Hemelgarns were in, knocked on their door, and, with a towel on his arm, pronounced, "Room Service! I'm here to give the morning foot massage."

Ron and Helen Hemelgarn fell in love with Mattie that morning, and Mattie with them and their family. For the Indy 500 parade, they had his wheelchair lifted onto a float. He then lunched with Ron and Helen, their adult children, and television stars Florence Henderson and Jim Nabors. He had a blast.

During the race the next day, the Hemelgarns' car was doing very well through the last five or ten laps of the race. Then, a driver with no chance of winning crashed, running the Hemelgarns' vehicle into a wall, knocking them out of the competition. Ron was beyond livid. Mattie wanted to talk to him, but Helen and the kids said to give him some space.

Mattie waited about ten minutes, then went over, put his arm around Ron, and said, "It's time for us to chat." Ron collected himself, swallowing his rage for Mattie's sake, and replied, "Okay, what do you want to talk about?"

"I want to talk about what it means to be a champion," Mattie said. "Of course we want to win. Winning matters, the money matters. This hurts, and you were wronged. It was a hard, unfair loss. But it doesn't mean everything. Besides, you're not cursing, you're not filing a complaint, you're not losing it. You *are* a champion. Where does *that* win fall in the course of your life?"

Ron just looked at Mattie. He seemed like he might have been about to say something, but he remained quiet.

"I think we need to do what matters most at a time like this," Mattie went on.

"What's that?" Ron asked.

"Go out and get root beer floats."

And we did. Mattie's message to play after every storm was put into action right there. His friendship with Ron and the Hemelgarn family only grew stronger after that.

After Indianapolis, Mattie and I headed to Detroit for another speech to a packed house. Once we arrived, Jeff Bouchard, whom we had met at the Verizon event a few months prior, followed through on his promise to give Mattie a good time should we ever come to Michigan. That week, besides playing with Jeff's two younger boys, Mattie went with them to zoos, concerts, and all kinds of other terrific events. He even got to throw out the opening pitch at a Detroit Tigers game. The Hemelgarns showed Mattie a good time in Michigan, too, where they returned home after the race.

We loved the companionship of our two new sets of friends, but Mattie and I also thoroughly enjoyed our time alone together, driving across vast expanses of the Midwest. We already enjoyed each other's company, of course—friends called us the Dynamic Duo. But there was something about spending as many as eight to twelve hours a day in that van together that brought us even closer. Mattie was never anything but my little boy, and I was never anything but his mom, raising him. We were able to relate beyond that, however, talking all the time and enjoying a free exchange of ideas—and having fun. He teased me on that trip that I would do anything to find a shortcut, no matter how long it took to find. And I indulged his penchant for buying decks of cards and collecting the jokers as souvenirs while giving all the other cards away.

There was also a fair amount of talk about cows, as we were not used to looking out the window and seeing them. The cows even reminded us of an incident that had occurred years earlier.

When Mattie was around four years old, I used to repeat a line from a soap commercial when I felt overwhelmed by the events of life: "Calgon, take me away!" But Mattie always thought I was saying something else—and finally confronted me about it. "Mommy, I thought we were Catholic. So why do you ask the 'cow gods' to take you away? I don't want you to go away. And if you do go away, please don't go with a cow god."

We laughed in the van over that misunderstanding, and also about everything else, singing silly songs and playing silly word games. No doubt much of our enjoying the insularity of those car rides came from the fact that once in public, we could no longer be anonymous.

Mattie had always gotten stares. He was small for his age and spoke with a maturity that didn't fit with his body size. Also, we were both in wheelchairs, an unusual setup for a parent and child. But now it wasn't the typical scenario of people trying to pretend that they weren't looking at us. We couldn't even pull off at a truck stop for a bite without people saying, "Oh my gosh, that's Mattie. That's the Heartsong Kid. That's Oprah's guy."

Everywhere we went he was recognized. People crowded him, wanted to touch him. People listened in on our conversations; we weren't really free to talk. "Mom, what if I burp?" Mattie would ask. "What if I say something that ends up twisted wrong on TV?" When Sandy traveled with us, she used to kid Mattie, saying, "Be good to me. I have the story 'Enquiring minds' want to know!"

Then, too, Mattie would go to a McDonald's restroom only to hear someone say afterward, "I saw that kid from Oprah using the bathroom." There was also a lot of "Can you sign my napkin?" "Can I shake your hand?" The handshaking was particularly nerve-racking for me because with Mattie's compromised immune system, dirty hands could be quite dangerous. It looked rude for me to make him clean his hands after every handshake, but in rest stops and places like that, I had no choice.

Even before we left for the Midwest, strangers had started coming to our apartment and calling us on the phone, which had begun to ring constantly. Most of the time it was to say something supportive or to thank Mattie for inspiration, but there were also people who wanted my eleven-year-old son to talk them out of suicide, come stay at their home, promise to call every week.

It was all exhausting for Mattie. He was an extrovert who drew his energy from other people; he could go into a book signing tired and come out energized. So for him to feel fatigued from the attention was significant. The unplanned public "viewings" had a whole different feel from the scheduled appearances. He had become a kind of peep show.

I told him in the van that he didn't have to continue to live his life on the world stage, that if he didn't want this, it was okay. He could go back to local public speaking, or no public speaking at all. But he said, "No, it's what I have to do. With every privilege, there comes a responsibility, sometimes even a burden, and you can't turn away from that if you're lucky enough to touch people you don't even know."

He did speak with Oprah, though, about how to deal with fame, e-mailing her the following:

> Is it sometimes hard for you to be famous? I know every-
> body must want to say "Hi" to you everywhere you go. . . .
> A lot of people recognize me now when we are out. This
> [can be] hard. . . . I asked my mom if people were in-
> spired by me because of my disability. Do people like my
> message because I am dying?

To which Oprah responded:

> The fact that I've become famous . . . is just part of the
> package. I've been doing television since I was 19
> years old, so all my working life I've been recognized
> in public. It doesn't bother me . . . except on days when
> I'm in a hurry . . . and just want to get something
> done and people keep stopping to say hello . . . but I
> always try to respond with kindness because I realize no
> matter what my focus is, when someone comes up to say
> hello or ask you to sign something, that is probably
> their one and only chance to do so. They will remember
> what happened in that moment. I try to make the moment a

good one. I also know that the only . . . thing that
changes [when you're famous] is people's perception of
who you are. You will be the same Mattie no matter how
many books you sell or how recognized you are. When you
start to get more money or a nicer van, or new things,
other people might think you're different, treat you
differently. But you will always know the truth. What
you have doesn't change who you are. A lot of people get
that confused.

As to your second question, I think a lot of people are
attracted to you because of the LIGHT they see in you,
not because they think you're dying. If that is what they
saw, they would be afraid of it. It's the LIGHT that is
so strong. People feel like, "I want some of that. I want
to be the kind of person who can face my greatest adver-
sity and still want to be a peacemaker." Those are actual
words that people have spoken to me about you.

I love you. Keep your strength. Have no fear.

Oprah

Those words were a great comfort to Mattie and really helped him get
through. He shared a lot with Oprah that spring, and her answers always
made him feel better. In another exchange, he wrote to her that when he
was younger:

I had kids force me to eat sand, I had a boy sharpen a
stick and stab me in the chest with it, and I got black
eyes and bloody noses. Lots of kids would push me because
I would fall easily because of my disability, and that's
how I'd get cut or bruised. They would say "Baby Walk"
and "Baby Talk" because my speech was not clear and I

fell a lot. It was sad. In school the teachers often made
me play on the girls' side of the playground so the boys
wouldn't hurt me. . . . Nobody invited me to birthday
parties or sleepovers. . . .

Oprah wrote:

I got your message . . . about kids not wanting to play
with you. It made me sad. You're such a delightful wonder
of a boy. . . . But . . . look at how blessed you are and
how many blessings you bestow on others through your
message. If you were just a regular kid, doing all the
mundane stuff regular kids do, you would not hold the
power and influence and credibility that you do now. . . .
In the end, you change the world. . . . I think that's a
Heaven of an exchange. I know it doesn't seem so to you
right now, cause you just want to play and be regular.
But let's face it. You're not. There's a huge calling on
your life. The Universe has big plans for you here, and
you're fulfilling them.

Those words, too, put Mattie's mind at ease—and made him feel better
about all the attention he was now getting. Still, he found it hard to be
in the spotlight when the spotlight was unplanned. "Mom," he said one
day as we were driving past farmland, "sometimes I wish I were a cow."

"Why, Mattie?" I asked.

"Because then I could just graze on the hillside with my friends and
kneel on the grass," he answered.

"Yes, I guess that would be nice," I told him.

We sat riding quietly for about five more minutes. Then Mattie turned
to me and said, "But you know, sometimes cows become hamburger."

"So you're not going to be a cow after all?" I asked him rhetorically.

Immediately, Mattie opened his journal and wrote the poem, "On Being Content," which is about how there's always going to be a pro and con to everything:

Sometimes,
I wish I was a cow,
Grazing on a hillside and
Lowing with my friends and
Kneeling in the soft grass to
Protect me from tears of rain . . .
But then I remember,
Sometimes, cows become hamburger.
Sometimes,
I wish I had a flat tongue,
Like that of a dog
Lapping water by the scoop and
Looking so very unique and cool . . .
But then I remember,
Sometimes girls don't like dog kisses.
Sometimes,
I wish I was a someone,
Or an anyone other than
The me that I am, who
Can not keep up and who
May not stay in but who
Will not give in, or up . . .
But then I remember,
Sometimes, that
I am uniquely cool and
I kneel in the protection of God,
Who created me to be,
Just who and as I am.[2]

---

2   From "On Being Content," in *Reflections of a Peacemaker: A Portrait Through Heartsongs,* page 113.

♥

We arrived home from that first long trip in the van on a Sunday. It was early June 2002. Our new service dog, Micah, was going to be arriving the very next day. We had received a call from Sue Hendrickson in March that a litter of puppies had just been born and that she'd reserve one for Mattie. I was thrilled that she had remembered Mattie and his desire for a dog, but I was nervous, too. At first I had cold feet, reminding her that Mattie and I were both in wheelchairs. "I can't potty train a puppy," I told her. "We have to charge our wheelchairs—we can't just leave the house when the dog needs to go."

Sue told me she'd wean the dog after six weeks and hire a terrific trainer who would work one-on-one with the puppy chosen for us, getting him housebroken and ready to go. She would even send the trainer to our house to help get us started teaching Micah commands.

I finally gave in, wondering what I had gotten myself into.

The night we arrived home, I dreamt that the trainer came to the door with a service *elephant* that could barely squeeze into the apartment. In the dream, Mattie was excited that he would no longer need a wheelchair because he could ride the elephant, while I was thinking that I could not clean up after the pachyderm if it had an accident indoors.

The next morning, the trainer, a man named Stacy Han, showed up with Micah, the ninth in a litter of ten golden retrievers. Micah had never seen a wheelchair, and by accident, Mattie promptly rolled over his paw. The dog started yelping, and Mattie began to cry and say that Stacy should take the puppy back because he wasn't going to be able to care for him properly. But Stacy assured us that all would be okay. "My guess is the dog's now going to respect the chair and never get himself too close to the wheel again," he said.

Stacy was right. Micah kept clear of the wheels from then on. He was amazing, in fact. Even though he was only eleven weeks old, he already went to the bathroom outside on command and sat still until his food was poured. The day after he came to us, we took him to a local sub shop and taught him "Under," meaning to lie under the table while we ate, and the day after that, he accompanied us to church, neither whining nor making any other sound during Mass. Within weeks, Micah learned to retrieve dropped items, help push doors open, and get my attention when an alarm sounded on Mattie's ventilator.

Still, I remained nervous. Here we were, a mother and son both with disabilities, left to do a fair amount of training on our own. And we had more road trips coming up, including a monthlong journey to the West Coast, and Micah would be coming with us. Two people in wheelchairs and a puppy traveling three thousand miles each way—it seemed like a crazy idea.

But it was too late to change our minds. Stacy had already left, and Mattie and I both had already fallen in love with Micah, who at that point was still small enough to sit on our laps. A summer chock-full of adventures awaited us all.

Mattie greeting large crowds during a book signing, spring 2002

CHAPTER 10

Believing in the Journey

Mattie and his service dog, Micah, ready to load for our cross-
country trip from Maryland to California, summer 2002

Thank You, God,
Not just for life,
But for our journey through life.
Life is a miracle,
And a journey through life
Is so full of so many more miracles
If we travel with our Heartsongs.[1]

"Oh, yeah, man, like you ever had the moves! What moves? She was way out of your league."

Chris Dobbins, Sandy's son, was being teased by a group of buddies about his girlfriend, Cynthia, and about how it took Mattie and his prac-

---

1 From "Prayer for a Journey" in *Journey Through Heartsongs*, page 1

tical jokes to provide an opening for Chris to talk to her when he first met her on the Outer Banks two summers earlier.

It was Guy's Night. Every once in a while, Chris would have his friends over, including Mattie, for an all-nighter during which they'd watch movies, play cards and video games, talk about girls, and shoot the breeze. Chris was twenty, and many of his friends were in their late teens. Mattie was just going on twelve, but he could hold his own. "All of my friends love Mattie," Chris told me on more than one occasion.

As did Chris. When Mattie was very little, Chris played the role of older brother to him, sitting with Mattie when he watched cartoons and playing Legos with him. Later on, despite the age difference, they were able to get on more as peers. Chris introduced Mattie to *Family Guy*, *Zoolander*, and *Monty Python and the Holy Grail*, an insane, funny film that made the two of them laugh all eighty-three times they watched it together. The two of them talked about dating. They talked about everything. When Chris said he wanted to switch from using his actual name, Christopher Newcomb Dobbins, to going with Christopher *Neptune* Dobbins because it sounded cooler, Mattie encouraged him to do so, which he did. Chris was way out there, and Mattie was right out there with him.

But their friendship was as solid as it was fun. Mattie even helped Chris through some hard times. A couple of months before one Guy's Night, Chris and Cynthia had a huge fight. Chris was miserable but didn't know how to fix things. Mattie finally picked up the phone and called Cynthia himself to pave the way. Then he told Chris what he had to do to show Cynthia that he was a good man.

With Mattie's mediation, the two were able to patch things up. "Mattie got me where I am today," Chris told me recently. And he meant it.

The morning after this particular Guy's Night, Chris, Sandy, and Mattie headed for Cynthia's high school graduation in Silver Spring, Maryland. It was a Catholic school, and the priest leading the Mass recognized Mattie and asked him if he'd come up and say a few words. Impromptu, Mattie spoke to the class about how they were on the threshold of their future and that going forward, they wouldn't always be able to choose their own realities—what happened to or around them. But, he said, they could choose how to accept, embrace, or deal with those realities, how to reflect them back out into the world, either with anger and misery or with grace and joy. Chris, Cynthia, and the whole class were moved.

After the graduation, Sandy brought Mattie back to our apartment. He wasn't home long when he started wheezing, having a hard time breathing.

I took him to the hospital. They admitted him, and he started feeling better right away without any intervention. But since they found his red blood cell count was borderline, they gave him an unscheduled transfusion before releasing him, thinking he always did better with lots of new red cells to carry oxygen. We had barely arrived back home, however, when the breathing problems started up again, worsening across the next couple of days.

The same scenario kept repeating itself. Mattie would have trouble breathing, go to the hospital, start feeling better soon after arriving, and be sent home again. Thank goodness for Laura, the ICU nurse who came to help me once a week. She was seeing the same pattern I was—it wasn't my imagination.

Despite the on and off breathing difficulties, the doctors said Mattie could go to MDA Summer Camp that year. They wondered whether his ups and downs might be emotional but felt that whatever the cause, I could always bring him back to the hospital if need be; the camp was just a few hours away. They were satisfied, too, that Mattie was going to be receiving good medical care during his week at camp. Because of his trach and ventilator, Mattie required round-the-clock medical attention, which I had been providing, with occasional respite from Laura or Sandy. But I couldn't stay with him at camp because parents weren't allowed. I spent nights in a nearby motel room and was allowed to "hide out" in the infirmary each day so I could change his trach ties, do an assessment, and make sure Mattie was stable. Laura was going to sit awake in his bunk at night to suction his trach secretions, if necessary, attend to any alarms on his monitors, and empty the water from his ventilator tubing. His bunkmates told him they were okay with her being there and said to Mattie that he had "the prettiest nurse ever."

Even during daytime camp activities, Mattie would have great supervision. Devin Dressman, the research doctor who had befriended Mattie in the PICU and who understood the medical situation, was going to be his counselor. Devin had undergone his own transformation. When he first met Mattie, he was uncomfortable about the prospect of entertaining a ten-year-old boy in the PICU. By now, though, he and Mattie had become close friends, and Devin was one of the full-fledged, out-in-nature counselors for rowdy twelve- to fifteen-year-old boys in the Cuckoo Cabin.

Mattie had a terrific time that week. It was hard at first because in years past, he had always been far more active, the Wild Man—somersaulting off the diving board, climbing trees, and doing a lot more than most of the other kids were able. But this year, his first at camp with his trach, he could not even go in the pool. He wrote about it in his journal, saying that when it was time for his group to go to the pool the first day, he decided to "let the world know I was not happy." He was told he could wear his bathing suit and get squirted with a squirt gun, but he said, "No." After five minutes of sulking, however, he decided, "This is not me," and began aiming the squirt gun at all his bunkmates. From then on, he resolved to make sure he had a great time, and did. He was applying his own message that you couldn't always choose your realities, but you could choose what you made of them.

Laura was thrilled to see Mattie in this new element. "You'd never know this kid lacked typical friends at home," she said, "and you'd never know he was a celebrity. This child who had tears in his eyes when neighborhood boys said they didn't want to play with him and who reached millions on television fit right in at camp.

"I loved seeing this *person* behind my patient," Laura added, explaining that watching Mattie at camp allowed her to realize, for the first time in her career, what the PICU staff was doing by trying to make children well again. They were trying, in effect, to help them become the children they were supposed to be.

Mattie's week ended with lots of happy memories and no medical complications, but within two days of arriving home, he was sick again. I was an hour from home at the university when Laura called to say he was blue and couldn't breathe and needed his trach changed. "I can do it alone," she said, "but it's better to have another person there." Luckily, Sandy was five minutes away and quickly arrived to do an emergency trach replacement with her. It didn't help.

As soon as I reached the apartment, we headed straight for the hospital, Mattie's respiratory distress not improving even though I upped his oxygen and changed his vent settings.

Once we arrived at the emergency room and the doctors started doing the workup, Mattie was fine again. Everyone shook their heads. "We're just not seeing what you say you're seeing," they told me.

"Well, *I'm* seeing it," Laura said. "This kid is dying in his home."

We took Mattie back to the apartment and this time, within minutes, he had difficulty breathing and turned bluer and bluer.

"You know, Mom," he said to me, "maybe I'm allergic to something. My carpet's still wet."

"What do you mean your carpet's *still* wet?" I asked him. Since we both got around in wheelchairs, our feet hardly ever touched the floor; we went straight from our beds to our chairs.

"It was wet a couple of months ago," he answered. "I sat at the edge of the bed one day. I thought maybe I spilled water by the foot of it. But, Mom, my whole floor is wet in there now. I checked."

I went in, leaned over from my chair, and checked for myself. The entire carpet near his bed was soaked. I told Mattie to go sit outside. I moved his martial arts trophies away from the wall—they were too big to sit on a desk—to find that the entire baseboard had turned black.

I didn't have the strength to pull the carpet away, so I called Don and Lorraine Retzlaff and asked them to come over. When they peeled back the rug, they said, "There's nothing but mold and mildew down here." It turned out something was leaking from the furnace right next to Mattie's bedroom, and that's what was making him sick.

I packed some bags, and Don and Lorraine scrubbed down all our belongings—we didn't have much: two hospital beds, two dressers, a ton of books, photographs, and some bookshelves—and put them into storage. The condo we would soon be buying with Mattie's medical trust funds was not going to be ready until late September or early October, and we were only into very early summer.

I phoned the hospital to explain the situation, and the staff started calling local hotels in search of good deals on wheelchair-accessible rooms. We couldn't stay at Sandy's because she had already sold her townhouse to buy a condo right next door to ours, and she and Chris, who still lived with her, were staying at Nell and Larry's house.

The hotels were wiping us out, even with the steep discounts we were occasionally offered to accommodate our situation; the money for Mattie's medical trust fund still had not come through. Fortunately, we had some overnight trips here and there for speeches Mattie was giving, along with a two-week trip out to the Midwest again, and our hotel stays and travel expenses for these excursions were covered by event sponsors.

The Midwest trip was for another big Harley-Davidson event in Milwaukee, where Mattie was also going to meet some people in preparation for the MDA telethon that September. On the way to Wisconsin, we visited once more with Jeff Bouchard's family and with the Hemelgarns. Jeff introduced us to singer Christopher Cross, who performed "A Walk Down Abbey Road"—a concert of Beatles songs at an outdoor theater there.

After the concert, we had dinner with Christopher, who took an immediate liking to Mattie and said that his children would love to meet him. Just as he had done with Jeff's children, Mattie called them on the cell phone right then, and he hit it off with Rain, a boy about his own age, and Madison, a girl two years younger. Detroit had now given us our third new family of friends.

Out in Milwaukee, Mattie did his usual book signings and interviews, in addition to a cover photo shoot for a Toys "R" Us guide for "Differently Abled Kids." There was also a cover shoot for *Parade* magazine with Jann Carl, cohost of *Entertainment Tonight* and a cohost of the upcoming MDA telethon. Mattie's speech to the Harley riders was followed by a meeting with then-Secretary of Health and Human Services Tommy Thompson. Having just talked to the motorcycle crowd, Mattie was in a Harley vest and gloves with no fingers, sporting a giant Wisconsin-style plastic wedge of cheese on his head, but Thompson, a Wisconsin native, loved it despite his own suit-and-tie Washington uniform.

Once back in Maryland, we continued our vagabond sojourn from hotel to hotel, waiting for our condo to get finished. It was during that time that Mattie helped launch the We Are Family Foundation with Nile Rodgers and his life partner, Nancy Hunt. Nile is a legendary producer, songwriter, and founding member of the band Chic, and he wrote "We Are Family" (along with many other hits). After 9/11, he heard from friends in a number of countries that the world needed to be reminded of that message—we are all one family. So he brought together two hundred celebrities—Patti LaBelle, Diana Ross, Joel Grey, Bernadette Peters, Phoebe Snow, Jackson Browne, and many others—to rerecord the song, and the gathering was filmed as a music video by Spike Lee.

Nile and Nancy then decided to start a nonprofit to further the cause of peace, and they wanted to launch their organization by presenting a peacemaker award. But to whom? When Nancy happened to see Mattie on *Larry King Live*, she knew the answer.

The next thing we knew, Mattie was being presented with the We Are Family Foundation's first peacemaker award at its inaugural event—held at the home of Mark Barondess, Larry King's lawyer, on a lawn overlooking the water in Maryland's capital, Annapolis. Nile, Montel Williams, and Larry's wife, Shawn, all presented the award to Mattie together.

After the We Are Family event, Mattie and I spent two weeks with my aunt and godmother, Mary Lou Smith, at her apartment in a retirement community. She would have hosted us the entire time we were without a place to live, but neither of her two bathrooms was wheelchair accessible. Because of the narrow hallway and tiny size of the bathrooms, Mattie had to disconnect from the ventilator attached to his chair to make his way in, and I had to crawl. Nonetheless, the time we did spend there was wonderful. Aunt Mary Lou was a terrific hostess, and we were able to reconnect with lots of extended family, since she had six adult children (one of whom was Jo Ann Stoddard, whom we had recently stayed with on our trip to Richmond). Her children had children of their own, adding to the socializing. By the end of the visit, Mattie was calling

Aunt Mary Lou "AML" for short. It was the first time he had met her, and they really hit it off.

From there we left for California—Mattie; me; Sandy, who shared driving the van; Chris, who helped carry luggage, filled the van with gas, and kept Mattie company in the back; and baby Micah, who slept on a little bed between Sandy and me in the front. Along with the passengers came the following: four large suitcases; four backpacks; two huge tanks, each filled with two hundred pounds of liquid oxygen; a smaller one-hundred-pound tank for emergencies; several portable tanks; several boxes with backup ventilators, chargers, vent tubing, trach tubes, medicine, and other medical supplies; a huge box of food that would get us almost all the way out west without having to pay to eat in restaurants; a cooler filled with ice and beverages (Micah learned how to open the lid, take ice for himself when he felt hot, then close the lid again); an enormous bag of dog food; and two power wheelchairs, which are bigger than manual ones and which don't fold up. Mattie even had a small duffel packed for his stuffed animal tiger, Tad, so that Tad could hang stylishly on Mattie's wheelchair as always, sporting anything from tie-dye to a tuxedo.

The van was huge, but riding in it now felt sort of like being in a space capsule. You were stuck in your spot—there was no getting up and moving around.

We left Maryland around lunchtime on a warm afternoon in early August 2002, singing "California, Here We Come" as loudly and atrociously as possible. That first day felt very exciting. But by day two, we were coming to grips with spending from before-sunrise to after-sunset together in the van's confines. At one point, Mattie leaned across the backseat, grabbed a potato chip off of Chris's plate, and said, "Can I have one?" while popping it into his mouth.

"I broke up with a girl because she ate off my plate," Chris warned. "I suggest you don't do that again."

Fortunately, the scenery soon had us mesmerized. Leaving the congestion of the East Coast behind and taking a more southerly route than Mattie and I had taken out to the Midwest, we truly were amazed at the beauty of our country—open fields, rich colors, farms without fences.

One day we treated ourselves to a bite at an Applebee's or Ruby Tuesday, and the waitress walked up and said, "Oh my gosh, you're Mattie!" Chris had seen that sort of thing before, but what he wasn't prepared for was the woman's question: "I just got married—any advice?"

Nor was he prepared for Mattie's answer. "I've never been married," Mattie said, "but I think it's a good idea to imagine that everything you say to each other is being videotaped for you to view later in Heaven. That will help keep you from saying anything in a way you'll come to regret. Also, never let the sun set on your anger. If you disagree with your spouse, before you go to bed, say a prayer and think of something you love about that person—and share it with them."

Chris was floored. Mattie's parents were divorced, Chris's own parents were divorced, and Mattie was only twelve years old, yet this woman asked him to give her marital advice—which he did! "I can't believe she asked you that," he said.

"I get all kinds of stuff," Mattie told him. "That's why I ask you to come to the bathroom with me and through the hotel lobbies. People are always coming up to me and asking me questions—advice for themselves, and lots of questions about me. They stare at me and listen in on everything my mom and I say. I like what I do, but I'm always glad if someone else is there."

Our first major stop was the Grand Canyon. We saw the Painted Desert upon arriving one evening in Arizona, then got up the next morning and drove over to the canyon itself. *Awe* is the only word I can use to describe it. The immensity, the colors, the topography were all almost otherworldly.

We could stay there only about a half hour. The weather was too hot and dry for Mattie's trachea. But we were able to watch a film about the canyon indoors, and Mattie picked up a deck of cards with new jokers from the souvenir shop.

From the Grand Canyon we headed to Las Vegas, crossing the Hoover Dam around sunset. By the time we reached Las Vegas, it was evening, which is the best time of day to arrive. What the Grand Canyon is to natural beauty, Vegas is to neon beauty. The sensory overload was spectacular.

Vegas was on our itinerary because Mattie was giving a speech on behalf of MDA to the International Association of Fire Fighters, who were gathering there for their annual convention. We arrived a couple of days before the event, and while Mattie couldn't go outside and enjoy the man-made beach with Sandy and Chris (it was 117 degrees, way too hot and dry for him), he enjoyed the pure luxury of the Mandalay Bay Hotel, where the firefighters put us up. He also enjoyed the hotel's making him an honorary member of the staff, which allowed him to help with tours of the indoor aquarium. Perhaps the biggest thrill was meeting Jerry Lewis in person for the first time, who was also there to talk to the fire-fighters. This was the man Mattie considered his role model for advocacy work, and Mattie had long wanted to meet him.

In addition to chatting about the upcoming telethon, they joked around together, with Jerry Lewis challenging Mattie to a race: Mattie's wheelchair against him on a luggage cart.

Mattie's speech was a rousing success. He had more than five thousand firefighters on their feet doing the Yonkers cheer in honor of the rowdiest team at the annual MDA softball tournament—"Give me a Y, give me an O. . . ."

Toward the end of the Vegas stop, Sandy's cell phone rang. It was Cynthia calling for Chris. Chris took the phone, and it soon became clear that something wasn't right.

Afterward, Chris privately told Sandy that Cynthia was pregnant, and he and his mother had a long heart-to-heart, with Chris laying out every possible scenario for how to go forward. He was scared. This was a twenty-year-old who had not yet gone out into the world, did not have a career, was not yet a responsible adult.

Sandy just listened until he finished. Then, once she understood that Chris and Cynthia weren't leaning toward abortion, which greatly relieved her, she told him he had two choices: Either be this baby's father—get a job, get involved, get married—or put the baby up for adoption. It would have killed her personally for them to give up her grand-child for adoption, but she felt the baby deserved the gift of a mommy *and* a daddy, and that Chris had to make a responsible decision to make that happen. She had already been both mother and father to her own children and was all too aware of how much they had missed because of that.

Across the next day or two, in between more talks with Cynthia and with his mother, Chris spoke with Mattie.

"You know, don't you?" Chris asked.

"I think so," Mattie answered.

"This is totally unexpected," Chris said, "totally unplanned."

"But is the baby *unwelcome*?" Mattie questioned.

Chris just looked at him. "I don't know what to do," he said.

"I don't have an answer for what you should do," Mattie told Chris after he spilled his heart, his fears. "This is your decision. But what I *can* tell you is that you have everything inside of you that it takes to be a wonderful father, and even more important, to be a wonderful *Daddy*."

Chris thanked Mattie. "I looked into his eyes," Chris told me later, "and I believed him." But there was still a lot of soul-searching to do.

Despite the challenging issue looming as we left Las Vegas, Chris decided to make the best of the rest of the trip and enjoy his time in California with us before going home to deal with his responsibilities.

We arrived in Los Angeles a full two weeks before the telethon. There was a fair amount of behind-the-scenes work Mattie had to tend to, including meeting with telethon hosts from around the country for briefings. He also did book signings up and down the Southern California coast; an interview with Oprah for her magazine; a segment for *Good Morning America*; and another taping with Larry King for Mattie's new book that was about to be released: *Celebrate Through Heartsongs*. Oprah had warned him not to release so many books in such short order for fear they would lose impact, but Mattie wrote to her, "*I have to do everything now. . . . I have to live fast. Unless I keep getting miracles,*" he told her, he wasn't going to be here long enough to share his message gradually. (That book, too, immediately hit the *New York Times* bestseller list).

The two pre-telethon weeks were filled with plenty of pure fun, along with the work. We went with Oprah's producer and now our friend Shelly Heesacker to Legoland—a theme park built entirely out of Legos, which Mattie of course loved. There were even Lego-made cities like Washington, DC.

We also spent a good deal of time with Christopher Cross and his family, who were becoming close friends, too. They took us to Disneyland, Universal Studios, museums, and a lot of other fun places. We met a host of celebrities as well, everyone from Nancy Sinatra to singer/songwriter Michael McDonald, Norm Crosby, Paula Abdul, and Elliott Gould.

Christopher also arranged for us to see a taping of *Everybody Loves Raymond*, a television sitcom that all four of us were great fans of. It was one of the few times being in a wheelchair proved an advantage. Usually, there are tons of hassles involved—no curb cutaway, no place to let out the lift from the van, doorways that are too narrow, no ramps. But that day, our being in wheelchairs got Mattie and me right onto the floor of the set rather than in the seats with the rest of the audience.

Staffers warmed up the audience by feeding them pizza and having people do "stupid human tricks" (Mattie, with his low muscle tone, won a T-shirt by wrapping his ankles behind his neck yoga-style, lying on his back, putting pizza crust in his mouth, and calling himself a bread basket). Then the first star came out. It was Peter Boyle, Ray's father, "Frank," on the show. His eyes widened as soon as he saw Mattie.

"You're him!" he called out.

"You're *him!*" Mattie shot right back. All the other stars also gave Mattie special attention, hugging him and signing his signature book, something he had started asking people to write in when he was nine years old, long before he began to meet so many famous people. The book was now filled with notes from celebrities like Oprah and Jimmy Carter, from friends like his doctors and summer camp buddies, and from members of various camera crews, right down to the key grip.

The cast gave Mattie a life-size cutout of Doris Roberts's "Marie" in a bridal gown that was used in the episode; Brad Garrett's "Robert" presented the prop to "Ray Barone" to razz him after Ray admitted that he wanted a wife who was more like a mother. After the taping, Ray Romano was nice enough to film a piece for a pledge drive that aired during the MDA telethon.

The 2002 telethon itself was one of the most wonderful experiences of Mattie's life. Beforehand, he tore around the parking lot of the set with

Entertainment Tonight host Jann Carl's daughter, Katherine Sears, in his lap; he met with cohosts Ed McMahon and comedian Tom Bergeron; he talked with Wayne Brady, one of Mattie's favorite stars on a television comedy show, who performed during the telethon.

The telethon that year earned more money than it ever had, and Mattie stayed up for all but two of the twenty-one hours it aired. He didn't want to miss a thing, saying, "When else am I ever going to have the opportunity to do this?"

Mattie did two planned segments with Jerry Lewis—one at the beginning of the telethon and one at the end. But after Mattie did his final segment and went back into the audience so Jerry could close the show by himself, as he does every year, Jerry asked him to come back up on stage. He pulled up a stool, sat right next to Mattie, and went completely off script, talking with Mattie not just as National Goodwill Ambassador for MDA but also as an advocate for hope and peace—we still were not a full year out from 9/11. He also articulated to Mattie his own philosophy—that you only go through life once and have one shot to make a difference, and he felt that Mattie understood this truth.

"Start the music," Jerry said immediately after, "I'm ready to sing." The producer's jaw dropped, as it was such a departure from the annual ritual; Jerry always closed solo. But right there he sang "You'll Never Walk Alone" straight to Mattie.

This had never happened in the thirty-six telethons before that one, and it has never happened since.

Mattie with Chris Dobbins, his
"kin-brother," fall 2001

Mattie with Jerry Lewis in Hollywood,
California, at the close of the 37th Annual
MDA Labor Day Telethon, 2002

CHAPTER 11

Choice Vows

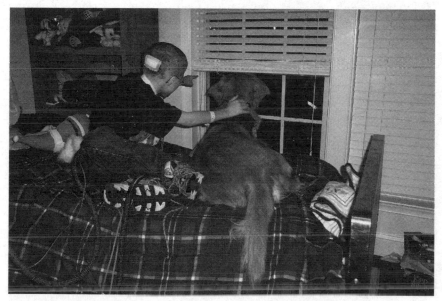

Mattie showing Micah their view of our neighborhood from one of eleven windows in our new home, fall 2002

. . . In the now, a bond is created, and it is good.
Yet, as it is with all things, a bond is a choice.
In each tomorrow, the future will be created,
And it can be good.
Yet, as it is with all things, the future is a choice.
As the love of yesterday binds the present into a touch
Towards every tomorrow
Do not vow to renew your choices
On your first, your fifth, or your fiftieth anniversary.
Rather, from this moment, go forth vowing.
Go forth vowing to choose gently, celebrating life each day.
Go forth vowing to choose wisely, playing after every storm.

Go forth vowing to choose fervently,
Never giving up hope in things that matter. . . .[1]

I don't know how we did it, but we left California on a Tuesday morning and dropped off Sandy and Chris at Nell's house in Maryland on Thursday evening. Mattie and I were on a mission to make it back in time for the kickoff of MDA's new fund-raising year—the annual softball tournament hosted by the International Association of Fire Fighters. It was the first anniversary of 9/11, and the opening ceremonies were going to pay special tribute to those firefighters who perished in the rescue effort.

There had always been an emotional underpinning to these tournaments, as much fun as they were. We were, after all, laughing our way through ball games, water balloon launches, "a dollar a squirt," "Luck for a Buck," and other shenanigans to raise money for people who were going to die without a cure. But that year, we were mourning people with whom we had high-fived at the closing ceremonies just a year earlier. There was a definite shift, and a realization of just how fragile and temporary anything in life can be, for anyone.

Still, the tournament was another success, and Mattie loved being with "the guys" he had known for so many years. As the weekend came to a close, however, he and I were still "homeless." It was only early September, and the new condo wasn't ready yet. Fortunately, Jeff Bouchard arranged for us to stay for a week at a Marriott hotel not far from where our condo was under construction, so that's where we headed next.

I hadn't said anything to Jeff about our living situation, but when we visited him and his family in Michigan that summer, Mattie told his sons, Kyle and Travis, about moving from hotel to hotel to get good rates. Jeff, friend as he was, stepped in, and the next thing we knew, we were the Marriott's guests, Micah included, free of charge for seven days.

When we arrived, the manager, Pam Follett, looked at all of Mattie's equipment and asked whether we needed anything special. I said he had

---

1 From "Choice Vows" in *Loving Through Heartsongs*, page 39.

some medications that required refrigeration and wanted to know if we could keep them in the hotel kitchen. In response, they had a refrigerator placed in our room to make things more convenient. When I said it was bigger than we needed, Pam explained that the hotel wanted enough space for food. "What does Mattie like to eat?" she asked. "What kind of milk does he drink?" They didn't want us to have to bother to go food shopping or down to the restaurant if we felt like staying in our room. They even offered to walk Micah if for some reason we couldn't.

The hotel's wonderful treatment didn't end there. The next morning, Mattie and I went downstairs and had coffee and bagels while we read the morning newspaper, and the morning after that, hotel staff brought our coffee and bagels to our room instead. The coffee was prepared just the way we liked it. They even delivered the newspaper.

At dinner, I'd tell Mattie to order from the kids' menu in the hotel restaurant and choose the cheapest thing for us to split. The hotel would not take our money for meals, and I didn't want to take advantage of their kindness. After the second or third night, the chef came out and said, "You don't like my cooking?"

"No," we answered. "It's great."

"Then why don't you order something other than a hot dog or chicken fingers?" he wanted to know.

We sort of fumbled for an answer until he said, "Look, this is not going to make or break us. You can't order a hot dog every night you're going to be here. We'll feel better if you get good nutrition." They made sure we ate beef and chicken and vegetables and dessert after that.

The hotel staff even let Mattie go behind the desk and be a greeter, welcoming guests. Being the extrovert he was, Mattie thoroughly enjoyed this.

On about day four or five, Pam asked to speak to me privately. I figured she wanted to know where we were going to go from there because the week was almost up.

"How much more time until your place is ready?" she asked.

"It looks now like it'll be the beginning of October," I told her.

"You can stay here until then," she said.

"Oh, no, we couldn't," I answered.

"Why not?" she wanted to know.

"Because early October isn't a guarantee. It could take more time."

Pam looked straight at me. "Consider this your home until your condo is ready," she said. "And if you move in and something is not right, if there's a medical problem like a material that's toxic for Mattie, you can come back here and stay until the problem is resolved."

I just sat there silently, astonished.

"Your son brings such a spirit to our hotel," she said. "Everybody seems happier. We like having you here, and now you're part of the Marriott family."

It was true that with Mattie around, the hotel lobby was always abuzz with conversation—he got people socializing who might otherwise have kept to themselves. The staff enjoyed his company, too. He hung out with everyone from the kitchen staff to the front desk workers, folding towels or doing whatever else was needed to help out. His good cheer was infectious.

A few days after my conversation with Pam, the hotel restaurant TV happened to be tuned to CNN while Mattie and I were eating dinner. Pam called out, "I'm taking off. Everybody set for the night?" when she glanced up at the television. Then she looked down at Mattie and back at the TV again. "And on my show tonight," Larry King was saying, "another visit from my special guest, and friend, Mattie Stepanek." There was Mattie's smiling face. He was waving to the camera.

"I *knew* I recognized you," Pam said. "Why didn't you say anything? Why didn't you tell us who you were?" All Jeff Bouchard had told them was that we were a family in need, with mold and mildew in our old place and medical complications that made it impossible to stay there.

"Why *would* I tell you?" Mattie answered. "You have done so much for us *not* knowing who I was. You wanted to help just because people were in need, and that makes what you did even better."

Life settled into a routine as the weeks wore on at the Marriott. Mattie started a new school year, and I started my final class as a doctoral student, with Mattie's nurse, Laura, coming once a week to help out, taking Mattie to see ducks in a pond nearby, roaming around the area with him, and, of course, watching out for his health. Laura had actually

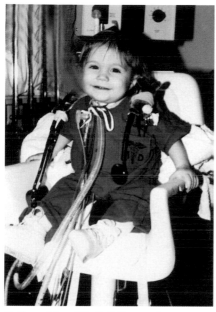

Kathryn Mary ("Katie") Stepanek
(12/10/1985–7/17/1987)

Steven Michael ("Stevie") Stepanek
(9/22/1987–3/24/1988)

Gregory James Jude ("Jamie") Stepanek
(2/9/1989–11/5/1992)

Matthew Joseph Thaddeus ("Mattie") Stepanek
(7/17/1990–6/22/2004)

Jeni and Mattie in the Pediatric Intensive Care Unit, where Jamie was also a patient at the time, Christmas Eve, 1990

Jeni and Mattie at the pumpkin farm, fall 1991

Mattie playing at a picnic, spring 1993

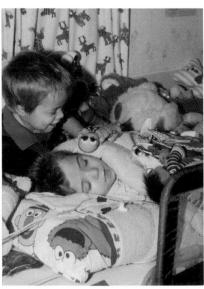

Mattie squeezing the caterpillar toy for Jamie, summer 1992

Mattie dressed up as a good shepherd, fall 1995

Mattie with Most Holy Rosary Church pastor Reverend Isidore Dixon after Mattie's First Holy Communion, spring 1998

Mattie practicing for his First Degree Black Belt test, summer 1998

Mattie with his new service puppy, Micah, summer 2002

(Left to right) Jamie-D Dobbins, Mattie, Heather Dobbins, Jamie Stepanek, and Chris Dobbins gather for a photograph just before Jamie (Stepanek) died, November 1992

Mattie with (left to right) Jamie-D Dobbins and Heather Dobbins, September 2003

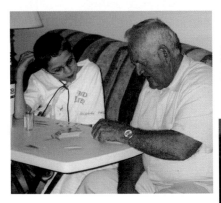

Mattie playing cards with "Papa" (Henry Newcomb), December 2003

Mattie and Chris Dobbins showing off their matching Santa gear, December 2002

Mattie getting a swim lesson from Jeni,
July 1992

Mattie enjoying being tossed into the deep end
of the pool by Chris Dobbins, July 2000

Mattie walking out onto a small fishing pier
on the Outer Banks, North Carolina,
July 1997

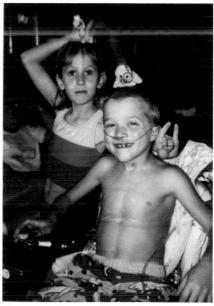

Mattie with his friend Hope Wyatt preparing
for the "duck on the head" practical joke,
July 2000

Mattie with "Aunt Flora and Uncle Paw"
Beaudet, New Year's Eve, 1998

Mattie with Shelly Heesacker (field
producer for Harpo) at Legoland,
California, summer 2002

Mattie with Katherine Sears (daughter of
Entertainment Tonight's Jann Carl) before
the 2002 MDA Telethon in Hollywood,
California

Mattie with Laura
and Annie Tresca,
spring 1998

Mattie playing gargoyles with legendary music producer Nile Rodgers, summer 2002

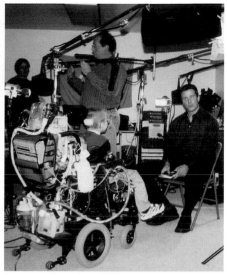

Mattie being interviewed by ABC's Chris Cuomo, fall 2001

Mattie meeting the *Harry Potter* actors (left to right: Emma Watson, Daniel Radcliffe, and Rupert Grint) on the set of *The Oprah Winfrey Show*

Mattie with his friends, a few members of the Hemelgarn family, spring 2002

Oprah Winfrey and Kaylee Dobbins (left) admire the bronze of Mattie during the dedication of the Mattie J.T. Stepanek Park, October 2008

Jeni selling Mattie's "Luck for a Buck" quotes for the MDA Mattie Fund at the annual IAFF/MDA Softball Tournament with Mattie's friends (left to right) Jimmy, Tommy, and Kenny Stack, September 2005

The Annual Heartsong Swim in Rockville, Maryland, raises funds to support the Mattie J.T. Stepanek Foundation, summer 2006

Children of Carlstadt, New Jersey, who study Mattie's message of hope and peace as a part of the school curriculum, celebrate the new "Peace Park" honoring Mattie, spring 2009

continued to help take care of Mattie every single week since we began wandering earlier in the summer, making her way to whatever hotel we were staying in. She loved being with him. "You'd never know this kid had such a rough life," she said. "He's honestly happy, and because of that, you're happy when you're around him."

Unfortunately, no amount of good feelings could keep Mattie's medical problems from ramping up that September. He had had a very stable spring and summer, mold and mildew notwithstanding. But his respiratory condition was beginning to decline again. One day, he was about fifteen minutes into a forty-five-minute keynote speech to some one thousand pediatric nurses and child life specialists when, through labored and choppy breaths, he interrupted himself to say, "I have to apologize, but I need my mother to come up here and check my ventilator and oxygen."

I rolled up onstage but wasn't able to find anything wrong. "Just give me a couple of minutes," Mattie said to the audience and was then able to continue after a bit.

The episodes of labored breathing began to occur more frequently, and I took Mattie to the hospital. Dr. Fink had moved to Ohio, and Mattie's new pulmonary specialist, Dr. Kim Witzmann, was wonderful. But she couldn't find anything specifically wrong at that time. We couldn't tell if this was just a brief spell, or if Mattie was headed into another dysautonomic storm.

It was around then that our old red van, the one we had stopped using when Oprah gave us our new one, was broken into. We were planning on giving it to another family with a child who needed a wheelchair lift, but were holding on to it until we moved into our new condo. Everything that counted to us we kept in that van, parked in Nell and Larry's driveway. We had been advised not to put anything of value into storage as it could get stolen. Inside the van sat our television, VCR, computer, Mattie's custody papers, my tax records, our wills, and, even more important, items of sentimental value: photographs, Mattie's journals, a number of his awards, and two new boxes of Legos that he had been given for his birthday in July but was waiting to open in our new home.

The items were all safe parked at Nell and Larry's, but at one point we had to use that van because the one Oprah had given us needed to be taken to the shop for a day or two for some tweaking. When the new van was ready again, Mattie and I drove down in the old one to pick it up. Sandy was going to meet us at the shop with Chris so that one of them could drive the old van back to Nell's while the other took Sandy's car.

Those plans went awry, however, when Mattie started to have difficulties at the shop—he turned gray and could barely breathe, so I had to drive to the hospital. I asked the mechanic if they could hold on to the new van for one more night. He said no, that once a van was repaired, they didn't have room to keep it on the premises. The shop was in a high-crime area, and I told him that if I put our new, expensive van from Oprah on the street overnight, it risked being vandalized, and if I switched vans, my old van that contained everything of value to us could be broken into. He said he was sorry, but there was nothing he could do.

I ended up switching vans before heading for the hospital because Oprah's vehicle had the electricity to provide the humidity Mattie needed. That came first. The old van with pictures of all my children and many other irreplaceable mementos sat at the curb. Once Mattie and I arrived at the hospital, he received a blood transfusion, new medications, and higher ventilator settings, all of which helped him to feel better.

The next day, when we arrived back at the curb outside the shop, which was closed because it was a Saturday afternoon, the red van was missing. "My photographs!" I said. "All my pictures of Katie and Stevie and Jamie! My videotapes of them. Gone. My tax records, court documents, your journals. Our TV."

"It's just stuff, Mom," Mattie kept saying again and again, trying to comfort me. "Stuff doesn't matter."

He was right, but I felt panicked about the pictures—I didn't know what I was going to do if I didn't have the photographs of my children. We started driving around, looking for the van.

All of a sudden, Mattie yelled out, "Oh, no, my brand-new Legos!"

"It's just stuff, Mattie," I said. At that point we both fell quiet for a moment, then burst out laughing. It was true. As devastating as it felt, it *was* just stuff. Mattie had just come through another health crisis that could have taken his life.

It turned out the van had not been stolen. The van shop had opened for a couple of hours that morning, and when the workers got there, the windows of our van had all been broken out, the doors pried open, and the vehicle vandalized, with papers ripped up, tax receipts torn into shreds, and the TV, VCR, and computer stolen, along with the video camera given to Mattie by Mia Hamm. The people who ran the company felt so bad about what happened that they towed the van into the shop and fixed the windows and doors at no cost.

Better still, while lots of things were ripped beyond repair and the more monetarily valuable items taken, most of the photos were still there—some ripped, some not. However, we also found that half of my tax records, several of Mattie's journals, a number of his schoolbooks, and many computer disks with speeches and other important documents were gone; some of that would need to be reconstructed.

And they would be—in the new condo. We finally moved in the first weekend in October, with the money coming through to the medical trust just in time to pay for it.

Mattie and I were thrilled. We were now living right next door to Sandy and Chris, with Nell and Larry just down the road. Not only that, but we were living in Rockville, Maryland, one of the best cities in the world.

Before we settled on buying the condo, Mattie and I had gone and sat in the van and watched people going in and out of the Safeway supermarket in the Rockville development we were considering, King Farm. What we saw was every shade of life, so many languages and dialects, people smiling and waving to each other. It was like a mini United Nations, and that's when we decided that, yes, we wanted to live there. We realized that King Farm was not just a series of buildings, of amenities. It was a community in the truest sense, with its residents interacting.

But the amenities were terrific as well. Right in our immediate area were restaurants, little stores, a coffee shop, a community center, parks, ponds, nature trails, "green" areas where grass was grown rather than mowed, even a community college right nearby. Mattie was finally free to go and explore. Where we had lived before, it was fairly rural—mostly houses (with steps leading up to the front doors) and no bus lines. There was no place for him to go and talk with people. Now he could roll right out of our condo building and over to Starbucks, to the ice cream shop. He could go to the Fontina Grille and talk to the kitchen help in Spanish, speak his rudimentary Korean with people from Korea. He could even take classes at the community college, we decided, rather than home-school with me for four more years. All he had to do was roll down the road.

Our condo unit amazed us as much as our new community. On the second story of a four-story building with an elevator, it had nearly 1,600 square feet—cavernous by the standards we were used to—with two bedrooms, two bathrooms, an eat-in kitchen, a dining room, and a little den off my bedroom. We purposely chose a unit above the garages; wheelchairs don't do well on carpeting, and we didn't want any down-stairs neighbors to have to contend with the noise of wheelchairs rolling across bare wood. We looked out over shops and a few trees, and that suited Mattie and me just fine.

Looking out over anything was astounding in itself; we hadn't had windows for years in our basement apartments. Now we had eleven—Mattie counted.

At first the windows made him nervous. He had even written to Oprah about it, saying that when he was little, "window" meant a place of light into Heaven, a place in your heart that connected your essence with your being. But once he started living in basements, he told her, windows became points of entry for people to vandalize your home and scare you, and he felt secure in his last apartment specifically because it had no windows. She e-mailed him back, *"Have no fear of windows,"* telling him that it was okay to go back to what windows had meant to him earlier in his life. Windows would now take him to new heights. Mattie was finally able to let go of his fear, writing to Oprah that the windows in the new condo let him look out on *"people and buildings and sky and life."*

It was going to be a while before we could afford furniture—it wasn't considered a necessity that would allow withdrawal of money from Mat-tie's medical trust. But it still felt like home, in no small part because of the generosity of friends, especially those we came to know through MDA. They moved our boxes in from storage, and when they saw how little we had, they brought us things like dishes, towels, even a new computer for Mattie. The condo echoed for nearly a year, but that was okay. Sandy put a card table and folding chairs in the kitchen, and we made out great.

Mattie set up his room with lots of books; Legos; stuffed animals; posters of tigers, *Lord of the Rings, Harry Potter;* his sunset glowing lava lamp; and his ever-growing rock collection. The collection included a heart-shaped rock found in South Africa by Oprah and Nelson Mandela and signed to him by both of them, and a rock that Jimmy Carter picked up for Mattie on a hill overlooking the sea in Oslo just after he won the Nobel Peace Prize.

I also gave Mattie the dining room as a "Bachelor's Pad," which contained his new computer; more books on everything from history and government to collections of poetry; lots of photos of friends and family members; games and art supplies; and a small table where he could sit with his friends to have a soda and not be in the living room with me.

As much fun as settling into our new condo was, however, Mattie's health continued to decline that fall. One evening, just as my class at the university was ending, Sandy called to say he was having a very hard time breathing. "I've suctioned him, but nothing's coming out," she said. "I don't know what to do."

I told her to change his trach just in case there was a mucus plug at the bottom. "Is there anybody around who can help?" I asked. This was not a routine trach change—Mattie was in crisis—and Sandy was going to need a second person.

But the only person around was her son, Chris, who had never even seen a trach change, let alone participated in one. Sandy showed him the shape of the trach tube, how they were going to slide the old one out and get the new one in at just the right curve while Mattie paused in his breathing. Chris was clearly scared. Mattie climbed onto his lap, put his arms around Chris's shoulders, and told him, "It's okay. I trust you. I don't have any doubts about your being able to do this."

That made Chris feel better, at which point Mattie added, "For those few seconds, my life is in your hands. But it's going to be okay." Mattie meant, "I believe in you," but the words sent Chris into an emotional tailspin, making him even more nervous than he had been. His heart was in his throat, but he *was* able to do what was needed.

After that incident, I called Dr. Fink. I had been wanting to contact him, anyway. "We need you," I told him. "We miss you." Dr. Fink had been Katie and Stevie's doctor as well as Mattie's. I had known him seventeen years. Not only that, he was the only physician who thought Mattie would survive back in the spring of 2001, when he had slipped into a coma. Dr. Fink had looked me in the eye during that crisis and said, "I don't think this is it. His body is going to *try* to die. But I don't think this is his time."

Dr. Fink never gave up on my son. When other doctors said, "Why are you giving this woman hope?" he would answer, "Because there always *is* hope." No matter how dreadful Mattie's condition, his response to his colleagues telling me, "There's nothing else," was always "There's nothing else, but we still have hope. There's nothing until something is discovered tomorrow." I really needed to touch base with him.

"You kept warning us about puberty," I said. "I'm scared."

"Because Mattie has done well recently," Dr. Fink told me, "his body is going to try to have a growth spurt. And his body finds growing very taxing. Where Mattie is now is the edge of a cliff. One foot has already slipped over the edge. The other is still on firm ground."

"So that's not too bad, then, right?" I asked him.

"The thing is, there's a banana peel where that foot is," he answered. "You just have to watch him. His future for the time being is going to be very stormy."

With that in mind, we went on as usual, celebrating life while bracing for a storm. Mattie applied himself to his studies and enjoyed exploring our new neighborhood. I went to school and work—and watched, as I always had.

A few weeks later, while I was working at the university and Mattie was at the condo with Laura, she called me to say someone was at the door from Best Buy delivering a TV. "Where do you want them to put it?" she asked.

"We didn't order a TV," I said. "Tell them to take it back."

They wouldn't take it back, though, insisting the TV was already paid for, at which point I said, "Just tell them to leave it in the living room. There's a mix-up and they've sent it to the wrong apartment. I'll deal with it after our trip." Mattie and I were headed that afternoon to Nashville for him to give a speech to thousands of employees of the oil company Citgo, another huge supporter of MDA.

While in Nashville, we met with singer Billy Gilman's manager. Mattie hadn't met Billy himself yet, but after seeing each other on the same episode of *Larry King Live* and realizing they were about the same age, the two talked on the phone and had become friends.

The aim of this meeting was to convince Mattie to set some of his poetry to music for Billy to sing. Mattie wasn't really interested—lots of people had already sent us demo tapes, and while it was a nice idea, it just hadn't worked. The music and the words never came together. So when Billy's people asked to stop by our room and play some samples, we said yes more as a courtesy than anything else.

The manager brought in three sample tracks, and, in a surprise turn, Mattie absolutely loved two of them. One was a song called "I AM/ Shades of Life," which was a combination of two of Mattie's poems.

Mattie asked if he could make some suggestions. "Could this part be spoken? Could this part be an echo in a child's voice?" They loved his ideas and named me executive producer of a CD they were planning so that we could have artistic control over the final tracks.

As we were getting ready to leave Tennessee, and Mattie was saying good-bye to his new friends from Citgo, one of them handed him an envelope. Out slid a picture of a TV with a built-in VCR and DVD player.

"Mom," Mattie said, "this is the exact same TV that was delivered to our house." We were thoroughly confused.

The man who handed it to us said that Citgo executives knew we didn't accept payment for Mattie's speeches on behalf of MDA but that the company heard we were moving and had had a little trouble with some of our belongings. I couldn't figure out how Citgo found out about the van incident until the man said that he got the information from an MDA executive when inquiring about us before we arrived in Nashville.

"It's a good thing we left for Tennessee when we did," Mattie told him, "because if my Mom had even one hour between coming home from work and leaving for this trip, the TV was going back to the store."

Soon after we came home, we were driving back from the university one day and saw police cars everywhere. Helicopters were overhead, too. We turned on the radio to learn that several people had been randomly shot and killed in the previous twenty-four hours while going about their business—getting off a bus, pumping gas, mowing a lawn. There was a sniper loose in our area.

News stations were warning people to stay inside; schools were having lockdowns. Our beautiful condo, our new space where we loved being able to go out and mingle with the world, was now unsafe. The last place the sniper shot someone was within a couple of miles of our development.

I was terrified. A child was soon shot outside a school. A kid in a wheelchair could easily make another "good" target, especially since the wheelchair lift on our van moved slowly.

A couple of weeks into what felt like an eternity during this crisis, Oprah called and asked whether there was any way we could get to Chicago by the next morning. I was beyond relieved to travel away from the area. We packed up and left right then.

Mattie thought he was going to do a follow-up taping with Oprah about his health and his life in general. He was playing with Oprah's dogs in her office when she said to him, "I hear there's a new *Harry Potter* movie coming out."

"Yes, in a couple of weeks," Mattie said. He was a huge fan and was actually sitting there wearing a *Harry Potter* wizard's cloak, and he had his Hermione Granger action figure on his wheelchair.

"We're doing a sneak preview tonight," Oprah told him, "a private viewing with other kids at a theater here in Chicago. Go, have a good time, and come back to the studio tomorrow. You'll be with all the kids in the audience who will have seen the movie and are going to review it."

Mattie was thrilled. He sat in the theater that night with other eight- to fifteen-year-olds, eating free popcorn, candy, whatever they wanted, all courtesy of Oprah. The next day, Oprah introduced "my guy, Mattie Stepanek," who was sitting in the audience, and together all the kids gave two thumbs-up to the movie. The highlight—a surprise to the entire audience—was that the actors and actress who played Harry Potter, Ron Weasley, and Hermione Granger in the movie all came out onstage. The children went wild.

More amazing was that "Harry"—the actor Daniel Radcliffe—knew who Mattie was. He even brought books Mattie had written for him to sign.

Oprah arranged for Mattie to meet Daniel and the rest of the cast backstage after the taping. She had asked them to bring something for Mattie that he wouldn't be able to get in the U.S., and they presented him with one of the wands that Harry Potter used in the movie. Perhaps an even greater gift was that Emma Watson—Hermione—kissed Mattie on the cheek. Posters of the young actress were all over Mattie's bedroom, and having a crush on her, he even kept his Hermione Granger action figure with him on his wheelchair. "Her hair brushed my lips, Mom," he told me afterward. He didn't want to wash his face for a week.

After Chicago, we left for a previously scheduled visit to Long Island, New York, where a youth group put on a peace rally, and Mattie had thousands of students on their feet engaged in his "Three Choices for Peace" chant. Then he gave a speech to about five hundred adults at a dinner and did an interview with *People* magazine.

On the drive back to Maryland from New York, an announcement was made that the two snipers terrorizing our area had been taken into custody. We could feel safe again at our new home.

Mattie received numerous awards during the fall of 2002, both for his advocacy work on behalf of people with disabilities and for his work as a peace advocate. He also delivered many speeches, perhaps none more exciting for him than introducing the Carters at a televised Kennedy Center event in November that highlighted the couple's humanitarian work. While we were roaming the Kennedy Center on the day of the affair, security asked us to leave because the Carters were arriving. Mattie kept trying to explain that he was Jimmy Carter's friend, but then President Carter walked through the door and called out, "There's Mattie!" The two hugged, and Mattie was allowed to stay.

Within a minute, however, the president was being advised that he needed to come away because the dinner was starting, and we were told to go to the waiting room and would be called when it was time for Mattie to give his speech.

"Mattie could come with us to the dinner," President Carter said.

"No, sir," he was told. "The dinner is for you and dignitaries."

"Isn't Mattie introducing me?" he asked. "If he is part of the event, he and his mother can be a part of the dinner, too."

"We haven't set a table for them," the president was then told.

"Put two extra settings at our table, and seat Mattie between Rosalynn and me," came the response. Then to Mattie he said, "I want you to hear what Rosie has to say. You'll be fascinated by her work in intergenerational caregiving."

Mrs. Carter spoke before the meal. Afterward, when the food was being served, I thought to myself, *Mattie, please, chew with your mouth closed. Don't spill anything. Don't drop anything.* Dinner wasn't dinner unless something dropped from Mattie's hands or mouth onto the floor. I was concerned about Micah, too—an eight-month-old puppy under the table of a former president and a bevy of top dignitaries. At one point, the president dropped his napkin, and Micah picked it up and gave it back to him. He petted the dog and went on using the napkin as if it had come from a white-gloved waiter.

Toward the end of the dinner, Mattie asked who "won" the centerpiece. He thought it was like a wedding, where one person at the table got to go home with the flower arrangement, which elicited chuckles all around. The president told him to go ahead and take it for himself.

"But it's on a Kennedy Center plate," Mattie replied when he realized it wasn't a prize item. "If I take that, isn't it stealing?"

"As a former president, I'm one of the people who practically owns this place," Jimmy Carter said, and he told the staff to take the centerpiece with the plate and put it next to our van.

After dinner, it was time for Mattie to introduce the Carters for the crowd. The president gave him a hug, asking, "Are you nervous, Mattie?"

"I usually don't get nervous," Mattie answered, "but I'm introducing my hero. This is the hardest speech I'll ever have to give."

"I know that whatever you say is going to be wonderful," the president said.

Those words were a great comfort. Mattie had been offered a stock speech to recite when he was first invited but received permission to rewrite it because, as he put it, "You can Google the Carters and get that information. I want to talk about them as people, tell the audience something they don't already know."

When Mattie finished talking, the president thanked him for "that intimate introduction," saying it was "the finest" he'd ever been given. He even asked for a copy.

Mattie then spoke again in early December—at Chris's wedding. Chris and Cynthia decided to marry and raise their baby themselves, and they asked Mattie to be their best man.

The wedding was supposed to be tiny, just Chris, Cynthia, Mattie, and Sandy and Cynthia's mother at the courthouse on a Wednesday, Chris's one day off from his new job at a credit union. But there was an ice storm that day that shut down the entire area, everything from government offices to the University of Maryland.

"What do we do?" Sandy asked. "They have a license. They need a wedding ceremony."

We pulled out the Yellow Pages, looked under "Weddings," and called the first listing, something like "AAA We Will Marry You."

In just less than two hours, Sandy, Heather, Jamie-D, and I planned a wedding held in Sandy's condo unit. There were flowers, a cake, folding chairs on either side of a makeshift aisle, and, when you looked out the window, a beautiful coating of ice on all the trees. Sandy's Christmas tree completed the effect.

Micah and Sandy's and Heather's dogs all wore bows, and Cynthia walked down the aisle in a beautiful white dress to the strains of Pachelbel's Canon coming from a CD, while I played photographer. At least twenty people were able to make it on the spur of the moment—Cynthia's aunts and uncles; her brother, Alain; Nell; Chris and Cynthia's friends—anybody who was close enough so that the drive through the ice storm wouldn't be too dangerous.

It was a beautiful ceremony, and Mattie sobbed his way through it, filled with pride, joy, and knowledge that his relationship with Chris would be changed now but that he'd have new "kin"—a "sister" in Cynthia and a new "niece" or "nephew" when the baby was born. He then read his poem "Choice Vows," which addressed the fact that a vow is not just for the day you make it but a choice you have to keep recommitting yourself to every single day for the rest of your life, even when times are rough. Chris and Cynthia loved it.

The rest of the afternoon and evening went wonderfully. Chris and Cynthia shoved cake into each other's mouths, the two new families mingled, and the memory of a real wedding was created.

Before bed that night, Mattie asked if I would snuggle with him. "Have I mentioned yet today how much I love you?" he asked me.

"Yes, you have," I assured him.

"Well, let me mention it again, because it matters that much to me," he said.

"I love you more," I told him.

"I love you even more," he answered back.

"I love you most," I said.

"I love you *mest*," he replied, which was our word for "most" and "best" together. "And nothing beats mest."

Soon after, he drifted off to sleep, not having said all the things I knew he was thinking—that Chris had something Mattie so wanted for himself, to be a husband and a father, but that he now knew he would never have. It wasn't that Mattie envied Chris; he was thrilled for him. He was just sad for what he was going to miss out on.

I lay there holding him. I already knew the pain of burying my own children, of burying my future through burying them; I knew there was nothing in the world heavier than an empty lap, empty arms. But that night, even as I was aware I was probably going to lose my fourth child, my grief was about what this felt like to Mattie—that he understood he was losing ground medically, that he was going to die, never grow up and have the seven children he had already named and fallen in love with. How hard it must have been for him, I thought, to sincerely feel the joy for Chris and Cynthia that he did, all the while knowing that joy was never going to be his. Tears fell as I lay in the dark.

Mattie serving as the Best Man at
Chris's wedding (left to right: Mattie,
Jamie-D, Cynthia, Heather, Chris,
and Sandy), December 2002

Mattie's "Bachelor Pad" in the new condo

CHAPTER 12

Ambassador of Humanity

Mattie enjoying a quiet moment with his service dog, Micah,
February 2003

Let our breath be gentle wind,
Let our ears be of those who listen,
Let our hearts be not ones
That rage so quickly and
Thus blow dramatically,
And uselessly.
Let our spirits attend and be
Most diligent to the soft
Yet desperate whisper of
Hope and peace for our world. . . .[1]

---

1 From "Resolution Blessing" in *Reflections of a Peacemaker: A Portrait Through Heartsongs*, page 135.

New Year's 2003 rolled in with Mattie becoming very ill. His blood chemistry was off, his blood pressure veered up and down, and he ended up in the PICU for an unscheduled blood transfusion. Something was just not right.

At the same time, he was named MDA's National Goodwill Ambassador for a second year—a great honor. Mattie wanted to use his notoriety to bring more attention to the organization as well as more donations for research, and to that end, MDA planned the first annual Heartsongs Gala, to take place in February. Mattie's vision for the event was not a black-tie dinner but a black-tie *party*—a real celebration with lots of fun rather than a staid affair. Jerry Lewis and then-president of MDA Bob Ross lent the idea their full support.

In the meantime, Mattie hosted a twenty-first birthday party for Chris on Super Bowl Sunday—a last big bash before he settled into fatherhood. The next day, I was suctioning his trach, as usual, when the secretions came up pink. My heart sank. I called the hospital, and they said not to worry—that the blood might be because Mattie coughed hard or because his trachea had been scraped during a trach change.

The day after that, *Larry King Live* producer Michael Watts came to get background footage of Mattie in preparation for the release of his fifth book, *Loving Through Heartsongs,* which he dedicated to Oprah and for which Maya Angelou had written the Foreword. Larry was going to be interviewing Mattie a few weeks later. During Michael's visit, he offered to take Mattie to a game arcade. Like Shelly Heesacker, Chris Cuomo, and everyone else who met Mattie, Michael had started out seeing him as a segment on a show and quickly ended up his friend. As weak as Mattie felt, he went, climbing out of his wheelchair and onto a Star Wars pod racer for a couple of hours of fun.

The next morning, January 29, Mattie called Oprah very early to wish her a happy birthday. She happened to be on the other line right then with Maya Angelou and put Mattie through on a conference call so the three could speak together. He was thrilled.

On the thirty-first, however, Mattie woke up coughing up skin and bright red blood. With dread in both of us, I told him to pack a couple of changes of clothes, some books, and his Game Boy for the hospital and wheeled next door to Sandy's unit.

"I'm scared," I said.

"They're going to have to do surgery," she warned me. "Go take him in. I'll get out of work as quickly as I can."

It was seven A.M., just getting light outside, and rush-hour traffic was particularly heavy that morning. I knew Mattie needed to talk, but I didn't want him yelling from the back of the van, which was quite large, because that would tax his throat even more. So when he asked if he could call Oprah, I said yes, even though it was an hour earlier in Chicago, a little past six A.M. They had just spoken around that time of day for her birthday, so I figured it would be okay.

Mattie called Oprah's private office number, and someone picked up to tell him she wasn't in yet. "Is this important?" the woman asked.

"I'm a little scared. I was just hoping to talk to her," Mattie answered.

Within seconds, he was patched through to Oprah.

"Hey, my guy, what's up?" she asked.

Mattie let her know what was going on, and she listened, talked with him, read him Psalms from the Bible, and sang to him, all of which helped him grow calmer. I was so grateful. It was six in the morning in Chicago, and she was taking care of not only Mattie but also me by letting me concentrate on what I had to do. It was not until months later that I learned it was not six in the morning for her but four—Oprah was having a couple of days of R&R in California and took Mattie's call in the middle of the night.

Mattie went for bronchoscopy surgery the same day we reached the PICU. The doctor who performed the operation said there was a complete ring of dead and denuded skin around Mattie's trachea.

"What does that mean?" I asked.

"We don't know," she said. "But I'm expecting that the remaining tissue is going to die, too. Once one area dies, the area around it dies. Over the next days, weeks, months, strips of airway are going to fall off. He's going to be in a crisis again and again. He will keep needing immediate attention to get out the pieces of skin so they don't block his airway."

In 2001, almost two years earlier, this same doctor had said Mattie's denuded airway meant certain death. Now she said that while there was no doubt in her mind that the entire airway was going to erode, she couldn't say whether there would be a regeneration of cells with new, protective scar tissue forming. She didn't know whether his body had enough strength to go through this a second time. In other words, she was no longer writing him off. She had already seen him come back from something she never expected he would.

Sandy and I had a family meeting with the doctors, nurses, social workers, and a child life specialist. There were more than a dozen people in the room, and we were given two options: Take Mattie home and let the condition run its course so that when his airway blocks, he dies; or remain in the PICU and suction out his skin when it drops off or force it in and then do an emergency bronchoscopy to get it out. That way, he wouldn't end up with an infection that leads to pneumonia. The big question with that second option was whether Mattie would *ever* go home again.

The decision, with Mattie's okay, was to stay in the hospital for the time being, at least for this current crisis, until all the eroding skin fell off. At that point, we could consider going home for the inevitable or staying longer. Again, it would be his choice.

In addition to the issue with Mattie's trachea, his body was suffering again from lack of oxygen. The hospital started searching for help from doctors all over the world. Why is this happening? Why is this child not processing oxygen?

Before any answers came back with suggestions for experimental treatments, it was Valentine's Day weekend and time for the Heartsongs Gala. Mattie felt, as sick as he was, that he had to go. "If I don't attend the first one," he said, "it won't go on after I die."

The doctors gave their blessing. The event was going to be held in a Washington hotel less than ten minutes from the hospital, and they felt that if worse came to worst, a physician could be sent to the hotel in an ambulance to perform an emergency procedure. They gave Mattie a "furlough" from Friday to Saturday night, when the event was going to be held.

Once at the hotel, Mattie met Billy Gilman in person for the first time. Special sound equipment was brought in so Mattie could record the spoken part of the songs set to his poetry—the CD was going to be called *Music Through Heartsongs*—and the two of them had a great time together after that, with Mattie introducing Billy to some of his practical jokes.

The next morning, Mattie continued to enjoy himself, loving the fact that he was staying in Room 666 so he could answer the phone, "Hello, Devil's Advocate. How may I help you?"

Once afternoon rolled around, *Good Morning America* producer Brian O'Keefe interviewed Mattie for his fifth book, which had been released the previous week. After the interview, however, Mattie told me he was having a hard time breathing. "I'm not sure I'm going to be able to stay for the event tonight," he said.

"Let's go back to the hospital," I responded.

"But what about the gala?"

"They have enough footage of you," I said. "It'll be fine." Larry King's producer, Michael Watts, was producing and organizing videos for the whole thing, gratis, for MDA.

"But we're supposed to be raising money. What if this fails, and we lose money?"

Someone from MDA piped up. "We will not lose money," she said. "There is no doubt about that. Even the tux for you is donated."

"You know," Mattie replied when he heard that, "I always breathe better in a tuxedo. Let's stay and see how I do."

I phoned the hospital, and they said it was my call to make, reminding me that once Mattie came back to the hospital, it was not clear whether he was ever coming out. Mattie stayed, and the Heartsongs Gala went beautifully. People came from all over the country, many flown in courtesy of the Hemelgarn family. The emcee, *Good Morning America* weatherman Tony Perkins, did make an announcement at the beginning of the evening that up to six inches of snow were expected so he was going to stick tightly to the schedule so people could get home or to the airport safely, but nothing was left out.

One of the highlights for Mattie was that Michael Watts and longtime MDA staffer Stephanie Goldklang had tracked down *Lord of the Rings* star Sean Astin and convinced him to do all the voice-overs for the event's videos since he was out of the country filming a new movie. The actor did introductions of people, explanations of the awards given out, and so on. It was a complete surprise for Mattie, who was not only a huge *Lord of the Rings* fan but also an admirer of Sean Astin as an actor. In the very first video segment of the evening, during which Sean introduced Mattie, he spoke directly to him, which brought Mattie to tears.

Toward the end of the evening, Tony Perkins announced that the snow was coming in quicker than anticipated so that if anyone had to leave, they should go right then. I called the hospital to see whether we should get back.

"How's he doing?" they asked.

"He seems good," I said. "I suctioned him, and he's doing okay." The hospital said to let him stay an extra night as it was becoming too unsafe for an ambulance to come, but that he'd be good for another day, especially since he had just had a transfusion.

The snow never stopped that night, nor the next. The storm track changed and stalled, dropping almost three feet of snow on Washington by Monday morning, and more in parts of Maryland. That left Mattie and me holed up in the hotel—with some two hundred of our closest friends. Mattie and his pals played poker in the lobby, had pizza delivered (on skis), and had a blast.

He had been scheduled to do a live Larry King interview Monday evening, but it had been canceled when he went back into the hospital a couple of weeks earlier. He still shouldn't have been able to do it—the roads to the CNN studio in DC weren't yet passable. But just across the street from the hotel was the ABC studio, and, in an amazing show of cooperation by competing networks, ABC let CNN use its facility. A path was shoveled in the deep snow from the hotel to ABC so Mattie could wheel himself over, and Mattie did Larry's show by live satellite feed to California. *Loving Through Heartsongs* became another *New York Times* best seller.

The next morning, we headed to the hospital with heavy hearts. We had literally played after the storm—even during the storm!—but now it was time to go back and face who knew what. Mattie's fingers, lips, and toes were beyond chapped by this point. They were also eroding. In addition, his blood pressure was all over the place. His whole system appeared to be in crisis.

Still, no one at the hospital was saying death was certain. By this point, Mattie was considered the Comeback Kid, and they were cautiously optimistic he would pull through once again. Mattie was less so. It was then that he expressed the desire to plan his funeral, talking about what should go in his casket, who should do which reading at the Mass, and playing out one final practical joke by having the fart machine placed in his casket. I didn't want to discuss these things but also knew Mattie had a right to talk about them, as well as make such decisions.

Within days of that discussion, Mattie had to be switched to a private PICU room because of his celebrity status. People would walk by his bed and try to take pictures, or announce to others in the waiting room, "I saw Mattie having a hard time breathing." Having his own room kept away gawkers. It also gave Mattie some quiet—he didn't have to constantly listen to the sounds of death in the unit.

At some point during the beginning of March, then-President Bush called the hospital one evening. Mattie had met Mrs. Bush several times, but now a sitting president, the leader of the free world, was on the phone with him.

Mattie came away from the call extremely excited. "Mom, there's not going to be a war! We're not going to attack Iraq! It's not going to happen!"

The president had already given Saddam Hussein, then president of Iraq, an ultimatum. People were bracing themselves. "How do you know, Mattie?" I asked. "Did he say he called it off?"

He then repeated the conversation. "I heard you're back in the hospital and having a rough time," Mattie told me the president said to him. "I want you to know we're praying for you because the world needs you. I want to thank you for the gift of hope and peace you've given to our world. Because of you, more and more of us believe that peace is possible. I get down on my knees every night and pray that I lead our country toward peace, and you are my inspiration." It wasn't a direct repudiation of war, but Mattie believed it was close enough to feel confident, positive even, that an attack would be averted.

Mattie moved through the next couple of weeks very optimistic—not happy about his medical situation but happy nonetheless. He was receiving a lot of visitors and cards to boost his spirits. Sandy would come and talk with him as usual. She'd exchange videos for him from home—but always left *What About Bob?*, a movie he watched every day, and *As Good As It Gets* to fall asleep with every night. She even began e-mailing a group of hundreds of people we had named the Prayer Warriors to keep them apprised of Mattie's condition; the hospital said it could not take hundreds of calls a week, as had been coming, on one patient's behalf. In an early March 2003 e-mail Sandy wrote:

> Every day he has episodes of respiratory distress. When there is tissue or blood blocking his airway, he desaturates and feels like he cannot breathe. Once they have suctioned out or he has coughed out the tissue/blood, his oxygen saturation goes back up, and he breathes better. His spirits are generally good. Both he and Jeni are tired of hospital life but are hanging in there. On most days he is able to do school work, although he did ask his mom why he needed to do his math if he was going to die anyway—to which she replied that if she had not taught him stuff every time in his life that he might have died, he would now be a very uneducated child, so back to math! He loves to play practical jokes on the staff, so they all want him home before April 1st!

Other visitors included Aunt Mary Lou, who was in her mid-seventies by that point but rode several buses and the Metrorail in each direction to get to the hospital, taking hours out of her day a couple of times a week; Devin Dressman, who now worked in Baltimore but would come to see Mattie in Washington at least weekly; Mattie's great-aunt Frankie; our friends the Retzlaffs; our parish priest, Father Dixon; and Nell, who was great company for me as well as Mattie. When Nell was there at the same time as Sandy, and Mattie had other visitors, the three of us Granny'olas would enjoy a little time over coffee in the hospital cafeteria. To be able to sit and laugh and reminisce even in the midst of all this pain and uncertainty was wonderful for my spirit.

Sandy's eldest child, Heather, came often, too. She lived more than an hour's drive away in Baltimore, where she was earning her Ph.D. in neuroscience, but she would visit for several hours at least twice a week. Heather was fourteen years older than Mattie, old enough to be another mother figure as well as a sibling to him. While Mattie called Sandy his "other mother," he called Heather his "other other mother." He had also nicknamed her the "Hedder Chair" when he was very little, before he could pronounce the *th* sound, because he and Jamie both spent so much time in her lap as infants and toddlers. She had the patience as a teenager to sit still with them for tube feedings and other procedures. She even learned how to suction Mattie and change his trach when he was a baby. Later on, she would visit his classroom and help the children do arts and crafts projects. Now, she would visit the hospital and chat while playing a Yu-Gi-Oh! card game with him—Mattie loved teaching this new game of strategy and luck to her—as well as help with some of his routine medical care.

On one of her visits to the hospital, she came out into the hallway when Sandy and I returned from the cafeteria and said she needed to talk to us about something. "Why does Mattie have a gay pride sticker on the back of his wheelchair?" she asked. "He seems as randy for girls as a boy entering adolescence could be, and I'm just asking, not judging, but if there's something he needs to share . . ."

"He doesn't have a gay pride sticker," I said. "What are you talking about?"

"There's a sticker of a rainbow that says, 'Celebrate Diversity,'" Heather responded.

"That's not a gay pride sticker," I told her. "Somebody asked to put that on Mattie's chair at a book signing. What better message from a peacemaker than 'Celebrate Diversity'?"

"That is a gay pride symbol," Heather explained. "Does Mattie know that?"

We all went back into Mattie's room together, and Heather asked him, "Do you know what this means?" pointing to the rainbow.

"It's about the mosaic of life," Mattie answered.

"No, Mattie," she told him. "It's actually the gay pride symbol."

"It is?" Mattie said. "Somebody asked me if they could stick it on my chair, and I said, 'Sure.'"

"Are you okay with having that sticker on your chair? With people wondering if you're gay?" she questioned.

"I don't think anyone is going to think I'm gay," Mattie said.

"Okay, then," she kept on, "now that you know what it is, and you are not gay, are you okay with it? Is this a statement you want to make?"

"God's love includes all people," Mattie answered. "It doesn't exclude anyone. I have friends who are gay. Now that I know what it is, I can't remove it, can I? What would that say to my friends? Jesus never judged love. Neither will I."

I was so proud of Mattie. So many people who are antigay point to the Bible to support the opinion that homosexuality is a sin. But Mattie understood that the Bible had to be read with an eye toward historical and cultural context. He never learned that; he just knew it.

I was so grateful for Heather's straightforwardness, too, on top of all the love and care she always showed Mattie. I appreciated that she could help my child with something about which I had been clueless.

A few days after that particular visit from Heather, Mattie was getting ready for bed when breaking news interrupted a sitcom we were watching (there were televisions in the PICU's isolation rooms where Mattie had been moved for privacy). Bombs were falling over Baghdad. Mattie let out a wail, put his head straight down on his knees, and began sobbing, shoulders heaving. His oxygen level suddenly dropped too low, his heart rate went too high, and his blood pressure started spiking and then dropping. Even his color changed. His nurse came running in, thinking he had coded.

"What did I say to make him think this is how peace is possible?" Mattie moaned. "What part of my message made him think this is part of peace?" He could not get control of himself—when the bombs starting falling, the pain of war affected Mattie medically. I climbed into bed with him, trying to hold and soothe him.

Across the next thirty minutes, Mattie moved from hysteria to shock. He stopped crying and just stared. Then he turned off the TV, closed his eyes, and started praying. After that his vital signs stabilized, but I stayed by his bedside that night rather than go out to the waiting room, as usual, to sleep on the bench. They couldn't *not* let me stay.

By the next morning, Mattie's optimistic demeanor of the past couple of weeks had completely changed. This kid who had been playing cards and having fun with visitors simply said, "I need to do my schoolwork."

I felt afraid. If Mattie lost hope for the world, he may then lose hope for life, for himself. If there was nothing he could say or do to make a difference for peace, he might then feel, "Okay, my time is up." His body had already reacted to the war in just that way.

Panicked, I left the PICU and called Sandy. "I don't know what to do," I told her. "He wants to be an ambassador of humanity, and he feels his efforts have failed."

"Does he still want to do a book with Jimmy Carter?" Sandy asked. Mattie and President Carter had discussed collaborating on a book about peace for at least a year by that point, talking on and off about how it should be structured and the content for various sections. But the talk had not by that point evolved into action.

"Yes," I answered. "But he can't get anything accomplished in the hospital. He doesn't have regular access to e-mail, to the outside world."

Sandy took it upon herself to contact President Carter on Mattie's behalf. "What do I do?" she questioned him. "He's got to believe in his own message again."

"Remind Mattie we're doing the book together," he said. "Tell him I need him now more than ever. We have to continue to move forward as peace advocates, or peace is not going to happen." He then wrote to Mattie himself:

> . . . With [the] beginning of what I consider to be an
> unjust and unnecessary war, all of us who are searching

for peaceful solutions to problems need to work even
harder. . . . I really need your ideas about what might
be done. . . . We can prevail with faith and determina-
tion. I'm in the midst this week of a conference with
Latin American leaders and will be lecturing at Emory
University, but it would be really great if I could talk
to you by telephone. I tried several times earlier but
was told you could not take calls in the ICU. Now that
you're doing better, I'll work with your mother on a
convenient time.

With love, Jimmy[2]

Mattie wrote back:

Dear Jimmy,

. . . I feel like [the] decision [was made] long ago
that [we were] going to have this war, and [people have]
spent so much energy carving out the trench that would
support [this] plan. Imagine if [they] had spent as much
time and energy considering the possibility of peace as
[they have] convincing others on the inevitability of
war . . . we'd be at a different point in history
today. . . . What happens after we "free" Iraq? Will we
then boast triumph while that country's citizens struggle just as the citizens of Bosnia and Afghanistan . . .
and how many other countries we have made "free" still
struggle today? . . . I want to look at patterns and see
if we can break the cycle

Love, Mattie[3]

---

2 From *Just Peace: A Message of Hope*, page 75.
3 From *Just Peace: A Message of Hope*, pages 75–76.

President Carter then responded:

> I don't have any way to understand your physical limita-
> tions right now, but would like to suggest a strong and
> powerful poem, expressing concern about the unnecessary
> war, concern about the innocent children of Iraq, and
> hope for peace. . . . Your love, wisdom, and insight re-
> ally mean a lot to me.
>
> Love, Jimmy[4]

Mattie penned two poems in response, one of which contained the following lines:

> *Seeping silently in the night*
> *Dark before the sun's first light*
> *The deuce of death not yet in sight*
> *Life awaiting dawn . . .*
> *Fires, fires, fires fell*
> *The horror, a sight straight from hell*
> *Why fire attacks, it will never tell*
> *Death before the dawn . . .*
> *Life cries out for help from friends*
> *Will the hatred ever end? . . . .*
> *The next day, what next . . .*
> *Live in fear or choose fight*
> *Live in fear or choose might*
> *Live in fear or choose flight*
> *Why choose any such sight*
> *For not one is right*

---

4 From *Just Peace: A Message of Hope*, page 77.

If we choose to count
On this and each night . . .
To wake with another dawn.[5]

The poetry writing was especially cathartic for Mattie during this time. President Carter's letting him know that they had to get down to work on the book—which Mattie decided to title *Just Peace: A Message of Hope*— restored his own hope and brought him back to his mission. He immediately started working out an outline for the book—and interacting again with others—his friends, his doctors and nurses.

Much had changed since 2001, when the medical staff looked at him strictly as a patient. Now they brought him coffee, sat with him as they filled in their charts just to keep him company, brought him food and treats from home.

There were always some new doctors, though, because Children's National Medical Center is a teaching hospital, with resident and fellow physicians rotating through different units every month. A fresh batch of them had just begun doing rounds one morning, a day before Mattie was scheduled to have another surgery to have a close look at what was going on with his trachea. Uncharacteristically, Mattie demanded to speak with them. He said he was outraged because while he had been told his surgery would be the next day, he was now being advised that he was on standby either for late that day *or* the next day and hadn't been given anything to eat. "I've been NPO [nothing by mouth] all morning," he complained. "I didn't eat much lunch yesterday and then skipped dinner because I was busy talking to a visitor. I'm hungry and *thirsty*! This is not fair. I at least need something to drink. Look how dark my urine is." He held up his urinal, a plastic bottle that male patients have by their bedsides.

The doctors tried to get Mattie to calm down, but he would have none of it. "You won't give me something to quench my thirst? Fine," he said.

---

5 From "Unfinished" in *Reflections of a Peacemaker: A Portrait Through Heartsongs*, page 104.

With that, he picked up the urinal and began drinking from it. One of the new residents leapt over the bed and tried to stop him.

"April Fools!" Mattie said. He had filled a brand-new urinal with apple juice. The doctors on rounds, being new, were unaware that Mattie's surgery had not, in fact, been pushed up. They were completely unprepared for his antics.

To soothe the physician's rattled nerves, Mattie said, "I'm sorry. Please allow me to make it up to you by letting me share my candy with you." He then handed the doctor a wooden box. When the young man slid open the top, out came a rubber mouse that literally jumped about a bit. Many of Mattie's practical jokes—lifelike rodents, rubber vomit, masks and costumes—came courtesy of the Hemelgarns.

Not all of Mattie's encounters with new people by his bedside were so much fun. The hospital was able to keep away hundreds of fans by compiling a specific list of who was allowed to see him and sending anybody else to the Public Relations Department, which then had to contact me for clearance; access to Mattie was extremely guarded. But one night, a very large man, more than six feet tall, walked into his room, shut the door, pushed me back into my chair when I tried to lean forward, and said, "Keep quiet." He then closed the curtain and said that he was a neurosurgeon from Philadelphia and needed to examine Mattie because he had been called in for a consult. "I need you to leave the room so I can take off his clothes and check him out in private," he insisted. Thinking fast, I told him that would be fine but that I'd like to give him some information about Mattie first. That way, I said, he would know what to look for. I suggested we talk outside the room because I didn't want Mattie to become alarmed by my discussing his condition. The man consented, and I got the two of us as close to the nurses' station as I could and mouthed "Help." Security came right away and removed the man from the hospital, catching his face on the security tape.

We were told they needed to move Mattie to a new room that night, and also to pick an alias for him. Only a handful of people ever learned that name.

A couple of nights later, the same man came back and hid in a first-floor bathroom for hours until he could get on an elevator. The elevators were blocked after visiting hours, so he had to wait for someone to come off one in order to sneak on. Unbeknownst to him, a security guard had been stationed in the far corner of the elevator, where he couldn't be seen from the door, and the man was apprehended. Fortunately, we never had an incident like that again.

April moved forward and, thankfully, many joyful things occurred. The CD with Billy Gilman was released, with about a dozen of Mattie's poems having been set to music, and Billy came to the PICU with *Good Morning America*, *The Oprah Winfrey Show*, and the *Today* show to do some publicity shots with Mattie. The CD debuted at number 15 on the music charts, with the music video from the "1 AM/Shades of Life" track making it to the Top 10 on Country Music Television.

Other famous visitors included Larry King, Quincy Jones, and one of Art Linkletter's daughters, Dawn. Christopher Cross came, too, with his wife, Jan, and his children, as did Jeff Bouchard and his boys. It could never be guaranteed that Mattie was going to have a good day, so young visitors would sometimes see Mattie with blood streaming from his lips, or his eyes looking like slits because of a bad reaction to a new experimental medicine that caused his eyelids to swell. I was so grateful that neither Christopher nor Jeff shielded their children from Mattie when he looked like that. It was hardest for Mattie to be alone when he was most scared, so their presence on those bad days was a great comfort.

Mattie received cards and phone messages, too—from Oprah Winfrey, Jerry Lewis, Maya Angelou—as well as letters from Christopher Reeve, who wrote, *"I'm very pleased to have an autographed copy [of your book] that I can keep and turn to whenever I want to be inspired by your words."*

Bill Clinton also contacted Mattie. He wrote at one point, *"I heard that you are going through a difficult time, and I want you to know I'm thinking about you . . . you are a wonderful person who brings joy into the lives of all who know you. I'm impressed by the courage you've shown in facing so many challenges."* At another point the forty-second president wrote to Mattie, *"You are the future of our country, and I encourage you to continue to use your creative talents so that you'll be prepared when your generation leads our nation."*

Mattie received telegrams from Ed McMahon as well, in addition to letters from writers with whom he had been corresponding across the years, including J.K. Rowling (who always signed her missives "Love, Jo"), *If You Give a Mouse a Cookie* author Laura Numeroff, and *Magic Tree House* series author Mary Pope Osborne. Mattie had been writing to book authors from the time he was five, sharing ideas with them and asking them about their own work. When he was seven, Osborne had sent him the following: *"By the way, your suggestion last year that I write [a book] on the North Pole did help me make the decision to write* Polar Bears Past Bedtime. *Thanks!! Keep up your great work, Mattie. Love, Mary."* In 1998, she dedicated her book *Dolphins at Daybreak* to him.

Communications from all these people cheered Mattie greatly, but a particularly wonderful blessing for him occurred on April 14. That was the day his "niece," Kaylee Renee Dobbins, was born. He was heartbroken that he couldn't go to see her, but six days later, on Easter Sunday, Cynthia and Chris brought her to Mattie, whisking her into the PICU even though infants weren't allowed. They put her right in Mattie's lap, where she grasped one of his fingers with her whole hand.

Chris Cuomo's first child was born around that time, too. Chris wrote to Mattie:

```
Hey Little Man, you asked about "being a Daddy." Bella
is now almost a month old, and I am overwhelmed with the
responsibilities, up to my eyeballs in diapers, and in
much need of a good night's rest. I love her dearly, but
I keep wondering what I have gotten myself into with fa-
therhood, and I worry about all the different ways I
might ruin this beautiful angel. And you want SEVEN? One
is taking all my patience, my energy.
```

To which Mattie responded:

```
Hug her, kiss her gently, and tell her you love her as
often as possible. Those are the things that matter
```

most. The diapers will subside, sleep cycles will return
all too soon as she grows up, and away. You are a great
Daddy already. Never lose sight of what really matters—
the moment at hand, which is the only time you can count
on for sure.

Mattie knew that last point all too well. Through all of these weeks, the doctors were trying different experimental drugs on him, different enzymes, blood products, anything and everything to keep him from bleeding and his skin from eroding. Some things made him feel better but for only a couple of days, and some immediately made him feel worse, causing him to vomit blood or undergo severe swelling. Finally, the hospital conducted platelet function studies and found that his platelets, which are supposed to help blood clot, were not doing what they were supposed to because of Mattie's underlying condition. It was suggested that he receive new platelets every other day from donors.

The call for platelets was put out, and people quickly came from near and far to donate. One minister flew in from California, allowed platelets to be extracted from his blood, then flew right back without even asking to see Mattie. People from MDA came also, as did friends, kin, some of those on Sandy's e-mail list of Prayer Warriors, even a busload of firefighters from Yonkers and Greenburgh, New York, who had to be turned away because the hospital could process only four platelet donors a day.

It was a perfect Heartsong circle. Mattie gave people hope, and now people were giving hope back to him. He thought it was terrific that inside of him were platelets donated by individuals from all over, those he knew and those he didn't know. "I always wanted to be an ambassador of humanity," he said, "and look at me. Now I represent everybody, literally."

Better still, the donor platelets slowed the bleeding. Mattie finally showed signs of healing on his fingers, toes, and lips. The doctors inserted a Broviac tube, or central line, into his chest, which went up into his neck, then dropped down into the top of his heart so he could get his platelets—and fluids, other medications, and red blood cells—that way instead of through the frequent insertion of needles, which caused him great pain. He had had a Broviac as a baby, as did Jamie, so this wasn't something unfamiliar.

But when the doctors went once again to look at his trachea, they realized that the platelets, no matter how they were delivered, were no more than a Band-Aid. All the skin had eroded, and he was still bleeding there. The hospital was at a loss for what to do. We were now well into May 2003.

"Mom," Mattie said, "it's time to go home."

"What do you mean?" I asked.

"I'm not better yet," he responded. "But what if I don't get better? Like Jack Nicholson says in that movie, 'What if this *is* as good as it gets?' I have to finish what I'm here for. I can't do speeches from here. I can't try to touch the world with a message of hope and peace if I'm sitting here waiting to die. I can't research the peace book or work with Jimmy Carter from the PICU."

"Mattie," I asked him, "do you feel the same way about leaving now that you did in 2001, that same sense that it's all going to be okay?"

"I have the same feeling that I'm leaving to live, not merely exist," he answered. "But this is different because I don't feel that I'm going to get another miracle. I think my time is marked, which is why I want to finish what I started before I die."

I was exhausted—I had been sleeping again on a bench in a noisy, well-lighted waiting room for months. I was terrified—what if Mattie's trachea perforated at home, I wondered, and he was in agony for his final twenty minutes, as I had been told he would be? But because of Mattie's belief that he had more to do here on earth, I was also optimistic. I thought of something Oprah had e-mailed to him a few months earlier:

> You have a big life, like I do. You, through your poetry
> and words of peace, will have a greater impact on more
> people than most people come in contact with in a life-
> time. Yours is a GREAT SOUL. And the way you've chosen to
> live and lead your life, through positivity and grace,

```
is the finest example one can give of a life well
lived.
```

Mattie wanted to follow through on that, to finish up his life in a way that mattered. It was a shot he had the right to call.

Before leaving the PICU, he wrote to Oprah, although with me typing for him since his fingers were still bleeding, and it hurt him to press on them:

```
I always live knowing I can die, and probably will die
young. But I am going home because they can't do anything
else here, and if I heal, it's because I'm meant to heal,
and if I don't heal, then my message is out there, and
it's time for me to go to Heaven. I personally am hoping
that my message still needs me to be a messenger a while
longer, but that's really in God's hands.
```

By late May, Mattie was back at the condo playing with Micah, whom he hadn't seen in months, eating ice cream from Maggie Moo's, the local ice cream parlor, looking out his eleven windows, and sleeping in his own bed. All the while his fingers, lips, toes, and trachea continued to bleed.

Mattie napping with Heather Dobbins (his "Hedder Chair"), spring 1991

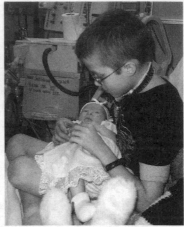

Mattie meets Kaylee for the first time in the PICU, Easter 2003

Mattie and Billy Gilman at the First Annual MDA Heartsongs Gala, February 2003

CHAPTER 13

Coming of Age

**Mattie celebrating his
thirteenth birthday, July
17, 2003**

*. . . We remember that sometimes,
Even if we don't understand why,
. . . . the rain falls for a reason.
We remember how important it is
To play after a storm, just because
We need to keep playing and living.
And, we . . . remember
To say thank You to God for our gifts.*[1]

Mattie Update 6/2/03

Hello to all and great news. Mattie . . . is bleeding
less and less. He is still on IV fluids at night. His
lips and fingers are better, but not healed yet. He is

---

1 From "For Mr. Thompson" in *Journey Through Heartsongs*, page 5.

enjoying visiting with friends and even an occasional
movie at the local theater. He is also busy with plans
for MDA Summer Camp. Jeni is delighted to sleep in a real
bed again. . . . As for me, and I'm sure you all share the
same feeling, I'm just so thankful that he is still here
to make a difference. As he was sitting in my condo last
week eating steamed-spice shrimp (with green surgical
gloves so the spices wouldn't burn his still raw fingertips), I was amazed. A month ago no one was sure he would
be here, and there he was, green gloves and all. He is a
constant reminder to all of us to remember that miracles
happen every day, and that common things like eating
shrimp with friends or enjoying a movie are miracles we
can have each day. Thanks to all of you who were faithful
in your prayers. . . .

Sandy wrote that e-mail to the Prayer Warriors less than two weeks after
Mattie arrived home. We did start seeing an improvement pretty quickly.
He never totally healed, but there was much less bleeding from his
trachea, fingers, and toes, and his lips went back to looking dark and
blistered rather than a mass of bleeding pulp.

Initially, we had to go back to the hospital every other day for platelets, and once a week for red blood cells. But across the summer, we
were able to ratchet down to twice a week for platelets and twice a
month for red blood cells, which was a great time savings. The ride from
the condo to the hospital took close to an hour—up to an hour and a half
if we became caught in rush-hour traffic. And the transfusion process
itself could take anywhere from three to ten hours, depending on the
platelet concentration of the blood from the donor and whether Mattie
was also getting red blood cells the same day. If he had a negative reaction to a donor's platelets, such as swelling, and needed an injection to
counteract the side effect, several more hours needed to be tacked on to
make sure the medicine worked.

But we were so happy for the treatments to be doing Mattie some good, and so happy he was home. He rested better there, without all the noises, alarms, lights, and constant interruptions in the PICU. The hospital was a safer place to have a crisis, but home was a better place to heal.

Mattie loved giving Micah random acts of kibble, as he called it, and holding baby Kaylee when visiting with Chris and Cynthia. He also enjoyed having regular access to e-mail, corresponding nonstop with his friends, including Oprah, who wrote to him within days of his homecoming:

Hey MY GUY!!!

We're all celebrating here . . . glad to know you're home.

Your letters to me are precious and a treasure. I've saved every one and often share your good thoughts with my friends. I love you dearly. I pray for you every day. I can't wait until you're better and we can "hang out." You can come to my farm and bring Micah.

Love-love you do, you know I love you.

Mattie got a kick out of Oprah's closing because, as he told her, "I am a huge Beatles fan." He proceeded to explain how he enjoyed:

. . . teasing my mom [because] she is a folk music type person. She likes John Denver . . . and Peter, Paul & Mary. . . . Sandy was a little more, well, a little more something as a teen than my mom ever was. My mom was more like an earth hippy, but Sandy was more into rock music. . . .

My boy was becoming a teenager, that was for sure. I wasn't even allowed to boogy in the van anymore when a song came on that I liked—unless it was dark out.

Before the month was out, Mattie would be leaving for MDA Summer Camp again, but late one afternoon, the fire alarm in our building started sounding. Sandy and I both went out into the hall from our apartments and smelled smoke. I yelled to Mattie to start filling portable oxygen tanks, then rolled to the refrigerator and grabbed his IV fluids and other medicines.

I could see the fear in Mattie's face. This was not going to be the first loss we were facing, nor even the first fire. Back in one of the basement apartments, there was a major house fire with flames shooting out of the walls. Mattie asked me then whether he could take his "stuff" with him as we raced out, and I told him, "Only what's between you and the door." He chose his Mr. Bunny fleece puppet and the family Bible. I grabbed computer disks and photographs before taking Mattie's oxygen tanks from the front hallway. This time, with Mattie on full life support, there was not a spare second to grab anything of sentimental value.

We rolled down the hallway to the elevator and pushed the button, but nothing happened. The elevator had done what it was supposed to do in a fire—gone to the first floor and stayed there with the doors open.

We then rolled over to the stairwell. I figured we'd sit in there—it was metal and wouldn't burn as easily—and wait for help. But we smelled even more smoke in the stairwell than in the hallway.

I told Mattie to go back to the apartment. Sandy would put wet towels under our door to keep out smoke and head downstairs to set up Mattie's backup ventilator system that we always kept in the van. It would take about fifteen minutes, and then someone would carry Mattie and me down. It was not possible for Mattie to be carried out before the ventilator system was ready. Everything he needed to live was attached to his wheelchair—he could not survive even a few minutes without it.

As soon as I sent Mattie back to the apartment, I heard the *ding* of the elevator stopping on our floor. The door opened, and I raced back to Mattie and told him to get on.

"Mom," he answered worriedly. "You don't get on an elevator in a fire."

"You always say I'm a woman of signs, Mattie, that I can spot a sign of something good," I reminded him. With that, Mattie made the Sign of the Cross and we got on, praying feverishly between the first and second floor: "Please don't let the cables burn and drop; please don't get stuck between floors."

The elevator went down to the first floor, the doors opened, and we rolled toward the exit. Then something even more baffling occurred. The doors remained open—the elevator had shut down again. To this day, there is no explanation for why that happened. The alarms were still sounding, and the smell of smoke remained heavy. An elevator is not supposed to work for a minute in the middle of a fire, then shut off again.

Mattie remained worried, even though we were now outside. I told him it was okay, that I could hear the sirens approaching. Sandy reassured him as well: "Insurance will cover any losses, Mattie."

It was at that point that I pulled Sandy to the side. "Our condo insurance covers everything right down to his Legos, right?" I asked.

"No," Sandy told me. "That covers the floors, walls, and ceiling. You have contents insurance, too, don't you?"

"No." The condo had been paid in full by Mattie's medical trust, and I hadn't stopped to think about contents insurance. If the building burned down, we would lose all our belongings: our refrigerator, stove, computer, brand-new TV, not to mention all of our photographs and everything we held dear.

Although I was whispering, Mattie overheard me. The fear left his eyes. He came over and hugged me and said, "We're fine, Mom. We've got each other. Remember, stuff doesn't matter." That same boy who was individuating from his parent in creating his own identity, as adolescents do, was now also taking care of her.

It turned out the fire was in the garage below my bedroom. Luckily, the firefighters arrived before there was a chance for the flames to do any major damage. The very next morning, I secured insurance for all our belongings.

Mattie never needed to be reminded that life was short and belongings temporary—he lived with signs of those truths his entire life—but the fire made him even more determined to enjoy every moment as much as he could. He couldn't wait to get to camp and start having fun with his friends.

On the third Sunday of June, we packed his things and left in the middle of the night so he could spend all the necessary hours at the hospital for platelets and red cells and be on time for the start of camp. Mattie was so thrilled to make it back to camp that he literally shook with excitement as we turned down the dirt road leading to the cabins. He was going to be in the Cuckoo Cabin for the second year in a row, with pretty much the same set of buddies from the year before. Devin was once again his counselor.

He didn't even care this time about not being able to swim. He knew that at least he'd get down to the pier for fishing and crabbing. Wheelchair campers typically were brought down a rather steep incline on a special lift, with their wheelchairs sent down separately, and Mattie couldn't be separated from his wheelchair because of the life support equipment attached to it. But he knew they'd find a way for him to join in—there was nothing MDA wouldn't do to get around a disability during summer camp week.

As soon as Mattie rolled away from the van, he was high-fiving his bunkmates—Neil, Lance, and the others. He then gave each of his "Lovely Ladies" from the Martin Cabin a small bouquet of flowers. The girls, in turn, gave him a button they had made that said MATTIE THE MARTIN MAN. Racheal Francis, the girl he bonded with years before when her sister died from the same condition she had, brought him a pimp hat with red and blue feathers glued to one side.

Each day brought more fun. There were campfires, a talent show for which Mattie did a spoof of Larry King, and contests both for cleanest cabin and cabin with the best theme decorations (that year the theme was wizards). Mattie's cabin never won for cleanliness, but there was a frenzied rivalry between the Cuckoo Cabin and the Eagle Cabin for wizard ambience. In the end, Mattie's cabin won, but not without a spirited contest on both sides that included Mattie "trading" Devin to clean the other cabin one day in exchange for some of their decorations.

There was also karaoke night, during which he sang "Soak Up the Sun" with the girls; "Man! I Feel Like a Woman!" with the guys; and

"Yoda" (Weird Al's parody of "Lola") with Devin. During a break in the crooning, Mattie spent time talking with Racheal. Much of their discussion was about typical camp goings-on, but they also talked about faith in God. She said she didn't believe in God anymore but still believed in Heaven and the angels. The two were going back and forth about the nature of faith and God and angels when Mattie's ventilator alarm started beeping. He wrote about it in a journal entry:

> *Racheal cringed, and asked me to make it stop. I did, and laughed, saying, "Yeah, I know, my machines annoy everybody." She shook her head back and forth saying, "No, it's not that. Before my sister, Rebecca, died, her machine beeped almost constantly. . . ." She . . . then told me that she misses her sister so much. I told her that I miss her, too. Racheal said that her sister would be 12 now. The same age as me. She started to look at a tree. I asked her what was up? She said, "You know the little holes in the trees?" I nodded. She told me, "My sister's last words in her diary were that the little holes in the trees were the stairs to Heaven." With that, the counselors started calling out that the break was over, and we headed back inside.*

Even with that conversation, Mattie wrote, he was able to have a good time and keep singing, although he recorded that he felt "a bit lonely . . . chilled." Still, he kept going, determined not to let all that the week offered slip away from him. He glued a sign to a monkey on a stick that said ALL HAIL THE SACRED MONKEY, which by the end of the week became a camp chant. He played wheelchair football, hid alarm clocks under another cabin that were set to go off at different times during the night, and sported a (temporary) tattoo when Harley riders and firefighters came on Visitors Day.

Like the year before, I'd hide out in the infirmary during the day and go to a motel twenty minutes away at night. But this season, I hired three nurses, not just Laura by herself, to rotate nights watching Mattie while he slept. On the third night, after the karaoke social, the nurse for the evening canceled at the last minute, and the camp director, Katie McGuire, said Mattie had to go to the motel with me. She apologized and even cried because she knew how much sleeping in his bunk with the others meant to Mattie, but without a nurse by his side, she had no alternative.

To cut into Mattie's time with his pals as little as possible, I let him stay with the others in his bunk until about one o'clock in the morning, when the boys started falling asleep. And I got him back by six so he could climb into his bed in time for wake-up and not miss a thing. Mattie didn't really get any sleep that night, but that wasn't what was important to him.

As we were reentering the camp, Mattie saw a vehicle going the other way. "Mom, that's Racheal's van," he said. "I wonder what she needed. Maybe a part of her wheelchair broke." We found out later that morning that Racheal had been having stomach pains during the night and was going home early that morning to have them checked out, just to be on the safe side. By the afternoon, the doctors could not find anything wrong, and she was set to come back that evening or the next morning.

Mattie spent that night with a new nurse whom neither of us had ever met, and she told him that if the alarms on his monitors went off before dawn, he should "run toward the light"—at which point all the kids in his bunk shouted, "No, Mattie. Run *from* the light! Don't go near it!" What could have turned out to be a very morbid moment became an eruption of laughter.

The next morning, I picked Mattie up at four A.M. for a drive to a local hospital so he could receive one of his twice-weekly platelet transfusions, getting him back just as the other campers were finishing breakfast. Racheal, on the other hand, had not yet come back, nor did she return that evening. The campers were concerned because they couldn't reach her or her parents by cell phone but still figured everything was okay.

Later that night, Katie, the camp director, called me at my motel to tell me that Racheal had died. Her parents were about to bring her back to camp when her heart simply stopped. It was heart failure, not indigestion or other GI troubles, that was causing her stomach pain. She was fifteen.

Katie asked me not to say anything to Mattie or any of the other campers because camp was supposed to be pure fun for them. I was right back at my Santa Claus discussion with Mattie a few years earlier, when I promised him I would never keep the truth from him. I was about to spend the last couple of days of camp holding back information that would be very important, even devastating, to Mattie.

On Saturday morning, the last day of the camp session, the campers each tied a wish to a balloon and let it float away. Mattie said that in years past he always wished something for himself—getting his message to Oprah or having his time with Jimmy Carter. But this year, he said, "My wish is for Racheal to be out of pain. She must be in a lot of pain if she wasn't able to come back." My secret was tearing me up.

On the drive home, with Devin along for a lift, we stopped at a fast-food joint, which was our end-of-camp tradition. Devin went in to pick us all up some lunch, and when he returned, Mattie started chowing down on a burger and asked that we call Racheal to see how she was doing.

I stayed silent.

"Racheal's not okay, is she?" he asked.

"No, Buddy," I told him.

"But she's still alive, right?" he questioned.

"No, Mattie. Racheal died. I am so sorry."

"When?"

"Thursday."

Mattie had known other children who died. Throughout his life he went to children's funerals. But this was going to be different. He had put a wish on a balloon for her to be out of pain. The two shared the connection of having a sibling predecease them from the very condition they themselves had, of watching their parents grieve the way they would be grieved over.

Mattie just cried and cried. When we arrived home, he wrote a poem called "Dear Racheal":

Racheal found the footholds,
The handholds in each tree.
Racheal climbed the laddered-stair,
Not grasped by you, or me.
I've seen the path
To Heaven's hold,
My fingers touched the wood,
But dear Racheal is
The one who passed. . . .
How I wish I understood . . . [2]

At the wake, after filing past Racheal's body, saying a prayer, and putting the poem in her casket, he started to roll toward the back of the room but completely fell apart. This child who had always been full of hope, hope that balanced my own hesitation, had been so slammed with loss after loss after loss that he just couldn't bear it anymore. The world was at war, a friend with whom he shared a special connection died seemingly out of the blue, and he himself had come home from yet another multimonth stay in the hospital without another miracle. He was more than well aware that his next crisis would be *the* crisis.

Across the next several days, he tried consciously to hang on to hope, but he felt he just didn't know how to play after the storm anymore. You can't play, he said, if the storms keep coming with no time between them, if the storm never ends. For the first time in his life, Mattie was hesitating, and I was the one desperate to offer hope.

E-mails from Oprah during that time helped, giving him something to hold on to when he couldn't find that something for himself:

```
My best friend Gayle and her children pray for you at
every family meal. . . . Prayer is powerful. I believe
you will be with us for a LONG TIME. I hope I'm around to
```

---

2 From "Dear Racheal" in *Reflections of a Peacemaker: A Portrait Through Heartsongs*, page 188.

see you grow up and have babies and win the NOBEL PEACE
PRIZE. You will be a most powerful man and father.

I love you. You love me.

Oprah

As for my own attempt to make Mattie feel better, I couldn't take away
his loss, but I did try to fill his days with as many moments as possible
that would give him reason to focus differently, to balance his pain with
as much as possible that *wasn't* painful.

We went out with Aunt Mary Lou and her daughter, Jo Ann, and the
rest of the family from Richmond, and other cousins. Jeff Bouchard and
his family came for a couple of days, too, just to play. And the Hemelgarns flew in from Michigan to go bowling with Mattie. Then, on July 16,
the day before Mattie's birthday, Christopher Cross flew in with his family to help celebrate.

"What do you want for your birthday?" he asked.

"I want to go out for Maryland crabs," Mattie told him. "I haven't had
crabs since forever."

"Done," Christopher told him.

That night, before bed, Mattie said to me, "This is it, Mom. Tomorrow
I should turn thirteen."

"Why do you say *should*?" I asked.

"I'm so afraid that during the night, something's going to come and
steal this victory from me, that I won't get to be a teenager. I don't think
I'm going to get *past* thirteen, but I at least want to get that far." I felt like
I had out on the pier three years ago. I believed him yet didn't want to
believe him. He's just scared, I thought to myself. Everything's okay.

"You *are* going to wake up tomorrow morning," I told him, "and you
are going to be a teenager. It's going to happen."

And sure enough, while I went to sleep with no small amount of ap-
prehension, it did.

Like we did every year on his birthday, Mattie and I talked about balancing the privileges of maturing with the responsibilities, and about lessons he had learned during the previous year. The biggest lesson he learned that year, he said, was that it was okay to be proud of his accomplishments as long as it was a humble pride and not a vain pride. That is, he was proud that he had had so many amazing opportunities to spread his message, but he was not empty with boasting that he had met famous people and been on television. He didn't let his notoriety go to his head. We talked about the fact that the word *humble* derives from an ancient word for "earth," that we all come from earth and will all return to it, no matter what our life experiences.

Mattie also wrote a poem, as he did every year on his birthday. But rather than being about sunrises and dolphins splashing, as his birthday poem usually was, it was about the distance that was to come between him and his mortality:

> *One day,*
> *Yet all too soon,*
> *My memory will*
> *Simply be a*
> *Silhouette in time. . . .*
> *One day,*
> *Still too soon and too near . . .*
> *My eternity will*
> *Forever and for all be*
> *The shape of the life*
> *Which I leave behind.*[3]

He never shared that poem with me; I didn't read it until I happened to come upon it myself nearly a year later. He was becoming very private by that point about his writing, whereas in the past he showed me everything he wrote as soon as he had written it. I think part of it was about

---

3 From "Coming of Age" in *Reflections of a Peacemaker: A Portrait Through Heartsongs*, page 190.

growing up, but part was also about keeping from me that which he knew I couldn't bear to read.

That night, despite the serious, contemplative mood in which Mattie had begun the day, we did go out for his birthday meal, which he thoroughly enjoyed. Christopher Cross had told me to gather the kin together, and he and his wife and two children took Mattie, me, Sandy and her children, and Nell and Larry for crabs. Poor Christopher had never seen Maryland crabs, and more to the point, had never seen them being eaten. In typical fashion, the restaurant staff spread newspaper before us and brought out wooden mallets, then dumped tray after tray of crabs right onto the table. We all started banging away, juices flying, extracting innards before plopping the lumps of meat in our mouths.

"Can you put a shower curtain around me?" Christopher asked the waiter, only half jokingly. "I'll pay for this, but I don't want to watch it."

We topped off the night at Sandy's condo, where we played games and had a chocolate ice cream cake that she made for the occasion. I gave Mattie his own cell phone in honor of his becoming a teenager.

The next week, on the twenty-fifth, I turned forty-four, and Mattie decided to throw me a surprise party. He planned it for the night before my birthday. Sandy told Mattie she'd cook "fried never chicken." I always promised Nell's husband, Larry, that I'd make him fried chicken for doing my taxes every year but never did, since I have never been a good cook. Sandy was finally going to make it happen. Mattie was going to pick up the cake.

"Here's the deal," he said to Nell, relishing the subterfuge it took to surprise me. "You drive by the King Farm Safeway heading south. I'll be heading north in my wheelchair. When we pass each other, toss me a twenty out the window. I'll go into the store and get the cake and other stuff. You go keep my mom busy—talk about taxes, whatever. When we're all set, Sandy will call out, 'Dinner's ready!' That'll be the signal to come on over to Sandy's condo."

That evening, Nell indeed came and went over my finances with me. She had been helping me keep track of bills and handle Mattie's fan mail during his long stays in the PICU, tasks I was grateful to her for taking on. The phone then rang; it was Sandy saying, "Dinner's ready," and I replied, "Okay, thanks," and hung up. Earlier in the day, Sandy had invited Mattie and me to join her for dinner, which we did often. But she hadn't told me she was also inviting Nell and Larry, and I didn't want to be rude and say, "Thanks for your help; now I'm going to go eat."

Sandy called two more times during the course of the next hour to announce, "Dinner's ready," finally coming to my door and saying loudly enough for Nell to hear, "DINNER'S READY! Why didn't you come when I first called?" she asked.

"I didn't want to be rude to Nell," I told her.

"There's enough for Nell," she answered, exasperated.

We finally went next door, and everybody yelled "Surprise!" I was really thrown for a loop—Mattie's caper had succeeded.

He spent much of the rest of the summer diving headlong into adolescence. He loved talking on his new cell phone, behind closed doors, to girls he had met all across the country. He sported a "look": black sneakers; black jeans or long jean shorts; a collared shirt, unbuttoned, over a T-shirt with a graphic; and his fishing hat. I could even see the hair on his legs beginning to grow coarser.

But despite the emerging teenage maturity, Mattie lost it every Tuesday afternoon during his Broviac dressing change.

He had always had adverse reactions not just to anesthesia but also to pain medications and sedatives. They would wreak havoc on his system, sending him into respiratory or cardiac crises or even causing hallucinations. That's why, from the time he was an infant, procedures for which another child or adult, would have been sedated, he was only physically restrained.

Among the procedures for which he was pinned down against his will were surgeries to insert or remove the Broviac tubes in his chest when he was an infant and toddler.

Now, when he was thirteen, cleaning the Broviac tube that had been reinserted the previous spring was not anywhere near the most painful procedure he had to endure, but it must have brought back distant memories of the extreme pain generated by the incisions all those years ago, and something puncturing his skin. Though he was stoic for much more invasive medical protocols, he would completely lose control as we scrubbed the insertion site with alcohol, panicking and crying. It was as though all the emotional and physical pain Mattie felt throughout his life was expressed during the Broviac cleaning.

Other than that awful weekly ritual, and despite all the loss Mattie was feeling, he spent the rest of the summer not only enjoying his entry into adolescence but also busy and productive. He attended MDA events and golf tournaments, did book signings and gave speeches, including a keynote speech on intergenerational caregiving for Rosalynn Carter. He also shared a keynote spot at a meeting of the International Society of Poets with Lucille Clifton, a poet who won the National Book Award and three Pulitzer Prize nominations. There he met Yolanda King, a daughter of Martin Luther King, Jr., and her friend Elodia Tate. They invited him to make a contribution to a book they were compiling with a collection of essays and poems on peace, entitled *Open My Eyes, Open My Soul: Celebrating Our Common Humanity.*

Other events that summer included working with the We Are Family Foundation on an upcoming peace event to be held at the United Nations, where Mattie would speak alongside Kofi Annan and other dignitaries. He also appeared again on *Larry King Live*, this time as a member of an "expert panel on angels."

September brought the return of the MDA telethon. It wasn't medically safe anymore for Mattie to travel to the West Coast, so, disappointed, he went back to conversing with Jerry Lewis via live satellite feed from Baltimore as he had done in 2001. It was the first time the telethon had a National Goodwill Ambassador who couldn't be there in person.

The day after the telethon, we headed to New York for the Emmy awards ceremony with *Larry King Live* producer Michael Watts. Larry told Mattie that if the episode with their first interview together won, he wanted Mattie to accept the Emmy.

Mattie loved the hullabaloo at the Emmys—the red carpet with all the paparazzi and the flashbulbs going off, the famous people that he knew personally being asked to "Look over here, please! Over here!" He also loved that these same people greeted him and hugged him hello.

Then, all of a sudden, someone in the paparazzi line started shouting,

"There's Mattie! There's the Heartsong Kid! Look this way!" Others immediately followed suit. Mattie was beside himself with excitement.

And while he didn't come away with an Emmy that night, he did end up with some new *Lord of the Rings* action figures. After the show, Larry and his staff took Mattie to the Toys "R" Us in Times Square, where Mattie hit the jackpot.

When we arrived back at the hotel where we were all staying, I headed up to our room exhausted, but Mattie went to the after-Emmy party at the hotel bar. Larry was there, along with Wendy Walker, his senior executive producer; Erin Sermeus, a publicist for Larry at the time; and others on his staff.

Someone started hitting on Erin, and one of the people in Larry's group suggested Mattie write a poem telling the guy that Erin already had a man in her life. Right there Mattie composed some lines with Shakespearean gush—"*Alas, I have another love*"—and Erin gave it to the man, who tried to write a sonnet in response but then gave up, saying, "Not fair. You've got the Heartsong Kid on your side." There were laughs all around. Glasses clinked. My thirteen-year-old enjoyed a truly adult moment in a world ten years beyond his age.

Mattie and I came home from New York in time for MDA's annual softball tournament. We were now two years out from 9/11, so the mood was a little lighter even though the pain was still there. As usual, Mattie had fun selling his "Luck for a Buck" quotes to raise MDA funds. The guys from Yonkers and Greenburgh, New York, and from Mississauga, Ontario, helped him launch water balloons on other teams and play all sorts of games under the beer tent. He even got to spend a night in the medic tent rather than return to the nearby hotel so he wouldn't miss a moment of the fun that extended into the wee hours of the morning. But he found saying good-bye at the end of the weekend particularly hard. Normally, he rolled around the bases high-fiving the softball players and calling out, "See you next year." This time, he just kept saying to everyone, "I love you. Don't forget I love you."

Mattie with friend and MDA Summer Camp
counselor Devin Dressman at MDA Summer Camp
Maria, summer 2003

Mattie reminding friends at the
annual MDA/IAFF softball
tournament to "Remember to play
after every storm!," September 2003

Mattie with Micah, fall 2003

CHAPTER 14

Afternoon Tea

Mattie playing a game of
chess, fall 2003

Mattie working on an assignment at the
University of Maryland, fall 2003

I feel the near-distance
Of Life in my life.
And though it feels sad
And lonely and large,
Even the silence of God
Gives me strength,
Turning courage into wisdom,
And wisdom into accepted
Knowledge and understanding. . . . [1]

The day after the 2003 softball tournament ended, Mattie was back at the hospital. He was going to have to start treatments with a drug called Desferal to reduce what had become severe iron toxicity in his body resulting from the frequent transfusion of red blood cells. Those cells contain iron, and too much iron can injure body organs.

---

1 From "Thoughts" in *Reflection of a Peacemaker: A Portrait Through Heartsongs,* page 191.

We were in a catch-22. He needed the red cells to enhance his oxygenation and thereby decrease the severity of his dysautonomia, but their iron, a sort of rusting agent in very high doses, could cause severe damage to his liver, heart, eyes, and other organ systems.

Before the Desferal treatment could begin, the doctors needed a baseline level on the status of Mattie's various organs. Conducting a scan of his liver would have required a lengthy trip to an out-of-town hospital where the specialized equipment was located and therefore was not a logistically wise option. But his liver enzymes were only mildly elevated, so they were confident he had not suffered liver damage, despite his extremely high iron levels. Remarkably, Mattie's heart seemed to be absolutely fine, too.

What they found in Mattie's eyes, on the other hand, was nothing short of shocking. He had worn glasses for years, but he had never been given drops of a drug called atropine that ophthalmologists use to dilate people's eyes and really look *inside* them. Atropine is a stimulant, and Mattie had bad reactions to stimulants. But the doctors told us that because of the initiation of Desferal, they had to get a look in his eyes to be able to determine whether the new drug affected his vision across time. Vision checks with eye charts, as Mattie was accustomed to, would not tell the whole story.

Mattie did have a bad reaction to the atropine—it sent his heart rate soaring and then plummeting—but what was found, to the astonishment of all of us, was that he had a significant visual field loss in both eyes. It was like he had a black box in the center of his vision.

This was a person who, from a young age, read hundreds of books a year, who loved looking at nature and absorbing his world visually, yet had spent most of his life seeing only from around the edges of vision. The doctors thought that it was probably a result of one of his early cardiac arrests—perhaps the one during which I performed CPR on the porch when he was a newborn.

At least now we had an explanation for Mattie's poor visual motor perception, for why it was hard for him to learn to drive a wheelchair or put together a jigsaw puzzle. Jigsaw puzzles are essentially all about vision.

After all the baseline readings of Mattie's organs, the game plan for the initial administration of Desferal was to admit him to the PICU and observe—and treat him should there be any negative reactions. Then, if possible, he would gradually be given the drug at the hospital without being admitted, and finally, switch to having it administered at home. It was infused into his body via his Broviac tube.

That first dose went pretty badly. Soon after the drug entered his bloodstream, Mattie experienced cardiac arrhythmias. Along with the irregular beats, his heart rate began running lower than normal. They needed to stop the Desferal after only about half a dose. The good news was that his urine started to become rust-orange in color—a sign that the drug was, in fact, removing excess iron from his body.

Across the next couple of months, the doctors found a dose Mattie could handle, and by the end of October, he received his Desferal treatments at home along with his nightly IV fluids, which he required due to blood pressure instability. He went back to needing to go to the hospital only for his platelet and red blood cell transfusions.

In the meantime, life continued to go on. Mattie started his third year of high school, taking six courses despite needing only one English credit and one science credit to graduate. Sandy and I had wrapped up our Ph.D. coursework in early childhood special education, too, and were now studying for the comprehensive exams that we had to pass before getting the green light to begin our doctoral dissertations.

In addition to all the academics, there continued to be book signings, speeches, and events. There were get-togethers with friends. There was the day Hurricane Isabel blew through, knocking out our electricity and leading to the Rockville Firefighters invitation for Mattie to sleep at the firehouse. He loved bunking down with his buddies rather than spending the night getting the electricity for his equipment at the hospital.

Mattie was also asked that fall to speak at the wedding of Nell and Larry's daughter, Erin. He read a poem and had a great time at the reception, dancing in his wheelchair with Micah running after him in circles. He was later presented with the garter by Erin's groom, who called Mattie "the studliest man here" and therefore shouldn't have to scramble to catch it.

As much fun as the wedding was, however, and the joy of sleeping in the firehouse and the various local events Mattie was able to attend, the downward progression of his health could not be denied.

The change was reflected by a shift in the nature of afternoon tea. Afternoon tea was something Mattie and I had been sharing from the time he was five or six, maybe once a week or so. We'd sit, talk, laugh—*be* together. If morning coffee was about making a to-do list after briefly reviewing the previous day, afternoon tea was simply about connecting, about being in the moment with each other rather than planning the next moment or checking off the previous one.

In the early years of afternoon tea, we often played board games, not just because they were fun but also because through playing, I could teach Mattie how to strategize, think ahead. And I could model how to win and lose, how to be good at both since both were going to happen in life. I never played my hardest, but I never lost on purpose, either. I let Mattie experience his own wins and losses. He even wrote about it in his journal when he was eight:

> *I made Mom coffee in bed again this morning. . . . In the afternoon, I made her tea. . . . Mom and I played cards today. She was winning, and I considered being a bad sport. I like to win when I play games, especially when there are so many things that I lose at, or just plain lose, like being able to really do Martial Arts, or like my brothers and sister. . . . I thought about it and then decided that even though I feel like sometimes, my life is about so many losses and I want to scream if there is just one more, it is not fun to play if you always have to win, or lose. My mom never complains when I win. She tells me I did a great job, and she laughs, and makes me feel good about winning, not guilty. . . . So even though I really wanted to win at cards today, I told her how happy I was that she won. And what is really funny and interesting is that as soon as I said that, and hugged her, I really WAS happy! It felt good to be making her happy, just like she likes to make me feel happy.*

By the time Mattie was thirteen, afternoon tea wasn't so much about playing games anymore. He knew plenty by that point about winning and losing. Instead, that punctuation mark to our day had morphed into something with a different kind of significance. We still used the time to connect. But by that point, tea had become a kind of substitute for sunrise on the pier.

Three summers had passed since we had been able to have our annual rite out at the edge of the water, and we missed that marking of time, that looking back across the stretch of Mattie's life and then forward to all the hopes and hesitations for the future. Having tea together allowed us to approximate that ritual of looking at the big picture and holding past, present, and future in the moment at hand—albeit on a smaller scale than out on the pier. Mattie called afternoon tea "a bookmark in our thoughts" or "our mental pause."

We needed that pause to ground ourselves in the face of all that was going on medically. And we needed it frequently; we were having tea together about five times a week by that point. On the pier, all it took was that one discussion. Now, with every day unfolding differently than we could possibly plan for, with so many medically unsettling things happening, we had to regroup often. Simply *being* was becoming so ephemeral that we took stock on a regular basis.

The emphasis of our talks changed, too. On the pier we reviewed the past quickly and spent the bulk of our time considering the future. Our feeling then was that despite whatever misfortune had occurred before, the future held the promise of something better. Now the tone was that, despite what the future held, we had wonderful memories of the past to relish, to recall in the present to sustain us. We couldn't put our trust in the future—it wasn't a place to go. To talk about what Mattie wanted to be when he grew up or about the seven children he wanted to have when the odds were so stacked against him would have been to be living in denial, even for the eternal optimists both Mattie and I were.

It wasn't that we ignored the future. We hoped for it and embraced it. But it held fewer options now. The focus of our discussions became the inverse of what it had been before. *That* was what was keeping us anchored.

We talked about all kinds of wonderful things from the past, sometimes serious things like accomplishments, but also very often light topics, memories that made us laugh. One of the reminiscences Mattie enjoyed concerned a story he wrote as a preschooler about "the child Jesus" wanting a swing set. It went as follows:

> *. . . They wanted to get Him a swing set, but there was no such thing as a toy store yet, or even a swing set yet. "Oh, bother," said Mary. "However can we give this gift to Little Jesus if it doesn't even exist?"*
>
> *"I know," said Jesus who was very young but also very wise. "Let's ask my real Father to create one for me, and for all the children of the future!"*
>
> *So, because God was also Jesus' daddy, He made stores and toys, so that Mary and Joseph could buy Little Jesus a swing set. But then, there was another problem. They were very poor. That meant they didn't have any money. "How will we ever be able to buy Little Jesus that swing set?"*
>
> *Mary said, "I know. We will sell the hay that He was born onto and that He slept on. Because He's special, people will buy the hay, and then we'll have money to get the swing set!"*
>
> *So they sold the hay, and got Jesus the swing set, and Jesus was so happy and said, "Thank you, thank you, thank you!"*

We also laughed about the time I told him that if we slept with a dirty spoon under our pillows, the Clean Dish Fairy would come during the night and finish our kitchen chores. And we got a kick out of remembering the evening I was putting Mattie to bed in our first basement apartment and he asked, "Mommy, are you afraid of anything?"

I thought he was broaching something serious that he needed to talk about that scared him, and that it would be an opportunity for me to teach him a lesson about dealing with fear.

"Well," I answered, "there are things I'd prefer not to encounter, but God is always with me, and I have choices even in difficult moments, so fear doesn't control me."

"You're not afraid of *anything*?" Mattie countered.

"No," I answered so he would understand about courage, "I think I could handle just about everything."

"What about spiders?" he wanted to know.

"I don't like them, but I could cope with one," I said.

"Even big, black hairy spiders?" he insisted.

"I'm still bigger than even the biggest, hairiest spider," I reassured him.

"So you're not afraid, then?" he persisted.

"No," I answered.

"Not even of the spider crawling up your leg?"

I looked down, screamed, and in a flurry of movement, swatted the spider off my leg with a book.

"So, I guess you *are* afraid of some things," Mattie said when it was all over. We laughed heartily at that one.

We played chess, too, although it wasn't to teach Mattie anything about winning and losing. It couldn't be—not once did I beat Mattie in a chess match.

He simply loved the game—and actually used it to do some of his own, most important, strategizing. It was while playing chess with me that he came up with the concept that a "just peace" is possible, which is how his book with Jimmy Carter got its title.

"Peace could begin simply, over a game of chess and a cup of tea," he said. "You connect with the person you're disagreeing with during this strategic configuration of knights and pawns and rooks. You could move across the board and meet in the middle—and stop there. You wouldn't have to finish. It would just be about coming to the table and staying in the game rather than about winning or losing, understanding why somebody felt it was necessary to make the move he did. And that could lead to mutual respect and accommodation and everybody coming away satisfied. There would never have to be another war."

Mattie spent a lot of time during afternoon tea telling me how the *Just Peace* book was progressing. While I now rarely saw what he was writing, he often shared what he was thinking. I already knew he felt that peace could be achieved when everyone's basic needs were met, saying, "When we are okay with who we are, it is so much easier to be okay with our neighbors in every corner of the world." Balancing needs could keep conflict from erupting into violence, and could nurture a view toward collaboration rather than conquering. But he was also now saying that to make choices that lead to peace, people have to *talk about* peace. To that end, he wanted the bulk of his book to contain interviews with people, with the same set of questions for all—conversations that readers could draw from to launch their own conversations not only with others but within themselves.

Mattie wanted to interview humanitarians, politicians, children in war-torn countries, nature conservationists, victims of violence, people of different religions and cultures. He wanted to know their thoughts on violence, on compromise, on life. If the questions and answers in his book could spark dialogue, he felt, peace would be possible. It was like a garden, Mattie said. If you don't tend to it and nurture it constantly, if you let it go, weeds take over.

The book had become a passion of Mattie's, and he felt rushed to complete it. That's how we discussed the future that fall during afternoon tea—not as something that might unfold in various ways as we considered options, but as tying up loose ends. The future had become almost like its own morning coffee to-do list, one that we didn't dare let go too far ahead. If we planned too far out, hope would have become too much of an illusion; we needed to keep it closer to the moment.

In that same rushed vein, Mattie said he wanted to publish one more collection of Heartsongs poetry. He was actually ready to move on from books of Heartsong poetry by that point, but he felt he had to lay the groundwork for something new first and give people a heads-up that he was ending the series, let them know that going forward they should listen for their own Heartsong. It was for that same reason that he told Oprah she shouldn't just end her show after twenty years, as she had been contemplating, but go five more years. "When you've given other people a gift that gets them thinking and changes their lives, you can't just disappear," he told her. "You need to teach them to find these gifts in other ways, even to be the source of these gifts for others."

The five volumes of Heartsong poetry Mattie had already compiled contained poems he wrote as early as age three, and he decided that the final volume should have poems spanning the ten years from when he was ages three to thirteen; he felt a decade of work made sense. If he had the opportunity to go on after that, he decided, he wanted to publish essays with poems interspersed as they related to the theme.

It didn't surprise me that Mattie wanted to wrap up his Heartsong verses. The themes of his poetry in many ways remained the same as they always had, but they had also evolved into something more developed; the mood was different. You could see an intended syncopation and hesitation in his lines now. He was so aware, in a way that was lost on me at the time, that he didn't know whether he was living his last year, his last month, or his last day, and his poetry reflected that. It was no longer a celebration of hope. It was more about how to finish living, even while still embracing hope as something real.

The difference was particularly clear in a poem Mattie wrote about seashells. One afternoon we were discussing sunrise on the pier, days at the beach, and how much we loved and missed those times. Mattie brought up seashells, saying to me, "You collect seashells the way I collect rocks." It was true. Rocks were symbolic to Mattie of the whole world. He wanted to go everywhere but couldn't, so picking up a stone from the earth or being sent one by people from far away became a kind of substitute for "touching" places. Seashells for me have always symbolized the essence of things that once were and the essence of the past that exists into the future. There is something sacred about them, and I appreciated how thoughtful it was of Mattie to recognize not only how much I, too, missed the beach, but also how much I felt I was holding in my hand when I held a shell.

I reminded him of a poem about living in a seashell that he wrote when he was seven. Called "Outer Banks Shells," it touched on the meaning of shells in a "pretty" and relatively straightforward way:

Shells are unique little gifts
Of beauty and symbolism.
If you consider a shell
With your heart,
Good dreams can be inspired.
Sometimes, I think I just
Might like to live in a seashell.
It would be great because
I could be happy, with
Hardened walls protecting me, and
Changing colors surrounding me, and
Songs of the sea heart lulling me. . . .

That very afternoon, after we finished our tea, he wrote a second poem about living in a shell that reflected where he was at age thirteen. He didn't show it to me then, and when I found it, it had two titles: "Sea Requiem" and "Requiem in Sea." I never knew which he had chosen, or whether he ever did choose one over the other:

Oh, to call the conch my home . . .
Stormy-smoothed tunnels of
Kaleidoscope walls spiraling into
Pearl-shimmered dyes,
Ever-changing with the light
Of the sun, of the moon,
Of the tide, and the gloaming,
And surging, and sighing,
Of the sea . . .
    Of that space
That calls to me
Beyond the Polished Pier,
Beyond the now, and here.
Echo of ocean breath,
Silhouette of Light,

Indescribable description
Passing, mortal fathoming.
Passion, ebbing into solace,
Upon realizing the sanctum
Of our perpetual Home
Along the shores of paradise,
No longer a distant horizon.
  Oh, to call the conch my home . . .
Such a lovely dwelling space
For the here, and the now.
Or perhaps,
A dove, an ark, a whelk, or
Any some-other lovely shell,
To be left on the shore
Like the hollows of driftwood
Or the gentle leavings of flower petal
Remains
  When requiem passage calls.

If I had seen the poem that fall, I would have understood even better where Mattie's thoughts were coming from, what was driving him. But even without full knowledge of how on the edge he felt by that point, he and I were still as close as we had always been.

Some of it, no doubt, came from our living such an intense life together. Either at the hospital or in the limelight, we were in a fishbowl, with people's faces pressed up against the glass, so to speak, to see how we were going to handle things medically or what the Heartsong Kid and his mother were *really* like. Some of it was that we were both in wheelchairs—that's not often something a mother and son share.

But I'd like to think that even had Mattie been healthy, had he gone to regular schools and spent more time away from me and enjoyed the same odds of having a tomorrow that other kids did, we still would have been close.

We truly enjoyed each other's company. I was always honest with him, too. There was never anything sugarcoated about our talks, despite the difficulties of our lives. I did my best to talk to him at a level appropriate for his age, of course—he was my child, not my peer—but I was sincere in what I said, in no small part so that he wouldn't be alone in his losses.

Being up front didn't mean we always agreed on things. But our arguments never devolved into personal attacks. They were centered on what we didn't like about what the other person said or did, not who they *were*.

That's a large part of why afternoon tea was always such a pleasure. There was mutual respect as well as mutual endearment. We liked each other as well as loved each other.

Even at that point in Mattie's life, however, it was important for him to have time away from me, to have fun. I would ask his nurse, Laura, to go with him and a friend to the movies rather than take them myself so he could have experiences with peers. I would let him roll around the neighborhood and into stores and apartments for conversations with others as much as he could handle. On Halloween, Mattie and Devin went off to an MDA costume party for teens, with Mattie dressed as a life-size whoopee cushion (courtesy of the Hemelgarns, of course), and Devin as a giant roll of toilet paper.

The reality of the medical situation kept encroaching, however. In early November, the height of Pumpkin Season because that month was the anniversary of Jamie's death, I took out four plastic bins, as I did every year at that time. Each one contained items saved from my children's lives, and Mattie would go through them. We always took out the Jamie box first, which contained things like Jamie's favorite book, *Put Me In the Zoo*, and his little moose toys. Then we'd get to the Katie and Stevie boxes and, finally, to Mattie's box. That year he said, "I think you might need a second box for me."

"Why would I need two baby boxes for you?" I asked.

"Mom," he responded, "we've always called them *memory* boxes, not baby boxes. Katie, Stevie, and Jamie each had a handful of months or

years for remembering. But you will have a few handfuls of years to remember me by."

By that point, Mattie was beginning to have more frequent adverse
reactions to the Desferal. Sometimes I couldn't give him the entire dose
because he would start to feel chest pains or his heart would beat too
slowly. At the same time, he was showing no signs of needing fewer
transfusions. In fact, he was showing signs of needing more. The bleeding in his fingertips had increased again.

Before anyone had figured out what to do, Mattie was asked to give a
speech to employees at the hospital who had worked there for any inter-
val of five years—five, ten, fifteen, or even twenty or twenty-five. After
the speech, a sweet one filled with humor, Dr. Christi Corriveau, the
PICU physician who first inquired about his "three wishes," came up to
him and hugged him, then went to squeeze his hand. But Mattie flinched,
closing his fingers over his palm. Christi opened them, only to find that
his fingers were cracking and peeling and had specks of blood on them.

She just looked at him in alarm and asked, "When did this begin?"

A few days later, when we came home from Sunday Mass and I
suctioned Mattie's trach, the secretions came out pink—and grew redder
through the week. The doctors decided to go back up to two to three
times a week on platelet transfusions.

Sandy's daughter, Heather, and Aunt Mary Lou both proved to be
wonderful matches for Mattie. He never reacted negatively to platelets
they donated, and they donated as often as was medically allowed. But
his negative reactions to many other donor platelets were beginning to
become more frequent and more serious.

We decided to keep Mattie home for as long as possible, knowing
there wasn't a lot left at the hospital as far as long-term solutions. Once
again I called Dr. Fink to apprise him of the situation. He told me, "I
wouldn't be surprised on any given day to receive a phone call saying, 'I'm
sorry, but Mattie Stepanek just died.' But I am not expecting it." As long
as Mattie's heart held out and didn't show signs of distress, Dr. Fink said,
we should keep doing everything we could.

The pulmonary specialist, Dr. Witzmann, kept the faith, too, saying,

"Let's keep going. Maybe his body will kick back in." She also supported our desire to remain at home, and to continue to do local events—but said there should be no more out-of-town travel; he needed to be within an hour of the hospital. Mattie was incredibly disappointed. He had been so looking forward to giving a presentation at the United Nations, an event that was just around the corner.

Thanksgiving came a week later. Mattie and I typically started the holiday by going to Mass. But that morning, he had to have a Desferal infusion. He seemed fine afterward but then said he needed to go to his room.

"Are you okay?" I asked.

"I always do Grace at Thanksgiving," he answered. "I really want to think about what I'm going to say today." Then he shut his door, which he never did except to talk to a girl on the phone, not even at night.

When he came out a while later, I could tell he was exhausted. We went next door to Sandy's nonetheless, for turkey dinner, and all of the Step'obbi'comb kin were there: Sandy and her kids; baby Kaylee; Sandy's parents, Mema and Papa, up from North Carolina; and Nell and Larry.

As usual, Mattie started the Thanksgiving prayer as the turkey was being carved because he could go on for so long, but we were surprised this time because he finished in less than a minute. He gave thanks for friends, for a few other things, and for "this moment," then ended with gratitude for what he called "the eternal feast."

Everybody laughed, assuming "eternal feast" was about the amount of food. We would always eat, watch football, then go back to the table and eat some more.

After the meal, Mattie said he wanted to lie down a little, so we went back to our condo. Before he went to his room, I told him how funny the "eternal feast" line was.

"It had two meanings," he said.

"What was the other meaning?" I asked, immediately sorry that I did. I knew where we were headed.

Mattie didn't answer my question. "The next time we go to the hospital for platelets," he said, "maybe they could check my heart. I have extreme pain that comes and goes, like my heart is in a vice grip. I was afraid I was having a heart attack earlier today but didn't want to ruin the holiday for everybody."

That's when I understood what "eternal feast" really meant. Mattie was telling us this was the Thanksgiving to remember him by.

Mattie and Jeni with their service dog, Micah, at the University of Maryland, fall 2003

CHAPTER 15

Silent Strength

Mattie sharing his "Heartsongs" poetry before a book signing, November 2003

The rising sun sends
Wisps of light through
Streaking clouds,
But the blackbirds play under
The empty willow tree.
The midnight of the fall
Is rising upon us,
And against us.
It is the dawn of winter.
There are things
In the clouds, and
We must be prepared.

We must be watchful,
As the blackbirds,
As the weeping willow,
As the waiting darkness.[1]

"They've taken Mattie off the Desferal. We're in a holding pattern."
I was talking to my friend, Diane Tresca from Rhode Island, on the phone, filling her in on the details of our hospital visit after Thanksgiving. The medical staff wasn't certain it was the drug that made Mattie feel as though his heart were being squeezed in a vice. Because Mattie's blood pressure was so erratic; because his fingers were bleeding more and his lips dark and bulging, ready to burst open and start gushing blood; because he was having hypoxic episodes even though we increased his oxygen; doctors believed that what felt to him like a Desferal-induced heart attack might just have been part of a larger dysautonomic spell—the one we were all bracing ourselves for as Mattie plunged deeper into puberty. But the doctors also felt that his body might not be able to withstand any adverse effects from the Desferal on top of the dysautonomic storm that was clearly gathering strength. What no one was saying but everyone was thinking was that if the dysautonomic storm didn't blow over, the Desferal treatments weren't going to make a difference, anyway.

"What can we do?" Diane asked.

"There's really nothing," I told her. "You're already praying. Just keep him smiling and laughing." The Trescas, particularly their daughters, Laura and Annie, chatted on the phone with Mattie every week and e-mailed back and forth with him all the time. And all of us together got along so well and could really laugh, not politely but with abandon—the kind of laughter that helps you find the strength you need to move into the next moment when you think you can't.

The next day Diane called me back and asked, "Can you pick up the four of us from the airport on Friday?"

"Aren't the girls in school," I responded, "and you and Sal working?

---

1 From "Before the Visit" in *Journey Through Heartsongs*, page 35.

How are you going to come? It's not Christmas break yet." It didn't matter, Diane said. More to the point, although she didn't say it out loud: It wasn't clear whether Mattie was going to make it to Christmas.

After the Trescas landed and we got them all to the condo, Diane remarked, "We're going to spend the next three days laughing into every corner of your home." And we did.

Much of our time was spent around the kitchen table. Even with the furniture we had finally gotten a few months earlier, we were never living room people; we were kitchen people, and so were the Trescas. Diane spent the weekend cooking and filling our freezer with baggies of meatballs, chicken cutlets, and other delicious meals that could be microwaved.

While Diane cooked, the rest of us sat at the table and played every game imaginable—card games, board games, word games, and everything in between. Mattie and Laura always had to be teammates because Mattie had a gargantuan crush on her. That left Sal and me to take turns being partners with Annie, who, being younger than the others, kept us all roaring in laughter with her creative efforts and answers in every game.

Along with sitting around the kitchen table, Mattie liked hanging out with the girls, particularly Laura, in his Bachelor's Pad. He had a keyboard in there that he was learning to play from books, and Laura was trying to teach him some basic songs that she knew from taking piano lessons. "You don't have to do it with both hands," she said to him. She could see his fingers were hurting.

"I want to do this," he answered.

"But look at your fingers," she told him. "Sometimes you even leave blood on the keys. It's got to hurt."

"Yes," he responded, "but I want to learn. And when my fingers hurt so bad that I can't use them anymore, I can still do this," at which point he leaned forward and bounced his nose around the keys, having pushed a button that would play a minuet no matter which ones were pressed.

One day we took time off from the game-playing and horsing around for Mattie to do a book signing a few miles up the road. The Trescas came along because they wanted to see Mattie in action; they had never been to one of his appearances. "Oh my gosh," Diane said when she saw the crowd. There were hundreds and hundreds of people lined up to see him, even though his latest book had been released almost a year earlier.

Diane knew, of course, that Mattie had achieved great success, but to see it in person was something else altogether. She also was surprised that one moment he could be talking with adults about serious matters, even dispensing advice, and the next, sitting in the van eating hot dogs and goofing off with Laura and Annie.

Before driving the Trescas back to the airport on Sunday, we all piled into our big brown van to go to Mass. Mattie was talking about summer camp, about how he, this little skinny kid, had sung "Macho Man" at a camp social. That led to him, Laura, and Annie singing that song and "Y.M.C.A." at the top of their lungs. When we arrived at the church parking lot and Mattie rolled out onto the wheelchair lift, he went into a "Macho Man" encore, hamming it up three feet off the ground on what was a essentially a little platform.

"Come on, Macho Man," Diane called out to him. "Mass is starting."

"*I'm* not your Macho Man," Mattie yelled out. "*Jesus* is your Macho Man." He started belting out his own on-the-spot "Macho Man" lyrics with the word *Jesus* in them as the platform descended. We were all laughing, including Diane, who said, "Hey, Nacho-Macho Man, the church doors are open, and everybody's looking at you."

We turned. The doors *were* open—it was an unusually warm day for late fall—and all eyes were on the spectacle before them. Mattie felt unbearably sheepish—for about a second. We all went into the church giggling.

But it was all foamy giddiness before the seriousness of the good-byes. By the time we reached the airport, the mood was decidedly glum. In the past, whenever we and the Trescas parted, we felt bad to see them go but happy because we knew the next time would be just as much fun. It was never a matter of *catching* up but *picking* up where we had left off, as if they had never gone away. This time, however, it was clear that by the next get-together, things would be much changed. "We'll pick up again," Diane said to me, "but it's going to be different."

With the hugs came tears. It was too obvious that what was now inevitable couldn't be stalled much longer.

Once the Trescas left, our world turned more and more upside down. Mattie's fingers continued to worsen, and we were going back to the hospital every other day like clockwork, leaving at 6:30 in the morning and frequently not coming back home till evening. There was no morning coffee at the kitchen table—we were both too exhausted to get up extra early for that—and no consistent afternoon tea. When Mattie was an inpatient, I could make tea at the hospital. As an outpatient, he had no place where I could store tea bags, mugs, spoons. We'd sit in the Hematology/Oncology infusion clinic with chairs lined up against the wall, cancer patients coming in for their chemotherapy, children with sickle-cell anemia coming in for their own infusions, Mattie waiting for his.

In the free time Mattie did have during which he wasn't sleeping, I wanted him to be able to do things that mattered to him. So I put away most of his schoolwork, went over math problems and Spanish flash cards just once a week, and let him focus on literature and history, which he loved, and which he also felt would help him fine-tune his *Just Peace* book.

Also, even during this time, I tried to make sure Mattie had fun. If he was up to it, he went to his MDA teen meetings, or to see his chess coach, Omar Pancoast. Coach Omar gave Mattie a roll-up fabric chessboard with a little bag containing small chess pieces so that when he went to the hospital, he could play a game of chess while waiting around. Omar couldn't have been more supportive, knowing Mattie needed something to focus on, anything, rather than what was going on.

Devin was wonderful to Mattie, too. Every year beginning in 2001, a new *Lord of the Rings* movie debuted in December, with Devin taking Mattie to opening night, and this December was no exception. Off they went to see the third movie in the trilogy, *The Return of the King*, both dressed in the elaborate *Lord of the Rings* costumes that Devin's wife had made them for summer camp. Mattie was Gandalf—the good guy— while poor Devin went as the Dark Lord, Sauron.

As the holidays moved closer, Mattie received his annual call from

MIX 107.3's Jack Diamond. But this time, Jack didn't want Mattie to just read his "December Prayer" poem on the radio show. He asked him to come in and be a guest DJ. Mattie was thrilled. He had grown up listening to the *Jack Diamond Morning Show*, a very popular drive-time program in our part of Maryland. From about five thirty in the morning till ten A.M. one day, he helped introduce the songs and participated in the between-song banter.

As the program wound down, Jack asked Mattie about his upcoming book signings, and Jack's cohost, Jimmy Alexander, told Mattie to mention his Web site so that listeners could log on and get information about his future appearances. When Mattie said he didn't have one, both Jack and Jimmy said, "Oh, one of our loyal listeners can solve that; let's get Mattie online," and the phone lines started lighting up. A week later, Mattie went back into the studio, and Jack and Jimmy helped him unveil Mattieonline .com with lists of his favorites (foods, authors, etc.), frequently asked questions, and so on. The Web site allowed people to reach out to Mattie and for him to touch back in a way that was easier to manage than phone calls and fan mail.

Although Mattie still had to go to the hospital nearly every other day, he continued to give a few local speeches. He did fund-raising for a new PICU at Children's National Medical Center, where he was so frequently a patient. In addition, MDA called and invited him to serve as National Goodwill Ambassador for an unprecedented third year. "Mom," he said excitedly when he hung up, "they believe in me! Even though I'm going to die, they believe in me and think I'm a good messenger for their organization."

Mattie also received a lot of awards that season. One was the Points of Light award from Children's Hospice International for his efforts to improve hospice care for children. The U.S. Department of Health and Human Services presented him with its humanitarian award, too. It really helped Mattie to receive these awards during that time. He knew his future was limited, but he also knew that people were beginning to recognize the full range of his message. And it allowed him to express how he saw his contributions. In his acceptance speech to the Department of Health and Human Services, he said:

I move forward sharing lessons with others, but many of these thoughts come from the people who have inspired me. . . . It might be natural for a child who has lived with many physical and financial and emotional challenges to forget humble roots and the things that matter most in life when suddenly being in a national, even international, spotlight. But I learned from my Mom that I am not at the center of the universe. The world does not revolve around me, nor does it revolve around any one person in particular. Instead, I, like every person ever created, am an essential part of the revolving world. I, like each person of every race, religion, culture, economic status, aspiration, and ability, am one unique and essential jewel in the great mosaic of life. And this mosaic is not complete without every single jewel, regardless of size or shape or location, or whether it helps give detail to the background or illustrates some image in the foreground. Every piece of a mosaic is necessary. I am a messenger, but my story is about the message. It's really about how my piece of the mosaic fits into the bigger picture. That is the real story for each of us, how together, we go round and round, with the world and with each other.

As much as Mattie was glad to be able to continue to make local appearances, he was disappointed about having to miss events scheduled out of town, like a youth peace rally he was supposed to lead in New York City, and an event put on by *People* magazine. He had been selected by *People* as one of "10 Heroes Among Us" in the fall of 2003, and each of the heroes was going to get a full page in the magazine to promote his or her advocacy work. But we couldn't attend the star-studded celebration to receive the award, and Mattie couldn't be photographed for the issue.

Sean Astin was at the celebration, though, and remembered Mattie from doing videos for the Heartsongs Gala earlier in the year. When he found out Mattie was too ill to attend, he asked if he could accept the award in his honor. The organizers of the event agreed. Sean then asked for Mattie's phone number so he could call him and tell him.

Mattie was ecstatic when the call came through. He and Sean chatted for a while and exchanged cell phone numbers.

"I'm going to make you two promises," Sean said to him. "One is that I'm going to meet you in person, and the other is that I'm going to make sure your message of hope and peace continues to spread, no matter what happens. I believe in you."

Mattie also received a great boost when he was invited to create a videotape to be played at a meeting in Rome for all of the living Nobel Peace Prize laureates, who would be coming together to discuss peace. For this recording, he gave a brief speech about why hope and peace matter, recited some of his poetry, and reminded people of his motto: "Think gently, speak gently, and live gently, so the whole world is touched gently by the essence of your existence." The video received a standing ovation, and Mattie was beyond thrilled. His vision was for people to converse about peace—around the kitchen table, around the conference table. In this venue, he had a world table.

As busy as Mattie was with all of these wonderful experiences, he was less busy than he had grown accustomed to being. He spent a lot of time in his Bachelor's Pad, tired. There was a silence growing about him, too. It wasn't that he was unusually quiet. It felt more like he was ruminating on something that he wasn't sure about, so he chose not to talk about it.

I had become used to Mattie being more private in his thoughts as he reached adolescence, but now this felt different. He seemed lonely, to be withdrawing somehow. It was as though something needed to be explored and discussed, but, uncharacteristically, he couldn't articulate his deeper feelings.

One night, when I was about to go to sleep, he told me that if I heard him on the computer in the Bachelor's Pad, not to worry. "I'm working on something," he said.

"Okay," I called out. I knew he could hook himself up properly to the equipment at his bedside.

Two hours later, when I woke by alarm as usual to drain the water that collected in Mattie's ventilator tubing, I found him not in his bedroom but still in his Pad, curled up in his large green recliner. The computer light was on, flickering, and I could see there was some work on the screen.

"Hey, Buddy," I said, "you need to go get some sleep." He nodded but didn't move.

I asked him what he was working on, and he answered, "My first novel. The title is *Eyes*. You're welcome to look at it."

From an early age, Mattie had written short chapter books for children, including a group that he called the Barry Tree House series, but this was his first work of fiction for adults. I felt honored that he was sharing work in progress with me again. The text included the following:

> . . . *Many of his acquaintances chose to alter time. It was an eternal summer with a light breeze, or autumn trees never ceasing to drop their orange rainbows. . . . But not for Stephen. For Stephen, seasons would come and go normally as they would in . . . life. . . . There would be days that would be miserably cold, or unbearably hot, or dull, wet, and gray. . . . Stephen wanted it that way, for he appreciated God's truth. . . .* [2]

Mattie was talking about Heaven, about Heaven being just like earth, because life on earth was that worthy, no matter what.

When I finished reading, he told me he was struggling for inspiration, going back to his own poetry and journal entries sometimes to figure out how to move forward. "I'm still optimistic about the future," he said, "but about the depth of my time, not the length. I have to draw hope from what fills each moment rather than from the number of moments.

"I know hope is real," he added, "but it's so silent right now. God doesn't speak into my heart anymore. He's still present, and even His silence gives me strength. But He's not giving me answers, and He's not asking anything else of me. I've shared the messages."

That's where Mattie's struggle was. He honestly felt his messages came from God but that God was no longer communicating with him. That's how he knew his life was over; he felt God was now simply walk-

---

2 From *Reflections of a Peacemaker: A Portrait Through Heartsongs*, pages 211–212.

ing through the rest of his days with him rather than inspiring him to share more.

I spent a near-sleepless night grappling with what Mattie was saying, as I always did when it came to the subject of his being a messenger for God. Had he had wonderful spiritual thoughts in his life that he attributed to God, or was it something else?

The next day we chatted some more. I knew he didn't want to drag me into his loneliness, but I also knew he needed to get something out.

"I know it's kind of futile, even selfish, to pray for another miracle," he said. "That's not what God wants for me. I'm not supposed to live longer. But my *body* is saying, 'Please, God, give me something else to do.' I'm stuck. I'm grateful that this is the life I got, but I'm also angry sometimes that this is my life, that my life is going to end. I love living, Mom. I want to go to Heaven, but it is so hard to feel ready. I'm thirteen, Mom. I'm *thirteen!* How do you live when every moment is wonderful yet intimidating, worth celebrating yet also worth despising?" He also wrote about it in his journal, comparing his life to that of a Dickens character:

> . . . the protagonist succeeds in spite of devastating truths. But the truth of my mortality will end sooner than the fictional heroes and heroines of so many books. I will not "defy the odds" again and "live happily ever-after." The truth that I know is that too soon, the last lines of my story will be those I used to write in my poems about Jamie when he died—I will live "happily after-After." I want to pray for ever-after instead, even though that is wrong at this point. Heaven and living after-After is a wonderful thought, but it should be a distant thought for someone my age. It is intimidating to think that my mortality is rising and setting simultaneously, and my spirit will soon be distant from this body. I love living, I want to go to Heaven, to see Jesus, hug Jamie and Aunt Margaret, meet Katie and Stevie and so many peacemakers of the past. But it is so hard to say 'Yes' to God about the apparent timing of this journey. I am spiritually preparing for it. But my body and mind are afraid and lonely.

♥

Across the next couple of days, Mattie talked to me more about God's silence in his life, and I better understood Mattie's recent silence in *my* life. He was still present with me but didn't feel he had anything to communicate; he knew that speaking his frustration out loud wasn't going to change anything.

Through all of this, we were edging closer and closer to Christmas. Sandy asked him if he wanted to be a volunteer teen at her church, Gaithersburg Presbyterian, helping the younger children build gingerbread houses. Mattie eagerly accepted. A young spirit, even a miserable one with little time left, is hard to keep down.

After the gingerbread houses were assembled, the group closed with a prayer service. Mattie asked Sandy if she thought the minister would let him sign "Silent Night" when the children sang. "It would really mean a lot to me to be able to do that for Jamie," he said.

The minister thought it was a wonderful idea, and Mattie so appreciated being welcomed into a church of a different denomination than his own. He wrote to Sandy:

> That's how the whole world should be . . . welcoming. . . .
> I believe that religion should be a structural framework
> to strengthen faith, rather than an organized force to
> divide, or even conquer, in the name of faith. . . . I
> firmly believe that we should never use our religion,
> our faith, our spirituality, or even our choice of non-
> believing, as a reason or basis to diminish the freedom
> or rights or faith of another person. . . . The struc-
> tured rituals of a particular faith should serve as a
> support during crises, pain, and difficult times in
> life, not as a battle cry.[3]

---

3 From *Just Peace: A Message of Hope*, pages 105–106.

♥

The visit to Sandy's church didn't sustain Mattie for long, however. He said to me, "The whole thing about Christmas is eternity, the eternal afterlife. This little baby comes to save the world forever. But the way it's celebrated, Christmas is about the here and now. I should be excited about that. I'm a teenager, but still a kid. I should be able to enjoy it. Yet I can't. There's something sad about Christmas for me this year. For me it *is* about the eternal afterlife."

He couldn't even write his annual Christmas poem that we included in our Christmas cards every year. He finally decided to look at an older Christmas poem he had written and use it for inspiration. He had never done that—recycled a theme for our holiday cards. But he was really struggling.

He looked to old essays he had written to inspire him, too:

> *Sometimes it may seem like God is not with us, or listening to us, or loving us, especially when life seems difficult. But God is always there for us . . . yesterday, today, and tomorrow. . . . We can't just pray for things to be exactly like we want them. We need to pray to be like God created us to be. We are created in God's image. God is all goodness. God is great. We, then, were created good and great. Let us remember this.*

Mattie was eight when he penned those lines. At thirteen they took on a haunting cast.

Part of me was hoping against hope that all his angst was about moving into adolescence. I wanted so much to chalk up this mood to his age and not the real reason he felt the way he did. But I couldn't. Even as he was more distant in his thoughts, he was more attached to me in his fear.

In the past, when I left to go to the university and Sandy or Laura was going to stay with him, he'd kiss me good-bye, and that was that. Now, I'd leave for a two-hour meeting, and he'd call as soon as it was over.

"Hey, how did your meeting go?" he'd ask in a casual voice. It wasn't immaturity; it was desperation.

Less than a week before Christmas, Sandy and I both took our doctoral comprehensive exams—two very long days' worth of testing. Sandy's older daughter, Heather, stayed with Mattie the first day, Laura the next. I came home exhausted at the end of the second day. Mattie was thrilled to see me, but I desperately needed to lie down. The heavy studying, on top of all the frequent trips to the hospital and getting up every two hours in the night to drain the water from the vent tubing, had caught up with me.

"Hey, Buddy, listen," I said. "I am so tired. I'm just going to take a nap. If I'm not up in an hour, come wake me, and I'll get dinner started."

"Sure, Mom," Mattie answered. "I'll hang out in my room."

The intercom was on, so I knew I would hear him if he needed me. I then promptly fell asleep—and started dreaming that I heard a snow plow backing up. We had had some snow a few days earlier, and the plows made a beeping sound while in reverse. In my dream, the plow wouldn't stop backing up; the beeping was incessant. "Did the snow plow hit a car?" I wondered as I dreamt.

All of a sudden it hit me. "Mattie, Mattie," I started screaming as I startled out of my sleep. "Your tubing's disconnected. That's your ventilator!"

It wasn't unusual for Mattie to beep. His tubing became disconnected all the time, and he'd plug it right back in. "You okay?" I'd call out, and he'd respond, "Yeah, I got it." The beeping never went on for more than ten to fifteen seconds. But this had gone on much longer.

I rushed myself into my chair and rolled into his room to find the top half of his body slumped over his bed, facedown, his legs dangling onto the floor. The part of his tubing that attached to his trach was disconnected.

I rolled him over—he was breathing, but shallowly and on room air rather than oxygen, and had turned a little gray—and reattached the ventilator tubing. I hadn't been asleep for even ten minutes.

After I turned up his vent settings, he opened his eyes and looked a bit dazed.

"What happened, Buddy?" I asked.

"I don't know," he said. "I was playing with my Legos on the floor, and when I tried to stand up, everything went dizzy and dark."

I called the doctor, who said it was a dysautonomic spell, probably from standing up too quickly and shifting his blood pressure suddenly enough to make him pass out. The tubing became disconnected as he fell over.

After that incident, Mattie's urgency to finish *Just Peace* went into even higher gear. The schoolwork was put away entirely, and the book was all he focused on. President Carter told him he shouldn't interview the one hundred people he had listed, that he needed to narrow it down to twenty at the most so the book would be digestible. Mattie took the list down to thirty, agonizing over the final cut.

Even with Mattie's feeling rushed to finish the book, and the recent scare of his passing out, we tried to make Christmas feel like Christmas. We couldn't go to Midnight Mass as we always had—it was too cold and Mattie was too tired, having gone that day to the hospital for platelets and red blood cells. But he and Chris got out their matching Santa boxer shorts and Santa hats, and Mattie made up a stocking for baby Kaylee.

On Christmas morning, Chris gave Mattie a giant cutout Gollum figure from *Lord of the Rings*, and I gave him two boxes of Legos—a large one and a smaller one. We went next door to visit with Sandy, her kids, Kaylee, and Mema and Papa, then drove to the cemetery to visit Katie, Stevie, and Jamie (a tradition we reserved for Christmas Eve in the past). Mattie couldn't go over to their graves this year because it was too cold, so we sang them Christmas carols from inside the van. Then we went to visit Aunt Mary Lou and some of our cousins for a little more Christmas cheer.

When we arrived back home, Sandy and the others were heading out to a movie—it was their Christmas tradition. They invited Mattie to come along, but he said he was too tired. I realized just how sick he was feeling when I saw that he hadn't even opened the larger box of Legos I had given him and was just fiddling with the smaller one. With his fingers bleeding and fatigue getting the best of him, the task of sifting through and sorting the pieces from the larger box would have been too much.

On New Year's Eve, Mattie wanted to have a party to welcome 2004. He had thrown one for Sandy and the kin the year before, but this year all of Sandy's children were out at parties of their own. It was just Sandy, Mattie, and me at Sandy's condo this time. I was so tired that I kept dozing off. Sandy entertained Mattie with movies and conversation. She listened to him read his end-of-the-year lists.

She and I had gone over our own resolutions earlier that day. Our theme that year was "Be careful what you wish for." We didn't talk about what that meant, but we both knew it was going to be relevant.

I knew I couldn't approach this point in Mattie's life the way I had in Jamie's. With Jamie I had said, "God, I'll take the empty shell; I just need a warm body, a living child." But then he suffered immensely, and I didn't really have Jamie for the last two years of his brief life. I did not know exactly how I would move through the end of Mattie's life, what decisions I would make when the time came, but I knew that it would be different.

On January 6, we all went to see the musical *Stomp* in Washington. It was Sandy's Christmas gift to the Step'obbi'comb Fam. Her children took the Metrorail into town, and she, Mattie, and I drove down in the van. Everybody had a great time. Mattie even seemed to have a little burst of energy and looked better than he had in a while. He laughed and clapped and thoroughly enjoyed himself.

"What a great night that was," I said as the van was warming up for the ride home.

"Yeah, it was. We Step'obbi'combs sure know how to play," Mattie responded.

"Hey, while I have the two of you together," he added, seemingly out of the blue, "I just want to remind you of my final wishes."

Sandy and I just looked at each other.

Mattie then talked very specifically about when to let him go, about the point at which we should stop heroic measures and let his body rest so that his spirit could be free, in case he was not able to make that decision for himself.

That was the crux of his final wishes—when to say, "Enough."

Mattie with (left to right) Laura, Diane, Sal, and Annie Tresca
during a visit, December 2003

Mattie and Devin Dressman ready for
the premiere of the latest *Lord of the
Rings* movie, December 2003

CHAPTER 16

Whispers of Peace

Mattie autographing book plates, winter 2004

Have you ever wondered
If some people will cry, and cry
And sigh after you die?
Have you wondered
If the people will cry and then
Try to move forward as time
Fades the wounds and
Dries the tears and
Gracefully blesses the soul?
I have.
I have so
Wondered. . . .
Have you wondered

> *If the people will wonder and then*
> *. . . . ponder the*
> *Essence of your echo and the*
> *Silhouette of your legacy that*
> *Spirits the memory after death passes?*
> *I have.*
> *I have so, so, so*
> *Wondered.*[1]

T he next morning, seven days into 2004, we left the condo at six thirty for what was supposed to be a routine trip to the hospital for plate-lets. We'd be home by afternoon or early evening. While Mattie waited in the Hematology/Oncology clinic for his infusion, I took Micah outside. When I returned, I was approached by a physician and a social worker who said they wanted to talk with me. My heart sank.

Mattie had had a blue spell while I was tending to Micah—his oxygen saturation went way down—and his blood pressure dropped precipi-tously. The doctor said, "We're not comfortable treating him as an out-patient at this point in time. We think he needs to be admitted to the PICU to get him back to a baseline we're comfortable with. He needs some round-the-clock observation so we can gauge what's going on."

"Every January or February we end up in the hospital," I answered. I had seen Mattie have blue spells at home, and had even told his doctors about them, so my first thought was that they were being extra cautious about something they were now seeing rather than simply hearing about.

For his part, Mattie said, "If I go into the hospital, I might never come out. Am I going to die in May or June this time instead of get to go home?" He did not want to repeat his too-frequent winter-into-spring PICU stay, especially sensing that his time was short.

A PICU doctor came to speak to us, assuring us that Mattie would come into the PICU for only two weeks to see if they could make a dif-

---

1   From "Final Thoughts" in *Reflections of a Peacemaker: A Portrait Through Heartsongs*, page 205.

ference. He'd be given platelet transfusions more often, as well as more red blood cells and IV fluids to keep his blood pressure steady. At the end of two weeks they'd reassess. "We're not putting him here to die," they told us. "Give us fourteen days and then we'll say, 'Here's what we can do,' or 'There's nothing we can do.' Either way, if you want to go home after that, you can go home."

Mattie was then readmitted to the hospital—a huge disappointment, particularly because he was supposed to be flying to Chicago toward the end of the month to surprise Oprah for her fiftieth birthday. Her producers had been working with us behind the scenes, trying to figure out a safe way to get him there and having a local hospital on call in case he had a crisis while visiting. Now, the fact that he would leave the PICU only days before he was supposed to travel made the plan all the more tenuous. Adding to our pessimism was that Mattie had a second blue spell as we were settling into the PICU.

We called Oprah's producers to tell them what was happening. They told me to give it a week and make a decision at that point about whether to continue to plan on coming to Chicago. If he can't come, they told us, they would send a film crew for him to tape his birthday message.

Mattie was not better after seven days. His blood pressure kept drifting. With a heavy heart—he hadn't seen Oprah in person in more than a year—he asked for a crew to come and tape him.

He did get to go home after two weeks—his blood pressure was stable by then, and he wasn't having blue spells—but the day he was discharged, he started running a fever. A blood test showed his white cell count was high, which the hospital attributed to stress rather than an infection. Still, as Mattie climbed out of his PICU bed and was getting into his wheelchair, he said, "I know I'm the one who complained about being here, but I'm not sure I should be leaving today. Something's not right. I really don't feel well."

The doctor told him that he always did better once he was home. "We'll leave the porch light on for you," she said. "If you need to come back, you come back."

A "Welcome Home, Mattie" banner stretched from our front door to Sandy's, festooned with balloons, and there were also balloons waiting for Mattie in his bedroom. Even though it had been only fourteen days, everyone was so happy to have him home again.

He was exhausted, however, and every time he tried to talk, he started coughing. Still, his spirit was indomitable. The next day, I went for a haircut just across the street, and Nell stayed with him while I was out. She told Mattie to practice his interviewing skills for the *Just Peace* book on her—she thought it would save him from doing most of the talking while she answered his questions—and the two of them ended up laughing hysterically at everything she said. That got Mattie coughing, but he didn't care. They had such a good time. Sandy wrote about Mattie's resilience to the Prayer Warriors:

> He knows his body is dying and hopes that process will take years. He also lives with the reality that it may take weeks or months. As always, Mattie is Mattie, and in the middle of a situation that would devastate many of us, he is busy winning Mario 3 video games and beating people in a game of Clue.

But his emotional resilience wasn't proving a match for his body. Five days after coming home from the hospital, he was once again back in the PICU, sicker than before, with more blue spells and more bleeding from his fingers, lips, and toes. At that point they decided to try infusing his blood with platelets every single day for a week.

It was tough for Mattie because that was the week he was supposed to have been in Chicago. He couldn't even call Oprah on her birthday because we weren't allowed to use the cell phone in the PICU. He also wasn't sure she received the three gifts he made for her. He had given them to the film crew, but they were freelancers, not part of Oprah's staff, and might not have realized how close Mattie and she were. A clock, a plaque, and a wind chime, all three made out of wood and fashioned with special messages from Mattie, could very well have gotten lost in the shuffle.

After a week of daily platelets, the hospital released Mattie once again, on Super Bowl Sunday, and we went home and over to Sandy's to watch the game with her kids. We were now into February.

A few days later, Laura came to watch Mattie so I could go to the university. While she was there, he had a blue spell like she had never witnessed before. "He has to go back into the hospital," she said. "I'm a critical care nurse, I work in the PICU and I've seen everything, and this is not something that can be handled from home."

When we arrived back at the PICU, we learned that Mattie had pneumonia. All the fluids he was being given stabilized his blood pressure and also helped slow his bleeding, but they compromised his lungs. Every time we worked to solve one problem, we were worsening another.

The hospital put him on IV antibiotics. Mattie felt awful—and worried. The second annual MDA Heartsongs Gala was now only about two weeks away. He feared he was going to miss his own event, just as he had feared the year before.

But by Valentine's Day weekend, a week before the gala, the antibiotics were clearing the pneumonia. Mattie also received a visit from the Bouchards that weekend, which lifted his spirits. And knowing that Mattie loved when I created little poems or messages for him, something I had been doing since he was three, I wrote him a poem. One stanza read:

> You are . . .
> My heart's jubilation
> Each day of the year,
> My own affirmation
> That God dwells right here. . . .
> You are . . .
> My life's celebration
> And reason for joy,
> My hope's inspiration,
> My own little boy. . . .

♥

Because Mattie was doing better, and though his medicine and intravenous fluid regimen was now more intense than it had ever been, the doctors allowed him to go home, for which we both felt grateful. He could attend his gala, which again was being held minutes from the hospital in Washington.

A few days later, the night before the event, Mattie enjoyed dinner with some of his MDA friends. Christopher Cross was there, too—he had flown in with his wife and daughter. Afterward, Mattie and I went straight to our hotel room. There were two king-size beds, and we needed to get to sleep to have enough energy to get through the next day and evening.

We plugged in our batteries to recharge as we switched from our wheelchairs to our beds, and as soon as my head hit the pillow, Mattie asked me, "Mom, will you please sleep with me tonight?"

"Oh, Buddy, I'm so tired," I answered him. "I've been sleeping on a bench in the PICU waiting room, driving back and forth to the hospital almost every other day when you are not in the PICU, and trying to do my work for the university on the side. I'm already in bed. How 'bout I do it another night?"

"Okay, Mom," Mattie said without a hint of disappointment. "No problem."

Within seconds, I crawled into his bed, held him, and said, "How about a snuggle?"

"Why?" he responded. "I know you're tired."

"I really love you, Mattie," I told him. "These beds are huge. I'll sleep fine."

The next morning, when I woke up, I opened my eyes and Mattie said, "Mom, it was a good thing you slept in the bed with me."

"Why?" I asked.

"You had a really bad dream in the middle of the night," he responded. "You were moaning and restless, and I rubbed your head to make you feel better, and you fell back to sleep. If you weren't here, I couldn't have taken care of you."

I could see that his lips had "exploded" during the night. There was blood on his face, and both lips had huge, pulpy scabs all over them. Here he was, in pain once again, yet glad that *he* could take care of *me*.

When Mattie made his way out of bed and saw himself in the mirror, he said, "I don't know that I can go tonight. I look so bad I'll frighten people. I look like a monster." He started holding warm, wet compresses to his lips to moisten the scabs, then peeled them from his mouth so people wouldn't be put off—but the process made it look like he had painted his lips bright red.

I could see that his cheeks had all kinds of red marks on them, too, in addition to the blood. "Mattie, are you using your skin cream?" I asked him. Since he hit thirteen, his face had become oily.

"Mom, they're not zits," he answered. "The skin on my face is eroding, just like on my lips, fingers, and toes. The skin is dying all over my body."

"You do not have to stay here tonight, Mattie," I said. "We can go back to the hospital." Just like last year, we were faced with this decision.

"No, this is my event," he said. "I want this to go on every year. I'm a people person. I'll be fine once I get downstairs with everyone."

And he was. His firefighter friends Bubba and J.J. had come to surprise him. Harley bikers came in business suits or tuxedos. Several hundred other people were there also, including Hope and her mother, Susan.

Mattie had had a crush on Hope when the two were little, but by the time he reached age nine, he decided that they were too much like family to ever date. That night, however, Hope came wearing what Mattie thereafter referred to as "the green dress" that fit her budding body like a glove. He looked at her and said, "Wow, you have turned into a young woman. I may have to take back what I said about how we can't date."

For the second year in a row, Larry King's producer, Michael Watts, donated his time to produce the gala, which was so successful, with so many tickets sold, that nearly $200,000 was raised for MDA. Also for the second time, Michael, in conjunction with the local MDA director Stephanie Goldklang, lined up a surprise for Mattie. It was a series of videos from Oprah Winfrey, Jimmy Carter, Jerry Lewis, Larry King, and

Maya Angelou. Each had a personal message for Mattie, and he cried during Oprah's, knowing what it meant for her to fit an extra videotaping into her packed schedule.

Dr. Angelou, in finishing out the montage, spoke verses from her poem "And Still I Rise," including this one:

> *Just like the moons and like suns,*
> *With the certainty of tides,*
> *Just like hopes springing high,*
> *Still I'll rise.*[2]

Then she said, "You are a poet, a humanitarian. This, Mattie, is you."

Afterward, Billy Gilman and Christopher Cross each performed. Once they finished, it would be Mattie's turn to speak. He was slated to give the keynote. But while Christopher was singing, Mattie rolled over to my table and whispered, "Mom, I don't know what to say."

Instinctively, I responded, "Of course you do. You always have something to say. Didn't you prepare anything?"

"Yes," he whispered again, "I planned a speech. But it's wrong. It's not the right message."

I didn't know what he meant and met his eyes with an "I don't understand" look.

"How do I go up and say, 'Hello, welcome, and good-bye—this event needs to go on without me'?" he answered. "How am I going to tell people I'm not going to be here next year in a way that inspires them to come back themselves and also doesn't bring everybody down tonight?"

I believed what Mattie was saying about not being there next year, even if I couldn't admit it to myself yet.

"Of course you'll be here next year," I answered. "You're only in the PICU for a week or two at a time now. You're doing okay."

He looked at me like he was about to cry. "I don't know what to say, Mom," he repeated.

---

2   From "And Still I Rise" in *And Still I Rise* by Maya Angelou (Random House, 1978).

I looked at him. I could see the skin on his face falling apart, his body dying around his spirit. I could see that he really might *not* be back here next year. But as a parent, you can never resign yourself to the reality that you're going to bury your child. You cannot, even as your child is fading before your eyes, anticipate it—even if you have done it three times before.

"Speak from your heart, Mattie," I said. "Speak from your spirit. Those words can never be wrong."

Mattie rolled back to his table. I didn't know it at the time, but Michael Watts, who was sitting next to him, said, "Okay, Mattie, you're up next."

"I can't do this," Mattie told him.

"Well, you have to," Michael said casually, knowing he was talking to a kid who was never at a loss for words. Then he looked at Mattie sitting there quietly. "I got goose bumps," he later told me. "He had just been laughing and fooling around with his friends, and when he was laughing, you didn't notice how bad he looked. But when he was silent, I could see he was so thin, so pale. He looked so alone, frightened. I had never seen him like that before."

"Are you okay, Mattie?" he asked after he had taken a second look.

Mattie looked up with tears in his eyes. "This is difficult for me," he said. "I don't do good-byes well."

With that he rolled up the ramp that led onto the stage. The emcee introduced him, and he rolled out to the middle, smiling, waving at everyone, looking like the Mattie we all knew and loved—the one who said we should play after every storm, the one who was in the business of always comforting everyone else.

He was handed the microphone, and only then could I see the hesitation. He put it in his lap and looked down for maybe fifteen seconds, readying himself to tell everybody it was going to be okay. Then, on the spot, he pulled the following out of his heart and spirit:

> *You all say I am a champion for MDA. I'm told I'm a champion*
> *for hope and peace. I'm told I'm a champion for so many reasons.*
> *But I'm not a champion. I'm a messenger. The champions are*

those who take the message, take the hope, take the peace, take the cause for something better and carry it out to the world—not because they have a disability, not because they're paid, but simply because they can.

Champions are able to balance blessings and burdens and always find a reason to celebrate life; they are the people who reach inside of themselves and find an ability to become part of the effort just because the effort needs them. Champions become the next messengers, the ones who choose to offer more opportunities for more people to hear and realize the message, so that the world grows with more messengers in it.

At this point, Mattie recited his poem "On Being a Champion":

A champion is. . . .
Someone who overcomes challenges
Even when it requires creative solutions.
A champion is an optimist,
A hopeful spirit . . .
Someone who plays the game,
Even when the game is called life . . .
Especially when the game is called life. . . . [3]

He finished by saying:

This moment, this event, this day, will end. But we know that other moments, other events, other days, will unfold with more opportunities to do good and to celebrate. And while those days and opportunities can never look the same as this one, nor should they, they can still be as wonderful if we remember why we gather at events like this, and what it means to be a champion

---

3   From "On Being a Champion" in *Journey Through Heartsongs*, page 20.

and remember that these moments are not about any one person.
They're about doing what's right and meeting the needs of any
other person. I love you all very much, and I'm so proud to have
been a part of this effort.

People clapped and cheered and cried, and didn't stop. Mattie had just
said good-bye, and we all felt empowered; we felt good. Carefully and
inspirationally, he challenged us to step forward. Yet we didn't want to
end our cheering because of the fear that it was the last time we *were*
going to be able to cheer for him. As much as we accepted his challenge
to embrace the next moment, we dreaded embracing it without him.
Would we get to clap for him next year? We didn't want to find out, and
if the cheering petered out and the moment ended, we would have to.

The next morning, nobody wanted to leave the hotel. That same joyful
sense of being with Mattie, mixed with foreboding that we might not be
able to come together again in the same way, stalled everyone. The
Hemelgarns, Billy Gilman, MDA friends, Michael Watts, the Crosses,
Nell, Sandy and her children, and others just milled around until Mattie
organized a quick game he learned at camp that left us all laughing.

Mattie and I eventually drove Christopher Cross and his family to the
airport. When it was time to part, Christopher leaned over and hugged me
and said, "Every time I hug Mattie and tell him good-bye, I wonder
whether it's going to be the last time. But I think this really *is* the last time.
I want to cancel my flight and just stay here. I don't want to let go."

"Neither do I," I said.

One morning a few days later, I found Mattie sitting at the kitchen
table, signing a huge stack of book plates. Usually book plates say, "This
book belongs to . . ." but Mattie's said, "Remember to play after every
storm." After he signed them, we would mail them to MDA, and they
would affix them to copies of his books. It was a way of autographing
books without having to travel the country for signings.

Mattie always tried to do ten a day, so I was surprised that he was
attempting to get through so many. "Why are you doing so many at once?"
I asked.

"I made you a list," Mattie said, not really answering my question. "This batch will go to people who get the *Just Peace* book after it comes out. "These," he said, pointing to another pile, "are for my final collection of poetry." A third pile was for specific people, like Sandy and the other kin, Oprah, Jimmy Carter, Maya Angelou, Jerry Lewis. Then, looking at a fourth stack, he said, "These aren't assigned to any particular group, but you'll know when someone should get one as you go along. I'm not going to be here to sign new books, so I want to get these autographs done now."

I was surprised. He actually seemed to be doing a little better now. His blood pressure was stable. But there he was, firm in the conviction that he needed to tie up these loose ends.

A few nights later, February 29, Mattie sat glued to the TV set, watching the Oscars while I dozed, and he cried when the *Lord of the Rings* folks went up to accept the eleventh of the eleven awards for which the movie had been nominated. "Now the world will get the message of what these movies are about," he said. "What *Lord of the Rings* teaches us is that war is futile. Good must prevail, or nothing prevails in the end." He then wrote Sean Astin an e-mail saying that he thought he "heard a broom, but it was the sound of sweeping" at the awards ceremony with all the Oscars the movie had won.

The very next morning, March 1, Mattie said he wanted to tell me about a dream he had had a few weeks earlier. "I dreamt that I died," he said, "but that God gave me a choice of whether I wanted to stay in Heaven or come back to earth for a while longer. I told God, 'You're the one who gave me the gift of life. I've always tried to serve You, to do Your will. What is *Your* choice for me?'

"Mom," Mattie then told me, "God reached out to my life and soul, and He just hugged me."

I didn't want to hear that dream. I was angry. I took God hugging Mattie as his welcome into Heaven, and I was frustrated because what my son was telling me was that God gave him a choice to stay dead or suffer longer, and he handed the choice back to God. He was saying, "I accept Your decision." I understood Mattie was coming to terms with his future rather than simply feeling resigned, but I wanted him to say, "Even though going back to earth would mean suffering, I want to be with my mother."

"That's a nice dream," I answered. "I have a lot of stuff to do today." I just could not bear that conversation, so I ended it. I realized, too, that that's why I had been so uncomfortable with "Be careful what you wish for" on New Year's Eve. I was wishing for him to stay alive for my comfort, at his own expense.

The next day, Mattie tried again. "Mom," he said, "we need to talk." He said it gently but was very serious.

I still couldn't bring myself to have the conversation I knew he wanted. I was afraid. I'm not a woman who lives in denial. But this wasn't the same as "This is what to put in my casket" or "Here's when to give up heroic efforts." Those conversations were therapeutic for Mattie. They were ways of helping him cope and feel some control in a situation in which there really wasn't any control. But I couldn't give him permission to tell me he was dying because I feared that in doing so, I'd be granting him permission to accept the truth. And even though he already was accepting the truth, he wasn't going to get the okay to do so from me.

"I'm sorry, Buddy," I said. "I told Sandy we'd have coffee this morning, so I'm going next door. We'll talk later." I had blown off my son a second time in two days, but I guess I figured that by withholding permission to say yes to death, I was keeping him alive. I felt horrible leaving Mattie alone with what he needed to say, but I hoped that after I came back in, he would have moved on to another topic.

While I was sitting with Sandy, recounting what had just happened, my cell phone rang. It was Mattie. I picked up the phone and said, "What's up, Bud?"

All I heard on the other end was beeping. Sandy started running— she could get next door faster than I could. She told me that when she reached Mattie's bedroom, he was at the edge of his bed, not unconscious but looking awful. He had had another dark and dizzy spell while trying to get from his bed to his wheelchair and, feeling weak, slipped during the transfer. He had reconnected himself to his tubing by the time Sandy made it to him, but he looked terrified.

"Are you okay?" Sandy asked.

"My stomach hurts," Mattie answered. "It has been really hurting for a week. You have to tell my Mom I'm dying," he added. "You have to help her prepare. I cannot leave her shocked."

Sandy didn't want to believe it, either. *Your home is at the edge of life*, she thought to herself. *You* are *the Comeback Kid*.

A few days later we went back to the hospital for more platelets. Mattie said to people there, "I'm dying. I'm in pain, especially my stomach. I'm frustrated. I don't think you all understand that *I am dying*."

They called for Terry Spearman, the child life specialist who had by that point worked with Mattie for three years, to come and spend the day with him. They did a chest X-ray and found nothing too concerning, just a little residual fluid from the pneumonia. His bleeding had also slowed considerably. He was actually looking somewhat better. "We can't find anything specific," they said. "We're going to send him home."

I was determined that he stay until they found what was hurting him, but they said, "We really think he's okay." So we had no choice but to head back to the condo.

"Mom, do you have any money on you?" Mattie asked. "I'm starving. Can we stop and grab some fast food on the way home?"

I counted. "I have seven dollars, Mattie," I said. "I have to check if I have a parking coupon. If I do, we can pay for the garage with that and use the seven dollars to stop off for food."

I did have a coupon. When we reached the garage, I handed it to Mattie and told him to give it to the attendant while I got the van ready. But he came over to me a minute later and said, "I'm sorry, but could I please have the seven dollars?"

"Why, Mattie?" I asked. "Just use the coupon."

"No," he answered. "You see that man with five kids? He doesn't have the money to get out of the garage. He must be here because one of his kids is sick. I gave him our coupon."

The next morning, I went into Mattie's bedroom, climbed into bed with him, and just held him.

"What was that for?" he asked happily.

"Just because I love you," I told him. "I'm going to go ahead and pour the coffee. Come on out to the kitchen."

When he rolled in, he stood up out of his wheelchair, which he rarely did anymore because he had gotten so weak, and put his hand on my shoulder. "Thank you for the hug, Mom," he said. "It really made my day."

I looked at him and realized, I'm looking *up* at my son. Even when Mattie stood, he had always been below eye level because his growth was so stunted. But he had had a growth spurt when nobody was looking and now stood nearly four and a half feet—still short for his age but significantly taller than he had been.

That is the coolest, coolest thing, I thought to myself. I had never had the opportunity to look up at any of my children before.

His dimples showed a young man's face emerging from a boyish grin. He looked like a teenager rather than a child. His blond hair had become darker, his blue eyes deeper. There was a light line of blond fuzz growing above his upper lip. *He's handsome*, I thought.

"Look at you," I said. "Mattie, when did you become a young man?" He smiled broadly. But then, when I reached up to put my arm around his shoulder and give him a hug, there it was. He was so thin. His eyes and lips were swollen. He looked so tired. My son was growing up and dying simultaneously.

That evening we were supposed to go to a cardiac foundation fundraiser hosted by Larry King in Washington. We were back and forth all day on whether or not to attend, given Mattie's health, but at the last minute, Mattie said, "I want to go. Larry does so much for me."

Larry introduced Mattie to James Brown, the godfather of soul, and to Dan Snyder, the owner of the Washington Redskins, Mattie's favorite team. He was beside himself with joy. Then Montel Williams, who had also become a friend of Mattie's, came up to him to say hello, and all of a sudden Mattie started having severe trouble breathing. He looked at Montel and said, "I'm sorry, I'm sorry. I've got to go. I can't breathe."

Michael Watts helped me get Mattie into the lobby, where I suctioned the secretions, but they were not bloody, just clear, like water. We went home right then.

Mattie felt better the next morning. He even went to an MDA teen meeting that evening. But he used the occasion to say good-bye. "Don't forget to turn off your wheelchairs if you're not rolling," he said to the other teens on his way out. "You don't want to run down your battery if you don't have to." To Devin he gave a big hug. There were no high fives, as there usually had been.

The day after, a Sunday, we went to the hospital for platelets and red blood cells. Mattie spent almost the whole day sleeping. His stomach was hurting badly. When he'd wake up, he'd say, "I think I'm dying. I think this is it. I don't understand why nobody believes me. Why won't anybody let me say this?" He didn't look especially bad—he wasn't blue—so it was easy to fall into a false sense of security, even then.

That evening, as we were leaving the hospital, I said to him, "Hey, how about a date? You and I have not been out just for fun in forever."

Mattie said, "Okay," so we stopped at a Ruby Tuesday. But he couldn't eat. His stomach was too upset. He took only a couple of sips of a chocolate shake.

When we reached home, I told him I would call his pulmonologist, Dr. Witzmann, the next day, that he should get ready for bed and I'd come in to say good night.

"Wait, Mom," he answered. "I have a thought I've been working with on and off today. I'm just going to go to the computer and finish it. I need to capture this." He then rolled to the Bachelor's Pad, typed something, saved the file, and turned off the machine. He clearly did not want me to see it.

When he went to his bedroom and lay down, he said again that his stomach was really hurting.

"Maybe a good night's sleep will help," I told him. "Call me if you need me during the night."

Mattie with his "AML" (Aunt Mary Lou Smith) at the Second
Annual MDA Heartsongs Gala, February 2004

Mattie with Hope in "the green dress"
at the Second Annual MDA Heartsongs
Gala, February 2004

CHAPTER 17

Sunset

Mattie, winter 2004

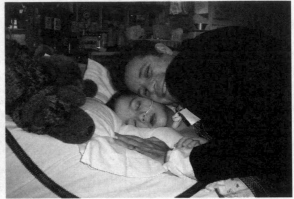

Mattie getting a visit from actor Sean Astin while in the PICU, spring 2004

Born of the
Dust of humility,
Spread on the
Wings of pride,
Carried by
Winds of hope,
I grow with the
Ebbing life tide.[1]

"Mom, please, I am in so much pain! *Help me, please!*"
It was a couple of hours later, around one A.M. on March 8, when Mattie called out. I went in, and he was doubled over.

"Where does it hurt?" I asked. "Your stomach? Are you hungry? Do you need some toast?"

---

1 From "Unfolding" in *Loving Through Heartsongs*, page 3.

"Yes, some toast, please," he answered. "I don't know what's wrong."

I started to head to the kitchen when I saw his back arch. He just rolled over, facedown, his body extended and unnaturally stiff.

"Mattie? Mattie! What are you doing? Are you okay?" I called out. I tried to roll him back over, but his body was too rigid.

After what might have been about twenty seconds, he relaxed, rolled over on his own, and sat up again.

"What happened?" I asked.

He had no idea what I was talking about. "I don't know. I think I fell asleep."

All of a sudden he cried out in pain again. "Oh, my stomach!" His lips had turned blue.

I grabbed the phone and called Sandy, who answered on the first ring. Like me, she had become hyper-vigilant about Mattie's situation. "Can you please come?" I asked desperately.

She was there in seconds. As she came into his room, Mattie rolled over and went stiff a second time. But again, some twenty seconds later, his body relaxed, and he lay on his back. He was alert but very weak, and hardly able to speak.

I called the PICU, thinking that maybe he was having seizures, and they said to bring him to the emergency room. Sandy called Chris, who came quickly and helped her dress Mattie while I filled his oxygen tanks and grabbed our toiletries, some changes of clothes, and his Game Boy. Chris picked Mattie up and lifted him into his wheelchair, but Mattie was too weak to sit, so Chris held him up and operated his joystick, enabling us get him down to the van.

"I didn't have anything to give him as hope that he would come home again," Chris later told me. "I wanted to hand him something that he would have to return to me. I needed to give him a reason to come back. I reached into my pocket. All I had was a receipt for window tinting on my car. I handed it to Mattie and said, 'I need this receipt back. When you come home, make sure you give it to me.' Mattie said, 'I love you, Chris.' I told him, 'I love you, too, Buddy.'"

Sandy drove while I rode in my wheelchair so I could hold Mattie up and do any suctioning if necessary. By the time we arrived at the hospital, he was feeling better, sitting upright on his own and chatting a bit. He even gave his own history to the ER staff, telling them what had just happened. Because there was the possibility that he had had a seizure, they did a CT scan of his brain. But all they found was old damage to his basal ganglia, the part that controls movement. That had been there for years.

Mattie was soon admitted to the PICU, where we were told not to worry. He'd be sent home the next day unless something specific could be found. But by afternoon, he became distressed, saying he wasn't feeling well again. Even Aunt Mary Lou, who had traveled a couple of hours to see him that day, could see that he wasn't up for a visit and decided to head home soon after she arrived.

"I love you, AML," Mattie said to her as she was leaving.

"I love you, too, Mattie," she told him.

Later in the afternoon, I noticed that his oxygen saturation had fallen to a range of 97 to 99 rather than 100—fine for anyone else but not for Mattie. I mentioned it to a doctor, a new resident who was not familiar with his case, who told me those numbers were "great." But another physician present who *did* know Mattie said that no, something was wrong when his oxygen saturation fell below 100 percent. Just as she said it, Mattie's blood pressure began to drop way down, and he started to lose consciousness. The doctor immediately ran a large dose of IV fluids into him to stabilize the pressure, and he became more alert but was clearly still in a bad way. They let me call Sandy from the nurses' station.

"He's not doing well. I think you need to come," I said.

Sandy had been up all night, had driven us to the hospital, then spent the entire day at work. It was now approaching evening. "I fell asleep driving home from my office," she answered. "I'll call Jamie and have her drive me down."

A few minutes before six, Mattie said to me, "I am so tired. I am so thirsty." I brought him some ice chips and spooned them into his mouth, a little at a time. After a few bites, he grinned and told me, "Thank you."

But within moments he was saying, "I am just so tired, and my stomach is in so much pain." Then he suddenly bolted to a sitting position with a look of fear in his eyes that I had never seen before. "Help me! Please, help me! I hurt! I'm scared!"

"We need help. Quick!" I screamed.

Doctors and nurses came running. I looked at Mattie and said loudly, to keep him alert, "I love you, Mattie! I love you! I love you!"

He looked back at me, let out a noise, then fell backward onto the bed. In seconds, the heart rate on his monitor fell from the 120s to the 60s to the 20s, then 0. "Clear the unit," the PICU clerk called out. "All visitors must leave!"

I thought I was going to throw up. I rolled my wheelchair backward from his bed so the doctors could move in and begin chest compressions. "I love you!" I kept saying. "I love you, Mattie! I love you. Oh, God, I love you. Oh, God, please, please, please, I love him so much. Please, God. Please. I am begging You. Please, God. I love you, Mattie. I need you. I love you. Oh, God, please!"

A few minutes later, Sandy was walking toward me. "We need you to come in," the PICU staff had said to her, even though the unit had been closed to visitors. The doctors were always relieved, when Mattie was in crisis, if Sandy was there to be with me while they tended to him.

Sandy saw that Mattie had coded, thinking "Oh, no. No! No!" and got a message out to her daughter, Jamie D, to phone Heather and Chris, Father Dixon, the Retzlaffs, and others. By the time she reached Mattie's bed, I was still staring at the monitors, at the mayhem of CPR, in shock and sickness, still calling out, "Oh, God, please. Oh, Mattie, I love you. . . ."

She put her arms around me. "Oh, Sandy," I cried. "I'm afraid he's leaving."

A very long twenty minutes later, Dr. Heidi Dalton, the PICU physician who was leading the code team, looked at me and said, "It has been a long time. We've even tried shocking his heart, with no response. There is a significant chance that even if he survives this, he will never wake up again. It would not be wrong for you to ask us to stop the CPR."

I couldn't say anything at all. I just sat and continued to stare at the monitors, at Mattie, his body now covered with tubes and needles and other medical paraphernalia. The CPR compressions continued.

At thirty minutes, Dr. Dalton tried shocking his heart with the paddles a second time. Again, there was no response. "You need to understand how long this has been," she said, "how serious this is. There is a significant chance that there is no brain function at this point."

By that time, Jamie-D had been allowed in, and Heather and Chris and Cynthia, all of whom had headed to the hospital shortly after I called Sandy. Each one went over to Mattie, told him they loved him, cried, and returned to the waiting room while Sandy and I stayed bedside, watching, praying, stunned. She, too, loved Mattie like a son.

Laura was there also. She had come in to work the night shift as the supervising nurse—she no longer gave direct care to patients in the PICU—but as soon as she saw the state Mattie was in, that he was being coded, she put on gloves and stepped in to administer the drugs for his heart and blood pressure, tears streaming down her cheeks.

After more than forty minutes of CPR, Dr. Dalton said, "Jeni, you need to know that short of some miracle, he is gone. We can try shocking him one more time, but I am not sure it is going to make a difference. What do you want us to do?"

Mattie had detailed his final wishes to Sandy and me just two months earlier. He told us when to stop heroic measures, which was when he was no longer able to think, communicate, or *be* Mattie. But for whatever reason, I could not at that moment, more than forty minutes into trying to rescue his stopped heart, say the word, "Enough." I could not be the one to make that decision.

"We're going to shock him one more time and do one more round of CPR," Dr. Dalton said. "When we pause to assess, if there is no heartbeat, we are going to stop the compressions, unless you specifically tell us *not* to stop."

They shocked his heart, did another two minutes of compressions, then assessed. I closed my eyes, bracing for the "I am so sorry" that was coming.

After what felt like an eternity, I heard Dr. Dalton say, "Wow, will you look at that? I can't explain it, but he's got a heartbeat." Every doctor and nurse on hand swung into gear to do everything they could to stabilize Mattie. Laura asked another nurse to supervise that night so she could care for Mattie herself. She wanted to be the one right there. She knew that she could tend to him best as the result of all her experience with him at home, and more important, she knew that if he didn't survive the night, she wanted to be with him.

Sandy's kids were overjoyed, staying in the waiting room and playing cards, awaiting more good news, while the Retzlaffs came with Father Dixon, who anointed Mattie. We had no idea which way it was going to go.

Shortly before midnight, Mattie's heart rate started falling again, then stopped completely for the second time. Dr. Dalton began the compressions, but after fifteen minutes of CPR, she started saying the things I knew she needed to say, that my son was dying and that at some point, CPR would have to cease. After five more minutes of compressions, however, his heart started to beat on its own once more.

Even so, an echocardiogram showed that neither side of Mattie's heart was functioning much at all. Dr. Dalton said I shouldn't get my hopes up, but they could try putting him on nitric oxide gas, which would come through his ventilator tube mixed with the 100 percent oxygen that he was now on.

The results were almost instantaneous. A repeat echocardiogram showed his heart function was improved, though his right side was much enlarged, which meant it was having to pump extra hard. The doctors also discovered that Mattie had a severe infection in his bloodstream, which very well may have been what led to the cardiac arrest.

Sandy and I kept vigil at Mattie's bedside through the night, her children coming in periodically to check on him, to say they loved him. Jamie-D, in her typical style, cheered him on, saying, "Go, Mattie! You keep that heart going!" But despite the fact that his heart was beating again, Dr. Dalton told me there was much less of a chance after the second arrest that Mattie would ever be himself again, or even regain consciousness.

Still, when morning came, I leaned over to him and said, "I love you, Mattie."

His eyes opened, and he looked straight at me. I cried with joy. The nurse on duty told him he needed to rest, and he closed his eyes again. But throughout the day, if I said quietly, "Mattie, do you hear me? I love you," he would open them for a moment or squeeze my hand.

Dr. Dalton told me that was a good sign, but that there's usually brain swelling after cardiac arrest that causes brain damage, and it sometimes takes up to seventy-two hours to occur. There was a chance this temporary alertness would be gone in a day or two.

The next night, March 10, the PICU had a television brought to Mattie's bedside because I told them he was an *American Idol* fan, and it was results night. Most of the staff was skeptical about his even knowing a TV was there, but I felt sure he would be aware. Also, I knew it would let *him* know that despite his closed eyes, I believed he was taking in his world.

When Mattie's early favorite that season was voted through to the next round, Mattie opened his eyes and emphatically called out, "Yes!" His nurse looked at him and said, "I assume he's your favorite." Mattie smiled, then closed his eyes again.

The next morning, Mattie was sedated and taken for a CT scan of his brain. Just moving him at that point was life-threatening, with tubes in him everywhere and medicines being administered for every vital function. But the scan was essential to assess the extent of damage from the two cardiac arrests, which left his heart unable to pump blood to his brain for more than an hour altogether.

"I can't really explain this," Dr. Dalton said when they brought Mattie back to the PICU, "but we cannot find any swelling or damage to his brain on his scan.

"We will do everything we can to keep him stable," she added. "But we think it's best to keep him sedated for a while in a medically induced coma so he can heal. We'll try waking him up in a few days, a week, to see where we are.

"You know, Mattie," she said, smiling at him and gently touching his hand, "I'm going to have a whole bunch of gray hair soon because of you, but I'll be proud of it. You really know how to scare a doctor, don't you?"

The next several days were touch and go. On St. Patrick's Day, Nell came to visit, and I went to the waiting room to make some calls. She came out a few minutes later, saying, "They need you in there right now. There's a bit of an equipment issue." Mattie had coded for a third time, and she couldn't bring herself to say that, in the few minutes I was out of the room, Mattie had another cardiac arrest. Fortunately, they were able to bring him back pretty quickly with compressions and not the paddles this time. But they determined that he now had pulmonary hypertension, which meant his heart wasn't pumping blood to his lungs efficiently.

During the next couple of weeks, there was not a single uneventful twelve-hour shift. If his blood pressure didn't dip, sludge formed in his gall bladder. His blood infection healed very slowly, and new infections set in. One day in early April, when the doctors reduced the sedatives to ready him to wake up, he writhed in pain, arching his back and tensing his arms and legs. They quickly resedated him.

I sat with Mattie day and night, resting only for a couple of hours if Sandy or Heather came and stayed with him. I played his music. I kept movies running in a portable DVD player. I talked to him, sang to him. I remembered his life, our life together, aloud and in my heart. I thought about how I performed CPR on him when he was an infant, his near-death experience three years earlier, and his waking up then to say that angels were much more magnificent than the way they looked on Christmas tree ornaments. I longed for sunrise on the pier with my son, morning coffee, afternoon tea, a word from him—any connection to him beyond my touching his broken body.

Not every nurse was okay with my constant presence, and sometimes I was forced to leave—or not be allowed back in if I stepped out for a quick bathroom break. That was devastating for me. Mattie needed me to be there if he woke up, or if he breathed his final breaths. I needed to be with him for the same reasons.

Through all of this, he was becoming addicted to narcotics, which he was given for his pain, and that raised the risk of another respiratory crisis. We were running circles trying to solve each medical dilemma.

Nell spent hours on the phone, working to secure a funeral home that would respect Mattie's final wishes—no morgue, no covering of his face. We were dealing with the eventuality of his waking up and the eventuality of his death at the same time. She finally found a place that understood our needs and said they would come to the hospital within three hours, day or night, so that he could be taken straight there and not be placed first in the morgue.

Sandy and I had family meetings with various teams of doctors. Some thought he would never wake up, regardless of medical support. Some said they didn't agree with my decision to keep Mattie alive but respected it. Others told me I was doing this *to* him, not *for* him. Ethical questions abounded, and all were frustrated, including me, and perhaps even Mattie, who had been clear on when it was time to let him go. But was it time? I heard him cheer for an *American Idol* contestant after two *long* cardiac arrests. And there was no brain damage on his scan. And when they tried to wake him up, he would cry, feel pain, look at me. . . .

One evening, Dr. Dalton worked on her charting and notes next to Mattie's bed while watching a basketball game with Sandy and me. I excused myself to take a break, and Dr. Dalton told Sandy, "I don't know that Jeni is going to let him go when he needs to. I don't know if we are making the right decisions for him."

To which Sandy responded, "When it is time to let him go, she will not force him to stay. But that time has not come yet. You need to trust her."

In the middle of April, a pain management specialist was added to the team. She came up with options for Mattie so that he could be weaned from the narcotics and woken without agony. They worked, at least to some degree. One day, as his sedation was wearing off before the next dose, his eyes opened, and he saw a photo of Kaylee with the Easter Bunny that I had taped to his bedrail. Sandy e-mailed the Prayer Warriors about the incident:

> I am so excited to be able to share the following news with you. . . . Mattie is beginning to be more responsive. . . . When shown the Easter picture of Kaylee, he smiled and said, "Oh, Happy Easter, Kaylee." He has also said "Hi" to a number of familiar staff when he sees them. He has been able to communicate by looking at a DVD or the TV to indicate a preference. . . . He's even asked for his mom several times in the middle of the night.

But the wakefulness was short lived. Mattie was soon unconscious again, from exhaustion as well as from one drug or another; from a new infection he developed; from the diarrhea, sweating, spasms, and fevers that came with narcotics withdrawal. More time passed. Then a new complication arose. His muscles started tightening, eventually to the point that his bones began breaking from the twisting and pulling, and his fingernails started pulling up from his fingers. The doctors didn't know what was causing this at first, but they soon found that Mattie had developed dystonia—high muscle tone that keeps the muscles from being able to stop contracting, to relax.

The doctors struggled to figure out a solution, to see whether there was a drug that could reverse the problem, or at least stop it from progressing. Bones continued to break as the muscles grew tighter all through his body. Sitting, waiting, I played more music, ran more movies, said more prayers.

One afternoon, there was a knock on the door. It was Sean Astin, who had flown in from California. "Can I come in and meet Mattie in person?" he asked.

I told him Mattie was comatose.

"Then you need to take pictures of me with him, kissing him, so that when he wakes up he'll know I was here. I promised I would meet him in person."

Sean leaned over and kissed Mattie, not even seeming to notice the blood that was trickling from his mouth and nose. He told Mattie, "I will be a messenger for you, no matter what tomorrow brings. Remember that."

Sean then said to him, "I brought you my home copy of *Return of the King*. It's not out on video yet—this is my publicity copy. Now it's yours. That way you can see it seven times before it goes to video, just like you wanted."

By May 7, Mattie was off all sedation and pain medication, as well as the nitric oxide gas that had been helping his heart since the arrests in

March. He still had not woken up, but I often had the DVD player running, and that day I put in a Monty Python movie. Mattie was facing away from me, and as soon as the opening credits started rolling, his shoulders started shaking. I raced to the other side of the bed, grabbing a suction catheter to clear whatever secretions were choking him, only to look at his face and find that he was not choking but laughing! On the screen were the words "A moose once bit my sister" and other typical *Monty Python* nonsense mixed into the credits, words that always made Mattie laugh.

I spoke to him, and he looked at me, but he didn't answer. He looked back at the movie, then closed his eyes again. But I knew *he was back*. He was waking up slowly, and reading *and* getting the humor, just as he got it before March 8, the day he coded.

I recounted the incident to the PICU staff, but they were skeptical. They hadn't seen it for themselves, so they doubted me. Later that night, however, a doctor had to remove a fingernail from one of Mattie's fingers. The muscles in his hands were fisted up so tightly that nails popped up and dangled and had to be taken from their nail beds. "OUCH!" Mattie said.

"Does that hurt?" the doctor asked.

Mattie looked at him. "It hurts really bad!" he said.

But again, Mattie went silent, and no other doctors had witnessed the exchange. Their skepticism remained high. But not mine.

The next morning I sneezed, and Mattie said, "God bless you, Mom." I just cried—with relief, with joy, with *fear*, too, but still with relief and joy.

The day after that was Mother's Day, and though his voice never rose above a whisper, Mattie began speaking again in earnest that day, making real attempts at conversation.

"Why can't I move?" he asked.

"Your heart was very sick, Mattie," I told him. "The doctors helped you sleep for the last two months while it healed, and it's in much better shape now. But your muscles are very weak, and tight. We are working on that. Do you understand what I'm saying?"

He paused for a second, then answered, "Yes, but I'm awake now.

What's for breakfast?" My Mattie, my true Mattie, was back with me. Later in the day, we exchanged "I love yous" many times over.

The following day, he still spoke infrequently but shared things with the doctors and nurses with whom he had a friendship before the March crisis. He even described his cardiac arrest to a nurse who was part of his code. "I was in pain," he said. "My mom yelled for help, and you held me as the doctors ran toward my bed. Then, I died."

"You are here, Mattie," I said. "You didn't die."

But he looked at me and said, "No, Mom, I died. I've been to Heaven. I've seen hell." He described Dr. Dalton doing CPR, Sandy and me together at the foot of his bed.

Soon after Mother's Day, he was doing so well that the doctors started saying it looked like Mattie would be able to go home in the near future, where further rehabilitation for his muscles could take place.

As she had been doing since early March, Sandy continued to come almost every day, even while working full-time and helping to take care of Kaylee as Cynthia and Chris went to their own jobs. Heather came two to three times a week. They usually visited at night so that I could lie on my bench in the waiting room for a few hours while one of them washed Mattie, watched movies with him, talked to him, read to him, even just sat with him in silence. Sandy's other children came, too, along with Nell, and Mema and Papa, who drove up from North Carolina one week. But nobody besides Sandy and Heather could give me bits of much-needed respite; they knew the monitors the way I did and could gently be with Mattie and reassure him with maternal love while alerting the staff if they anticipated a crisis.

Some of the doctors, while they had heard that Mattie could speak, were frustrated that he would not speak to *them*. Some even questioned whether he was really alert or if it was "the family's wishful thinking." One day, when Heather was watching him, a few of the physicians were trying to get him to talk, but he just stared ahead at the TV, never responding. "We're not even sure if he knows what's *on* TV," they said. "He's just staring."

Heather looked at him and told him, "I love you, Mattie."

He turned to her and responded, "I love you, too, Hedder. It's just so hard to speak," at which point Heather explained to the doctors that it was hard for him to say words and that he used the breath and energy he had to communicate only what was important. And what was important, she said, "was love, inspiration, and amusement."

Mattie spoke to Devin, too, who visited once or twice a week. But Devin would do most of the talking, keeping him up to date on goings-on in the world. Mattie said to him, "I can speak, but it's so difficult that I choose not to, unless there's something I really need to say." Devin understood completely and was just so grateful that it was truly Mattie and not some shadow of his former self. At the same time, he found it painful to watch this talkative child not be able to ramble and chitchat, as he loved to do.

To help Mattie along, speech therapy was initiated in addition to the physical therapy. At the first session, the therapist told Mattie, "You look like a man of many thoughts."

"And many, many words," Mattie responded in his own, inimitable fashion.

At one point I showed Mattie the pictures with Sean Astin. He smiled and asked, "Is that really *him*? He really came and visited me in the PICU?"

Sean soon contacted him to ask if he could do an interview with the *Lord of the Rings* Fan Club magazine. Mattie was thrilled. The magazine called the PICU, and I relayed Mattie's weak whispers. He loved the idea that he was going to be with Sean in the article.

I encouraged other people *not* to come to visit, even though so many wanted to keep Mattie company now that he was awake. I wanted him to rest, to heal, and not try to comfort others about the state of his body, twisted as it was from the muscle tightening, about the weight he had lost yet didn't have to spare. Comforting others remained what Mattie was all about, even in his condition. One day he heard a baby crying in the next bed and, brow furrowed, called out to a nurse, who ran to him, worried he was in crisis. "Please hold the baby, love the baby," he pleaded. "Sing to it. Babies are God's gift to the world."

Despite my advice to people to stay away, some insisted on seeing their friend. One was Christopher Cross. Mattie didn't speak to him, but he looked at Christopher as he sat there and blinked him a clear "good-bye" as he was leaving. By then we had worked out an eye-blinking system so Mattie could communicate without talking, to save his strength.

Good Morning America's Brian O'Keefe and Chris Cuomo came, too. Later, Chris told me:

> I had developed a false sense of comfort with Mattie's condition. He was always dying. I'd get a phone call or an e-mail from Sandy about his dangerously low blood pressure or oxygen levels, the bleeding episodes. But then I would get a phone call or an e-mail from Mattie, who would somehow make light of a dark situation, telling me his latest practical joke or talking about the bleeding with a writer's graphic and gory description. But when I saw him, he was so weak. And I knew he was scared. I could see it, and feel it, even though his words, his manner, were still that of a messenger. Everything he said, I would think, "Oh, yeah, I need to remember this."
>
> Faith is not supposed to be easy, and in true form, I asked God, "Why?" I found no consolation in the whole "Jesus suffered and died for us." It was okay for Jesus, this grown man who gave us Heaven. But this was not okay for Mattie. It was so hard to see him like that, to see him suffering, even as he continued his service as a messenger.

Terry Spearman, Mattie's child life specialist, came by as well, asking Mattie if he wanted anything. He asked for some chocolate ice cream. She bought it that day but was never able to bring it to the hospital. She was afraid, after seeing him, that he would be taking his last bites of a favorite treat, and she just couldn't bring herself to see him do his last anything.

Aunt Mary Lou continued to visit twice a week, as always, and for every crisis, the Retzlaffs raced to the hospital with Father Dixon, who anointed Mattie more times than I could count.

Mattie's best friend, Hope, too, came to the PICU. I told Susan that this was not how she was going to want to remember him, but Hope insisted.

She had always been a very quiet child, with Mattie doing the talking for both of them across the years. But that day, while Hope's mother, Susan, and I stepped into the hallway to give the two friends some time alone, she chatted the entire hour she was there. Mattie never said a word but stared straight at her the whole time, his eyes filled with a million thoughts. When she stood up to leave, she hugged him. He could not move to hug her back—his tightened muscles left him essentially paralyzed—but he said, "Good-bye, Hope. I love you."

Still, even with all that, there continued to be talk of Mattie going home by the end of May, or perhaps early June. He was clearly awake, eating his own food now in addition to being fed by tube, making requests as he read the hospital menu. He was even choosing TV programs and requesting specific movies. He still wasn't chatting much, but he was truly and clearly Mattie, and improving each day.

Laura, now pregnant with her first child, began recruiting more PICU nurses to do home care with Mattie when she went on maternity leave. The list was growing each day with nurses wanting to cover a shift or two a week, with a general feeling of "How can we make this work?" Mattie, meanwhile, told Laura how excited he was that she was going to have a baby, so thrilled for the upcoming joy.

But by early June, things had again taken a turn. Mattie ended up with yet another infection in his blood and needed more IV antibiotics. He was feverish and distressed. He began growing weaker again, his muscles twisting even tighter, if that was possible. The doctors inserted a catheter into his spine with medicine to try to loosen the muscles, but more bones continued to break from the strain. And his chest muscles had become so tight that even on high settings, his ventilator was not able to fully expand his lungs. He was beginning to have bouts of severe respiratory distress as a result, triggering more dysautonomia. His body would not even regulate his blood sugar anymore, and he had to go on an insulin pump, like someone who had had diabetes for years.

Particularly distressing was that Mattie developed high muscle tone in his jaw and tongue and was losing the ability to speak, sometimes barely able to utter a single yes or no.

In an e-mail to the Prayer Warriors, Sandy wrote:

```
Mattie survived the arrest that should have been impos-
sible to survive on March 8th. He woke up and talked to
his mom again in spite of all odds that he should not
have. And after all of this, Jeni now has had to watch
him decline and lose all ability to move, to communicate
easily. When I left [the hospital] a few nights ago I
felt as if I had seen a glimpse of hell. . . . The stakes
are as high as they can get. Some days I don't even know
what to pray for. I'm just thankful that when "we don't
know what we ought to pray for, the Spirit intercedes for
us with groans that words cannot express . . . because
the Spirit intercedes for the saints in accordance with
God's will" (Romans 8:26-27).
```

I had a "When is enough?" conversation with Mattie, asking him, "If we can resolve the pain and you can't move but can talk and think, would that be okay? Would you be okay with moving forward like that?" We were still in early June.

He said that as long as he could think, could share and be a part of the world, he wanted to live—but to *please* stop the pain, which was excruciating.

I begged him to put up with the pain while we searched for a solution, promising him that when he got better, we would go anywhere in the world he wanted. "Where?" I asked.

He smiled and answered, "Hawaii." It was the only place I hadn't taken him with me once on a business trip. The nurses immediately started a sign-up sheet for who would accompany us.

One morning during this period, Sandy received a gift. "Every day I awoke with dread that this would be the day Mattie would die," she told me, "but that day, in the middle of that same ominous feeling, I felt a message come into my heart, my spirit, saying, 'Yes, he is going to die, but you do not need to be afraid. Do not be afraid for him.' Instantly, the dread vanished," she said. "I was sad. I knew I would grieve and miss him. But I knew something wonderful was awaiting him."

At the same time, Mattie told me, "Heaven is a wonderful place."

I answered him, "Heaven will always be wonderful. It can wait for you while you are here with me. I will make this a wonderful place for you. We are working on fixing your muscles. You won't always be in this pain. You may not be able to stand again, but you will talk and write. We'll play after this storm, okay?"

He said to me, dripping in sweat and with strained and broken breaths, "Mom, promise me you will choose to inhale, and not breathe simply to exist."

"Mattie," I responded, "I don't want you to leave me. I need you. I love you. You are my best friend. I can't go on without you. I am going to make it all better for you. Please, can you hang in there for me? Please?"

"Mom, do not lie down in the ashes of my life," he said. "Take my message forthward. Make it part of your own message. I'll live through the message. I will be with you."

"But, Mattie," I pleaded, "we are going to Hawaii, remember? There is so much to do. Please don't leave me. I love you so much."

By mid-June another brain scan showed that the part of his brain that directed movement was devastated, with no hope for improvement. His ability to think, reason, remember, feel, and love—to be "Mattie"—were all intact, but there was no scientific hope for the severe muscle strain, or dystonia. The gnarling of his body would continue to worsen, with the pain only intensifying. With that information, I made the awful decision that there would be no more heroic measures. He was to receive full support to *avoid* a crisis, but not to get through one.

I encouraged him to rest, to close his eyes. I left for bathroom breaks only if he was sleeping. I showered only if Sandy or Heather was with him. I even defied a nurse who caught me dozing by his bed one night, refusing to leave even though parents are not allowed to sleep in the PICU. "Call Security and let them drag me out," I told her. She complained to the supervising nurse, who simply said, "Let her stay with him."

I asked Mattie what I could do for him. "Be with me. Talk to me," he said. He was very afraid of dying alone.

I told him stories from his own life: "Do you remember when you tried to impress a girl at the pool and did a flip off the diving board but forgot to unwind your tubing and the whole oxygen tank followed you into the water? Remember your Lovely Ladies at camp?" I talked about his favorite cartoons and movies, our Dweeb Tape of silly things we had done.

Tears welled up in his eyes. "Please stop," he said. "It's making me so sad."

I was ripping apart from the inside. All of our memories were packed into a definite past; there were not going to be any new memories, and the moment at hand was filled with physical pain and emotional anguish. What could I say to him?

I said, "I love you," and just began to sing to him—"Amazing Grace," our "I'll Love You Forever" song that we had made up, Weird Al songs, Beatles music, John Denver tunes I had sung to him when he was younger, Christmas carols.

One day he asked me, "Have I done enough? Will it last? I haven't finished the book, the interviews."

I had no clue where he was with the *Just Peace* book. Sandy contacted Jimmy Carter, who told her, "Mattie's done more than enough. The book is close. The message will get out there. Mattie has done more for humanity than he realizes."

Mattie felt so reassured when Sandy gave him that message. He then told me where to find his computer files, his loose papers, his notes, journals. "You will take my message forthward for me," he said. "I trust you. I believe in you."

For months I had been praying to God to save him—novenas and litanies and any other prayer to convince God to spare my son's life. Finally, I told God that I was ready to "be careful what I wished for." I prayed for Mattie to have the grace of peace. In my mind, I hoped that would mean a physical miracle for my son. But in my heart, I knew that I was beseeching God to give my son the hope and truth and wonder of Heaven.

One day, Mattie whispered that he wanted to receive Communion. Father Dominic Eshikena, the hospital chaplain who had ministered to Mattie for several years, came to his bedside, prayed with him, and gave him the Holy Eucharist. Mattie could handle only a very small sliver of the wafer, the host, by that point. But I could tell he felt the grace of receiving the sacrament.

He was not done living yet, however. He wanted to see the new *Harry Potter* movie, still in theaters and not yet out on video. Sandy e-mailed everyone on the Prayer Warrior list: "Can *anybody* make this happen, quickly?"

Nancy Hunt, president of the We Are Family Foundation, worked with an organization called the Lollipop Theater, and they pulled it off. On June 19, a Saturday, dripping in sweat, gasping, and in great pain, Mattie thoroughly enjoyed every minute of the film, holding the magic wand given to him by the *Harry Potter* actors on the Oprah set.

By the twenty-first, Mattie leaked spinal fluid from the catheter insertion site where the doctors were trying a new drug with the hope of relaxing his muscles even a bit. He began to spike very high temperatures. There were now two different bacterial infections in his trachea. I spent the entire night wiping down his sweating body with wet cloths, trying to comfort him, singing to him and speaking softly. I asked if anything I was doing was helping at all, and he said, "Yes," loudly and clearly.

"I heard that!" his nurse called out.

I sang him "Amazing Grace" again and then recited a prayer aloud. He looked at me and said, "AMEN." I knew he was ready. But I wasn't. "Mattie, I love you so much. I need you to stay here with me . . . please." He looked into my eyes and blinked "yes."

On the morning of June 22, I called Sandy and told her he wasn't doing well. "Is that him in the background?" she asked. His gasping was worse than ever.

She was there an hour later, and I asked her to please keep wiping him down, talking to him. I needed to close my eyes for just ten minutes.

Two hours later, I jumped awake. I had fallen into a deeper sleep than I meant to. While I had been resting, they performed another echocardiogram. The pulmonary hypertension had increased. By noon, Mattie was clearly in agony, gasping and sweating profusely while his heart rate soared into the 200s.

I talked with Sandy. If they gave him a dose of pain medicine now, with his heart functioning so erratically, it could cause an arrest—and I had already made the decision that there would be no more heroic measures. Thus, there'd be no CPR, and I would have brought on his death by allowing the drug.

Aunt Mary Lou came in at that point, not knowing Mattie had gotten so much worse. It was simply her day to visit. "Should I leave?" she asked.

"No, you should stay," I told her. "He loves you."

By 1:15 in the afternoon I knew Mattie had to be offered relief. A nurse drew up a dose of pain medicine that would go through an IV line. A doctor came in, in case I changed my mind about not doing CPR.

The nurse began to wipe the IV site with alcohol before injecting the needle, and I said, "Wait. I need to talk to him first."

I rolled up to his face and leaned in close. "Mattie, I need you to look at me," I told him. "I need to tell you something, and I need to know that you are listening to me." He opened his eyes and looked into mine.

"Mattie, I love you very much. I want you to know that you can rest now. I will be okay. I will choose to inhale. Do you understand what I am saying to you? I am saying that it is okay for you to rest now."

He opened his mouth, but nothing came out. He tried to smile.

"You can rest, Mattie," I repeated. "It will all be okay. Do you understand what I have just said to you?"

He blinked "yes," closed his eyes, and stopped gasping.

I turned to Sandy and the doctor and asked, "Am I wrong?"

"Of course not," the doctor answered. "You told him to rest, so he is relaxing. Look, we haven't even given him the pain medicine. He doesn't need it. You calmed him down."

The doctor misunderstood. I looked at Sandy. "Am I wrong?" I asked again.

"No," Sandy said. "This is the right thing."

"Look," the doctor said, "his heart rate is finally coming down to a normal level."

I climbed into bed with Mattie. Even when he was ready to go, he stayed to take care of me until I was ready, until I said I'd be all right. I held him in my arms. I began saying, "I love you." He opened his eyes and looked at me. His heart rate was now in the low 100s—normal.

He closed his eyes again, and I put my hand on his chest, where I could feel his heart beat slower and slower.

In those few moments, I remembered his fascination with God's answer to Moses' question: "By what name shall I call You?" and the answer was "I AM."

Mattie loved that humans were each created in God's image, so that we can each, like God, say, "I AM." I remembered that, at age nine, he wrote that "because we are each made in the image of God, which is good . . . if we are then as good as we can be, if we just do our best . . . we will have lived God's will, our Heartsong."

"I love you, Mattie," I kept saying to him. "You were the best person you could be. You lived a good life, and that is all God asks of any of us. You are just as God created you to be. You are good, you are good. I love you, Mattie. I love you."

At 1:35 P.M. on June 22, 2004, I felt the last beat from my son's heart. I leaned into his face and inhaled as deeply as I could, gathering his last breath into me, making his essence part of my own. I would take his message forthward. I began kissing him. I must have kissed him a thousand times or more, enough, I hoped, to last until I could kiss him again, beyond the thin space.

But my moment alone with him was short lived. Within minutes, the hospital's Public Relations Department said they were sorry but they needed a statement. Mattie's life, his belonging to the world and not just me, was already going forward without his body.

Dozens and dozens of people came by as all the local television stations interrupted their programming to announce Mattie's passing. Jeff

Bouchard later told me he heard the news in Italy, where a television show was interrupted minutes after his death.

We waited for Micah to be brought to the hospital. He had been staying with my cousins the Stoddards in Richmond during the long months of this whole last crisis, and a storm snarled traffic and slowed his arrival. After he came and licked and sniffed Mattie and then sank down in despair, Mattie was taken to the funeral home, where his body was still warm hours and hours later.

The next morning, I did an interview with *Good Morning America* from the condo so there would be "no guesswork" about Mattie's life and death. I knew stories were going to be aired, and Mattie deserved the dignity of accuracy.

Next door, both Sandy and Heather had a phone in each ear, responding to questions from the media and others. By late morning, top-tier MDA administrators had begun to gather in Sandy's condo, too, along with representatives from the International Association of Fire Fighters and Harley-Davidson, asking, "What do you want? What did *he* want? Just tell us, and we will handle every detail."

A few days later, Sandy, Heather, and I went to the funeral home to cut his hair, dress him, and tuck him into his casket with all the items he requested, along with a few others of which I thought he might be saying, "Oh, I should have this, or that! I hope my mom thinks of it."

The wake was held June 27, at the church where the funeral Mass would take place. Before Mattie's casket was lifted onto the fire truck outside the funeral home, a taxi dropped off Sean Astin at the curb. "I didn't know where to go," he said, "so I just came here." He looked lost—which was the way we all felt. I told him to ride with us in the van.

A twenty-minute video loop of Mattie's life played at the back of the church while a never-ending line of visitors slowly filed through. Hope handed out hundreds of "Sunset Ribbons of Hope" that she had made to celebrate Mattie's life and message. Other teens, including those from MDA Summer Camp, handed out Mattie's little slips of one-liner Heartsongs, aphorisms he had given out across the years to brighten someone's day or help them through a hard time.

That evening, Sandy's apartment was filled to bursting. People from

Larry King Live and *Good Morning America* came, not to get "a story" but in friendship, to share memories and grief. Celebrities came: Sean Astin and Billy Gilman. MDA friends, firefighters, bikers, kin, others, all gathered.

After the world learned of Mattie's death, after the media, the interviews, the trips to the funeral home, the wake, I went back to my apartment next door. It was so close to Sandy's, and had always seemed so when Mattie and I lived there together. But now, Sandy's place seemed an eternity away. I felt so alone, as I had all five nights since the day of Mattie's death. I comforted myself that at least I would see, touch, Mattie's body one more time the next morning before the funeral. But I was lost. I rolled from room to room, looking for something, I didn't know what, perhaps some sign that Mattie was still with me. I had been away from home for almost four months.

I ended up in his Bachelor's Pad and remembered that Mattie told me where to find various pieces of writing. I sat there thinking—of all the lessons, the inspiration, the challenge to humanity in calling us *all* to be messengers, the challenge to choose and follow through on our own peaceful vision for living.

I found some poetry I had not seen before, including "Coming of Age," "Purple Moon," "Unfinished," and "Final Thoughts." The last was the one he told me he needed to write down on March 7, the evening before he went into cardiac arrest.

All I wanted in that moment was a single touch from him, nothing more. No wisdom, just a touch. A reminder that while he was the world's Heartsong Kid, he was my son, my best friend, my everything.

It was then I saw an envelope that read, "Mother's Day, 2004." Inside was a card with a poem dated December 8, 2003, the same day I had found him curled up in the green recliner, working on his novel. He had titled it "Dear Mommy—":

> *For thirteen years, you've gently taught me,*
> *You've celebrated life with me and brought me*
> *Each strength and joy that a child could know,*
> *All guided with love—a maternal rainbow.*

It was God who made me to be who I am—
A messenger with Heartsongs to offer His lambs.
But then it was you who said 'Yes' to our Lord,
And chose my first gift—the chance to be born.
My spirit then bodied could finally see
The mosaic of life and humanity—
A fabric of wonder, a kaleidoscope!
Yet, in need of a gift, a message of hope.
You shaped my being from God's humble clay—
You led me, inspired me, with wisdom each day.
And like the glory of sunrise at dawn,
You led me from darkness, and held me upon
Your lap when I feared—when I most needed shelter,
You kissed my tears, fading hurts, calming welter.
Like a brave shepherd, you've been my life's guard,
Witnessing peace through your heart—loving ark.
We've played and prayed through the storms and the good,
Together we've grown just as God knew we would.
And I am who I am, now, because of your touch—
And for that, I am grateful, and I love you so much.
I could never say thank you, or I love you enough,
I could never fit words in a note—even stuffed,
That capture your role for my essence in Life—
So nurtured and tendered by your guiding light.
Oh, my dearest mother, please hear what I say:
I wish you the happiest, Each Mother's Day!
May you realize true peace beyond mortal replevin—
As my echo and silhouette linger past Heaven.

Your loving son,
Mattie J.T. Stepanek

Mattie and Jeni, fall 2003

Epilogue

A firefighter looking at photographs just before Mattie's funeral, June 2004

Mattie's grave marker at Gate of Heaven cemetery in Silver Spring, Maryland

Our life is an echo
Of our spirit today,
Of our essence
As it is,
Caught between
Our yesterday
And our tomorrow.
It is the resounding
Reality of who we are,
As a result of
Where we have been
And where we will be,
For eternity.[1]

"**I** AM . . . I AM . . ."

Mattie's whisper came echoing through the church. After Oprah

---

1 From "Eternal Echoes" in *Journey Through Heartsongs*, page 62.

and the others finished their pre–funeral Mass testimonials, the song "I AM/Shades of Life" played through the loudspeakers, the uplifting strains of the melody and Billy Gilman's beautiful singing woven with Mattie's own voice, reverberating, fading.

When the music ended, Sandy and I followed the casket forward from the back of the church, taking our places for the service. Micah was by my side; Tad, the stuffed animal tiger, hung on the back of my wheelchair, dressed in a tuxedo, just like Mattie in his casket.

Mattie had chosen "How Can I Keep from Singing?" for the processional hymn, not a funeral song but, rather, almost a reassurance, a sense from him that said, "I'm not really gone. I'm just different."

Sandy, Aunt Mary Lou, and MDA camp director Katie McGuire led the readings. We received permission from the Catholic Church for Sandy to read Mattie's "Psalm of Tad 358" instead of a psalm from the Old Testament:

> Lord, You have
> Saved me from sadness,
> And lifted me to light.
> All my life,
> I have been haunted
> By the darkness,
> Only my dreams gave me sight.
> But my Savior
> Has now turned me
> Back to light,
> No longer do I dwell in shadows. . . . [2]

Father Dominic Eshikena, the hospital chaplain and one of more than ten celebrants helping to lead the proceedings, read from the Gospel according to Matthew 19:13–15:

---

2 From "Psalm of Tad 358" in *Loving Through Heartsongs*, page 52.

*Then little children were brought to Jesus so that He might lay
His hands on them and pray for them. . . . Jesus said, "Let the
little children come to me, and do not hinder them, for the kingdom of heaven belongs to such as these."*

Father Dixon gave the homily, followed by Paula Beckman, my advisor
from the university, who said the offertory prayers.

The altar servers, friends of Mattie's, were the children of firefighters.
The gift bearers—the ones who brought the bread and wine to the altar
for Holy Communion—were also children: Hope; Christopher Cross's
daughter, Madison; Jann Carl's daughter, Katherine; the Bouchard boys,
Kyle and Travis; and several others. They didn't just carry what would
become the body and blood. They also brought every one of Mattie's
books, the CD of his poems that had been set to music, a peacemaker
bumper sticker. All meant for God, they had been chosen by Mattie and
therefore offered up by him during his own funeral Mass.

It made the ceremony transcend what it otherwise might have been.
I was still in shock, still in those raw, earliest stages of grief. I had seen
and touched my child's body for the last time and would never have that
gift again. But because of Mattie's own hand in the funeral, it wasn't sad,
the way funerals usually are. It was truly a celebration of his life. It was
personal. It was wonderful. It was an amazing mix of liturgical music and
prayers with Mattie's songs and psalms, his touch, folded in.

I was so glad that others were experiencing it the way I did. I still felt
more alone than I can describe, even with more than a thousand people
surrounding me. Bob Ross, MDA president at the time Mattie died, used
to say, "Mattie and his mom are so close, they are like two bodies with a
shared spirit." How I ached for that part of my spirit, how I missed it, and
nothing could fix that. But because of the communion among all of us
that Mattie engendered, I didn't feel isolated. All of us were carrying
forth his gift, his inspiration, together.

After the Communion hymns, Billy Gilman went up to the altar and
sang "For Our World," one of Mattie's poems that had been set to
music:

We need to be silent.
Just silent.
Silent for a moment . . .
Before we forever lose
The blessing of songs
That grow in our hearts. . . .
Stop, be silent, and notice . . .
In so many ways, we are the same.[3]

Then Jimmy Carter gave the eulogy, in which he said:

> *. . . I traveled around the world. In fact, since I left the White*
> *House, my wife and I have been to more than 120 nations. And*
> *we have known kings and queens, and we've known presidents*
> *and prime ministers, but the most extraordinary person whom I*
> *have ever known in my life is Mattie Stepanek. . . .*
>
> *When I won the Nobel Peace Prize . . . as soon as the cere-*
> *mony was over at the hall in Oslo, I went by myself to the top of*
> *a little hill right behind the place, and I found a rock, and I*
> *inscribed on it and I sent it to Mattie, because I felt that he*
> *shared the honor that I had received. . . .*
>
> *He wanted to leave a human legacy . . . family descen-*
> *dants, but Mattie's legacy, obviously, is much greater than*
> *that . . . because his Heartsongs will resonate in the hearts of*
> *people forever. . . .*
>
> *I always saw the dichotomy between Mattie as a child and*
> *with the characteristics and intelligence and awareness of an*
> *adult. Just as we see the dichotomy of Jesus Christ, who was fully*
> *a human being at the same time as truly God.*
>
> *I would say that my final assessment is that Mattie was an*
> *angel. Someone said that to him once, and he said, "No, no, I*

---

3   From "For Our World" in *Hope Through Heartsongs*, page 49.

*am simply a messenger." He was very modest. But really, in the
New Testament language, angel and messenger are the same,
and there's no doubt that Mattie was an angel of God, a messenger of God. . . .*

After President Carter's eulogy came the final blessings. It was much
harder for me following my son's casket out of the church than following
it in. I knew that when we reached the cemetery, I was not ever going to
see it again. Every tangible aspect of my son's body would disappear.

The fire truck was parked right outside the church doors. Mattie's six
kin pallbearers—Heather, Jamie-D, Chris, Cynthia, Devin, and one of
Mattie's favorite PICU nurses, Ian Crumbley—handed the casket to the
six firefighter pallbearers, who included Bubba and J.J. People began to
make their way to the back of the church and started to file out, both
flooding the driveway and knotting up at the door.

Usually, once a funeral service is over, there is small talk, murmurs,
some bustling. And there should have been even more of that than usual
at this particular funeral, with cameras and television crews everywhere.
But there wasn't. Instead, there was silence, a graceful silence. It was
like we were following the instructions in Mattie's poem to "stop, be silent, and notice" rather than just whisk by and forget that we are all together in something bigger than any one person.

In the quiet, with rows of firefighters standing at attention, the white
pall that had draped the casket during the Mass was removed and re-
placed with the United Nations flag. Then, just as the firefighter pallbearers lifted the casket onto the fire truck, bagpipes began sounding
"Amazing Grace." Nothing could have been more mournfully uplifting.
It was like a weeping willow tree translated into song, the song I sang for
Mattie so many times.

The road from the church to the cemetery was crowded with still
more people, bowing, saluting, making the Sign of the Cross. We were
preceded by a police motorcade, helicopters overhead, the road closed
to all but the vehicles going to the burial.

At the cemetery gates, two fire trucks were waiting, each with a ladder extended. A large American flag hung down from where the raised ladders met in an inverted *V*.

Once inside, we could not take the direct route to the burial site. We had to wind our way up and down the narrow cemetery roads to make room for the hundreds of cars. As we were giving everyone time to make their way over once they parked, we began to hear a long, low rumble. Hundreds and hundreds of Harley-Davidsons had arrived behind the cars and were wending their way through the cemetery paths, giving Mattie a planned "Rolling Thunder" memorial tribute. It would become louder, then softer, then louder again as the motorcycles wove a little closer toward us, then farther away and back again as they came up the next row. The tribute was made all the more beautiful by the crescendos and decrescendos, like thunder from Heaven growing louder and softer and louder again.

As the Harleys made their way closer and people were gathering at the burial site, Devin came over to me and whispered, "I made a promise to Mattie that I would follow through on the joke he wanted to help everybody play after the storm."

I was torn. I so wanted to let Devin honor Mattie's wish, the wish for the fart machine to be sounded, but it seemed far too irreverent.

"Look," Devin said, "there's lots of noise now with all the motorcycles. Bubba and J.J. are up there on the fire truck with the casket. We could do it just for them, and nobody else would have to hear. It's now or never."

"Okay," I answered.

With that, Devin pressed the trigger. Bubba and J.J.'s eyebrows went up. They looked at the casket. They looked at me. I shrugged my shoulders, making a don't-ask-me grin. They had been very serious, stalwart, albeit with tears streaming. Then, these two men, who had put Mattie up to so many practical jokes during softball tournaments, started laughing. Nobody knew whether they were laughing or crying. *They* didn't know whether they were laughing or crying. Mattie had gotten the last laugh after all, and had begun the healing.

After Father Dixon performed the burial rites, said the prayers, and blessed the gravesite, Devin stepped forward holding a huge bunch of balloons by their strings.

A year earlier, he explained, Mattie's fellow MDA camper, Racheal Francis, died during camp week, just like Mattie had this year. MDA had decided not to tell the campers the previous summer because they didn't want to spoil their week. But the kids let the camp director know that was not okay, that they did not want to go for several days thinking everything was all right with a friend when it wasn't. So when Mattie died, Katie McGuire gathered the camp teens together to tell them.

"They grieved, they cried, they shared memories of Mattie," Devin said. "They talked about how he always made them feel good, made them laugh. Then, while they were talking, a fierce storm kicked up. The wind was howling like crazy, and there were blasts of thunder and lightning. It was out of nowhere and intense. But just as quickly as it began, it stopped.

"'Mattie always told us to play after every storm,' one of his friends said. 'Do you think this storm is like a reminder that we need to finish celebrating camp week in his honor? That we have to play hard?'

"They rolled outside, where they saw a huge rainbow arcing across the sky, one end to the other. 'Okay, now Mattie's just showing off,' one of them said."

Everyone laughed, at camp and now again at the gravesite.

Then Devin explained the significance of the balloons, describing how, every year at camp's end, they were released into the sky, "representing all our wishes, all the things that matter." Most of the balloons—orange, green, pink, yellow, blue, red—he held with one hand. In the other he held a lone purple—Mattie's color for hope.

He put it together with the others and let go of them all at once. They rose immediately, twenty, maybe thirty feet, and all kept going, except for the purple one. It sort of paused, hovered, danced a little to the right, then the left, playfully bobbing up and down a bit. This went on for almost a full half minute, until all of a sudden it shot up, racing higher than all the others and taking one last pause before leading the way skyward.

Mattie celebrating the sunset, summer
1998

Forthword

The bronze statue of Mattie and his service dog, Micah, in the Peace Garden at the Mattie J.T. Stepanek Park in Rockville, Maryland

Hundreds of bricks from people around the world serve as a mosaic walkway in the Peace Garden at Mattie's Park

> . . . *And all of the pages would*
> *Have lots and lots of words, filled with*
> *Mattie's thoughts and Heartsongs.*
> *And they would live and teach*
> *Saying "Hooray for Life" forever,*
> *Even after I am gone.*[1]

It has been said that when an old person dies, a book has been lost. My son, Mattie, did not die an old person. He himself called his life span "a few handfuls of years." But I can only imagine how many books were lost with his passing just weeks before his fourteenth birthday. Yes, his chronos—the dash that marks time from birth to death—was brief. But

---

1 From "The Mattie Book" in *Journey Through Heartsongs*, page 60.

his kairos—the depth of the moments he lived, and what grows from them, even today—is full and rich. He embraced every opportunity to learn, to be inspired, and to share his message, his *Heartsong*, thereby touching the world with a gentle strength.

When Mattie was barely a month old and medical professionals suggested I not bond with him, that I place him in an institution and let his disease run its course, I followed my heart, not the advice. I'm not the only one who is glad for that decision.

If you consider the details of Mattie's life—his disability, the deaths of all his siblings from the same condition he had, his mother in a wheelchair from the time he was four, his parents' divorce, the years of reliance on church food pantries for enough to eat, his having to look his own death squarely in the eye from a very young age—you might feel very sad. But every person I've ever met, or heard from or talked with about Mattie, has focused not on the tragedy of the facts but instead on the triumph of his essence. Each has taken to heart Mattie's belief in hope and peace, his desire for people to get along and act collaboratively and cooperatively, rather than in rancor and warring rage. Remembering that message from my son makes people smile; it reminds them to listen for and share their own Heartsong, to always embrace the next moment with the best of intentions no matter what the circumstances of the moment they're in.

For years I wanted to tell the story of Mattie's life, of this boy whose greatest wish was to inspire people to be their best selves, in no small part because I think it's a really good story. But I hesitated because I wanted to make sure I could do it right. I didn't want this to be a story about my grief, or simply about the details of Mattie's life, which *were* often sad. I wanted to relay the *jubilation* that was Mattie's life, the wit and wisdom, the spirit and celebration that was and *is* the essence of my son. I held that story, Mattie's story, in my heart as I considered how to do that.

Then, one day in the early fall of 2008, about a month before the formal dedication of the Mattie J.T. Stepanek Park in Rockville, Maryland, I received inspiration. A life-size bronze statue of Mattie and Micah was being installed, and people started coming over to look. Children were petting the dog, and everybody, children and adults alike, wanted to touch Mattie and hold his hand. One four-year-old boy stood and pondered the statue with his arms folded across his chest, finally saying, "Mommy, that boy makes me feel happy inside."

"That boy's name is Mattie," the mother answered, "and that's exactly what Mattie wanted. He wanted people to feel happy—and he wanted to spread peace."

Other small children began to gather, asking about the nature of peace and what it meant that Mattie wanted to "spread" it. By the end of the conversation, more and more children were saying *they* wanted to make people happy and spread peace, to *be* peace, just like Mattie.

I realized then that years after his death, Mattie is still giving happiness and love that lead to hope and peace—still touching the world with his Heartsong. I realized then that the new park, a tangible aspect of his legacy, was already beginning to inspire people. And I realized it was time to articulate the inspiration in the pages of a book. Yes, Mattie is the Heartsong Kid, Oprah's guy, my son, and someone who faced uphill challenges between every single one of his 5,089 sunrises and sunsets. But he also reminds people that we each have a reason to be, something within that allows us to believe that hope is real and peace is possible, and that these truths begin with an attitude. That is, while the facts of your life may not be your choice, the attitude with which you deal with those facts *is* entirely your choice, and therein lies your capacity to make a meaningful difference in the world, to leave behind an echo and a silhouette that can gently and beautifully shape the future.

This book offers the story of Mattie's choice, his decision to celebrate life and perceive it as a worthy blessing even during the most painful moments. It would be his hope, and mine, that his example now serve as a reminder that while we can't always plan our future or choose what becomes our memories, what happens doesn't have to define us, or limit us, or control us. We can always find something good in the moment at hand, in whatever comes next, and even in how we reflect on the truth of things past, and in that way, help shape the world. That is his essence, his legacy. As Mattie wrote:

Blessed are those who
Bear the torch of hope,
For they shall have peace!

But how *do* we bear the torch of hope? How do we shape the world? That's the question Jimmy Carter asked at the end of *Just Peace: A Message of Hope*, which did in fact get published after Mattie's death (and in 2007 was awarded an IPPY Gold Medal for outstanding Peacemaker Book of the Year), along with a final book of poetry, entitled *Reflections of a Peacemaker: A Portrait Through Heartsongs*.

President Carter also supplied the framework for the answer, explaining that *forthword* and *forthward* were Mattie's own terms for going to the next step. "It was [Mattie's] dream," the president said, "that the encapsulation of his ideas and poetry into [books] would not represent the final achievement of his influential life, but rather that it would launch his spirit into the future."

It all starts with Mattie's conviction that if we all take care to identify and share our Heartsongs, their combined strength and beauty will carry us forward together into a better future.

There's nothing unique about the concept, of course. It's the universal message: Live your best life, be your best self, give what you wish to receive, and in so doing you will connect with others and receive fulfillment.

But how Mattie *packaged* the message, how he mined the sadness and celebration of his life to remind people that we all have within us the capacity to be messengers and that his job was just sowing seeds, made his concept of "Three Choices for Peace" not just believable, but *doable*. He stripped his message down to something that everyone could embrace within themselves, and then gently touch the world and be touched back. In this way, we each become part of the global effort to move us all *forthward* together in peace. That is the reason his legacy matters, the reason it continues to have resonance and ripple farther and farther outward.

The first ripple began right in his own community of King Farm in Rockville, Maryland, where upon his death an article in the local newspaper said the following:

> *We miss waving to him as he whizzed down the street or seeing his bedroom light on at night. . . . The employees of Safeway miss his smile as he rolled around the aisles bargain shopping. Maggie Moo's folks knew his favorite flavor of ice cream. Those at Starbucks knew how he liked his coffee and hot chocolate. . . . Mattie taught us how to love and play no matter what our challenges. He believed in people helping people and learning to live together in peace, which is also what it means to be a good neighbor. . . . The next time you help someone or speak to a neighbor as you pass by, remember Mattie, and know that a part of him lives on. . . .*

Soon after Mattie died, local citizens established the Mattie J.T. Stepanek Foundation, a nonprofit organization run on a volunteer basis, with a mission of making Mattie's message available to people across time and space. One of the most important projects the foundation is presently gearing up for is to create curricula for use in classrooms from the pre-school level to universities, using Mattie's writings. Many school systems, including Montgomery County, where Mattie lived, already use his poetry to teach and inspire students. The curriculum programs developed by the foundation will expand on this effort, using Mattie's words to help young people find the Heartsong within themselves and make use of it to create a just peace among all peoples.

The formal development of these educational programs will support schools like Carlstadt Public School in New Jersey, where Mattie's books have been used since 2001, when they were first published. For example, students there write essays to compare and contrast peacemakers on Martin Luther King, Jr., Day, applying Mattie's ideas about what it means to be a peacemaker. At the same time, according to Carlstadt middle school English teacher Michael Mangone, who first introduced Mattie's books to the school system, they are "engaging in personal introspection" about how they, too, can cultivate a peaceful attitude and peacemaking habits. One parent whose child attends school in Carlstadt has said that Mattie's influence in the lesson plans has "been able to put the children in touch with feelings they never knew they had before."

Every May, Mattie Stepanek Day is celebrated in Carlstadt, with the flag flown at half-mast—until Mattie's vision for world peace is achieved. The citizens of Carlstadt have also dedicated a Peace Library in Mattie's name, as well as a Peace Park with reflective quotes and a bust of Mattie. The town's mayor has said that every state should dedicate at least one open space to peace.

The idea for the Peace Park came from Rockville's Mattie J.T. Stepanek Park, for which ground was broken on the first anniversary of Mattie's death, with hundreds of firefighters, Harley-Davidson riders, politicians, and other citizens showing up to turn dirt in Mattie's honor. The twenty-six-acre recreational facility, which has playgrounds, ball fields and courts, a dog park, and abundant green space, was dedicated in 2008, with speeches by Oprah Winfrey, politicians, musicians, and others. Pepper Choplin, a renowned creator of spiritual compositions, synthesized words from one of Mattie's final peace speeches to music, and the resulting song, "Look Up, Way Down," had its debut performance during the park dedication with a choir of one hundred voices singing:

> . . . *Seek peace, and make peace,*
>   *and bring peace to every place.*
> *Know peace, live peace, be peace in every time and space.*
> *Peace bringer, peace singer, make peace a reality.*
> *Share peace with everyone you meet*
> *In your world, in your home and community.*
> *Look up way down, look up way down the road.*
> *We're not there yet, but it's where we wanna go. . . .*[2]

---

2 From "Look Up, Way Down," lyrics by Mattie J.T. Stepanek, music by Pepper Choplin (Alfred Publishing, 2009).

In the Peace Garden at the center of the park is a life-size bronze statue of Mattie in his wheelchair with Micah by his side. This area of the park, which has won design awards, was based on imagery from Mattie's *Just Peace* book. Rippling out from the statue are concentric "circles of support, rivers of kindness," chess tables, and mosaics of bricks, many engraved with messages from people in nearly two dozen countries around the world. Visitors can also listen to Mattie's voice via an information soundpost. And outward from the Peace Garden throughout the park, quotes from Mattie can be found on benches and plaques. It's a palpable expression of Mattie's belief that when we come together, when we act as the mosaic of gifts we are meant to be, something beautiful is created. And, the park itself is a literal aid to help people play—after storms, between storms, and even when it appears that there is no storm on the horizon.

In addition to putting people in touch with their Heartsongs at parks and in school programs, Mattie's legacy has been rippling out to provide hope—real, tangible hope that is being put to good use. The Heartsongs Gala is still put on every February in Washington, as Mattie challenged everyone to do, and at this point has raised millions of dollars for research toward cures for neuromuscular diseases and for MDA Summer Camp, which lifts children's spirits as they await those cures.

There is also the MDA Mattie Fund, established after Mattie's death, which has raised several million additional dollars for research on *childhood* neuromuscular diseases in particular, including fellowships that focus on mitochondrial diseases like the one that took Mattie and his siblings. Mitochondrial diseases are so variable—no two look alike—making it difficult to allocate research funds. That's why a certain percentage of money donated to the Mattie Fund is earmarked specifically for learning more about them in the hope of eventually finding a treatment.

Hope also comes in the form of four scholarships that Rosalynn Carter gives out every year in Mattie's name to people seeking to further their education or work in caregiving. And Mattie's lobbying efforts on behalf of Children's Hospice International so that parents "never have to choose between hospice care and hope for a cure" is well on its way to bearing fruit as a new law. Championed by Virginia congressman James

Moran, the "Mattie and Melinda Bill" will grant hospice care to children without their having to give up their right to lifesaving efforts.

Initiatives for peace, too, continue to ripple out, to echo, from Mattie's spirit. The year after he died, the Children's Peace Pavilion in Independence, Missouri, where Mattie first shared his "Three Choices for Peace" concept, devoted the two-room entrance space of its museum to his message with a "Peace Is Possible" exhibit.

In addition, the town of Lapeer, Michigan, has taken up Mattie's call on page 71 of *Just Peace* to commemorate September 11 by celebrating what he called World Trade Day. Every September 11, the aim is to *trade* something—a thought, a photograph, a book—with another person, perhaps even with a stranger. In that way the citizens of Lapeer, as well as those of other cities that are also embracing this tradition, foster a message of hope and peace.

Mattie's push for peace also continues to ripple through the We Are Family Foundation, which presented him with its first Peacemaker Award in 2002. Today, that organization, still headed by Nile Rodgers and Nancy Hunt, partners with the Lollipop Theater to bring Mattie's Movie and Poetry Slam Day into hospitals around the country.

Children don't only watch the just-released movies that they wouldn't otherwise get to see while in the hospital. They also talk about Mattie's poetry and poetic expression and then have their own poetry slam to express themselves.

In 2005, We Are Family renamed its Peacemaker Award "The Mattie J.T. Stepanek Peacemaker Award," annually presenting it to someone who uses his or her gift to better humanity, to meet people's basic needs and thereby promote peace from the ground up. Recipients thus far have included Maya Angelou, Quincy Jones, Paul Simon, Deepak Chopra, and Desmond Tutu.

In 2007, We Are Family, which also raises funds to build schools in African and Latin American countries, named a school in Mali, Africa, after Mattie, and in 2008, the inaugural Just Peace Summit, based on the tenets of Mattie's final book, was held in New York. The summit is part of We Are Family's "Three Dot Dash" initiative. In Morse code, three dots and a dash stand for the letter *V*, which is the international hand gesture

Acknowledgments
(Thank yous!)

First, thank you to Dr. Maya Angelou, Mattie's friend and mine, for contributing such a poignant and powerful Foreword to this book. Your words truly set the tone for why this story matters. Although I have written or edited many professional publications, I am really more of a storyteller than a story writer. Thank you to Larry Lindner for embracing my detailed vision and notes for this book, for recording every story exactly as I conveyed it, and for your contribution as a word weaver as each chapter came together. Thank you to Chris Lewis for believing in the ongoing inspiration and power of Mattie's story, and for believing in me as both a storyteller *and* a story writer. Thank you to Oprah Winfrey for your friendship, and for allowing me to share excerpts from your personal communications with Mattie. And thank you to Carrie Thornton at Dutton and Dan Strone at Trident Media for your encouragement and enthusiasm.

Thank you to all who shared personal stories of how Mattie touched your lives, and for allowing me to weave such wonderful memories into this book. If I were to share the *complete* story of Mattie's life, the publication would be in volumes rather than pages. So, I offer a special thank you to those who not only were touched by my son, but who also profoundly touched my son's life yet whose names are not on these pages— simply because of space, and not because of significance. This includes Veronica "Granny" Wheeler, Valerie Etherton, Jim Hawkins, Jimilu Mason, Ann Armstrong Dailey, Sue Moi, Patty Pfleiger, Jeanne Myers, Judy Marlow, the Mox family, and Daniel Boda. My appreciation also goes to members of our MDA and IAFF family who are not mentioned by name, including Jerry Weinberg, Mike Blishak, Annie Kennedy, Randy Sisulak, Vito D'Anna, Roger Claxton, Mark Duval, Gina Clark, DJ and Tom O'Connor, Donnie Simmons, Kevin Reilly, the Crisman/Stack families, and many, many others. And my appreciation goes to countless physicians, nurses, and staff members (especially at Children's National Medical Center) who loved and cared for my son, and for me, especially Terry Orzechowski, Pauline Barnes, Marilyn Hill, Terence Flotte, Kim Fenton, and Dr. Matt (aka "Dr. Evil" from *Austin Powers*).

Most of all, I offer my eternal love and gratitude to the kin-family that celebrated life with Mattie and with me—especially members of the Step'obbi'comb Fam as well as my many cousins and aunts and uncles. A special mention goes to the youngest members of the Step'obbi'comb Fam (including Leah Marie, Collin James, and all the little grand-kin yet to be born); I know that you will come to know and love your "Uncle Mattie" just as he already knows and loves you.

Finally, I am thankful to my four incredible and cherished children— Katie, Stevie, Jamie, and Mattie—for making me a "Mommy," which always has been and always will be my favorite title. And, thank you to God, for the gift of my children, and for the gifts of tangible hope, amazing grace, and eternal peace.

In hope and peace,
Jeni

for peace. This program helps achieve peace by mentoring teenagers from around the world, teaching them how to get information, apply for grants, produce public service announcements, edit photographs and videos, and give speeches so they can work on or create projects that help people get their basic needs met and thereby become peacemakers themselves. The first thirty Global Teen Leaders, as they are called, have already touched more than four million people with their projects and have been honored in a Forthward Ceremony. Thirty teens will be trained each year, sowing more and more seeds as they go.

Thus, what was most important to Mattie—that his message not die with him but be taken forthward by others—is being realized. We are giving breath and voice to the words and message of "a poet, a peacemaker, and a philosopher who played." We are becoming a *world* of messengers through our peaceful choices.

In sharing Mattie's vision, Jimmy Carter said, "We will continue his journey together. If we heed Mattie's message, then we know where to go from here."

Mattie's mom, Jeni (far right), with the thirty teens from eighteen countries who attended the 2008 We Are Family Foundation's "Just Peace Summit," where they learned about Mattie's message of hope and peace and created their own peace projects to be implemented during their year as a "Global Teen Leader."

For more information on Mattie-inspired projects, programs, and initiatives, please visit www.mattieonline.com.